100 THINGS ARIZONA FANS SHOULD KNOW & DO BEFORE THEY DIE

Steve Rivera and Anthony Gimino

TRIUMPH
BOOKS

This book is available in quantity at special discounts for your group or organization. For further information, contact:

Triumph Books LLC
814 North Franklin Street
Chicago, Illinois 60610
(312) 337-0747
www.triumphbooks.com

Printed in U.S.A.
ISBN: 978-1-62937-018-7
Design by Patricia Frey
Photos courtesy of AP Images unless otherwise indicated

To Cameron and Trey, two of the best boys and young men a man can have as a father. This is for all those years dad worked at his home away from home—McKale Center.

—Steve Rivera

To Leila and Nico, the family that has to put up with a sportswriter's crazy hours, missing weekends and all those games on TV.

—Anthony Gimino

Contents

Foreword

One of the first things I said after being hired by Cedric Dempsey in 1983 was that fans should get their tickets now, because it wasn't going to be so easy to do so a few years down the road. The program was coming off a tough time, but the fans came roaring back with us and they have helped fuel many of the success stories you will read later in this book.

There were great Arizona basketball players, coaches, and stories before I arrived in Tucson, and writers Steve Rivera and Anthony Gimino have covered those, too, in this book. I'm proud to say that I was part of Arizona's program as its coach for a quarter of a century. What a ride it was. And I'm proud to see the success Sean Miller has had in the past five years. He runs a classy program and is committed to creating a family atmosphere at Arizona, which is what my staff and I always strived to accomplish. Sean is creating many more chapters in UA basketball lore.

Fans should be familiar with the work of Steve and Anthony. Steve started covering us in 1991 and hasn't stopped. He used to joke with me that there was a period of years in which he saw more Arizona basketball games in person than I did. He may have been right, but I used to joke right back that he could never keep up with me on any of my power walks. Just ask him about the ibuprofen he had to take a day later. And, I have him by a number of years. Anthony has covered the Wildcats sports scene for just as long as Steve, and his fairness as a columnist at the *Tucson Citizen* was evident to those around the program.

I spent time with them on multiple occasions for this book, providing further detail on some of the classic players and stories of the past 30-plus years, and I'm confident our super fans will be even more knowledgeable about the Wildcats after reading this book.

—Bear down!

Lute Olson

1 Olson: The Program Builder

What would have occurred had Iowa defeated Villanova on that March day back in 1983? "I don't think I would have [taken the Arizona job]," said Lute Olson, then the ever-popular Iowa coach who had led his team to the Final Four just three years earlier. For Arizona, it was the best thing that ever happened. It started a chain reaction in the hiring of Olson in what would later turn into a quarter century of success that has become Arizona basketball. Today, Arizona is one of the best programs in the country.

After UA fell to Villanova in the Elite Eight in the tournament, then–UA athletic director Cedric Dempsey sauntered up to Olson to inquire about UA's opening at head coach. "Gee, Cedric," Olson told Dempsey after the loss, "this isn't a great time right now. Why don't you give me a call tomorrow?" So Dempsey, Arizona's athletic director for less than a year, waited. He had his man...but he needed to be patient.

A day later, it became a family affair with the Olson family meeting Dempsey in his hotel room. Soon after, Lute and Bobbi, his longtime wife, jumped on a private plane and headed to Tucson.

It had been a year earlier—when Arizona was looking to replace Fred Snowden—that UA had first inquired about hiring Olson. But Olson declined after he had spent time fund-raising for a new arena for Iowa, a team that was rolling with talent and had a bright future. Months earlier, USC had inquired about his availability. Stanford, Washington, and Cal had asked, too. But he turned them all down.

How was Arizona going to lure Olson, who in essence had a lifetime contract at Iowa, to move to Arizona, and a program that could only offer year-to-year contracts? The coach had 24 hours. Time was of the essence in part because Dempsey already had his backup ready. (It was Gene Bartow, the former UCLA head coach. And he, too, was in the hotel.)

Iowa wanted him to stay, but the Olsons' hearts eventually tipped the scales. "I think both of us were ready to move," Olson writes in his book *Lute! The Story of My Life*. "It was everything, the lack of privacy, being with family, returning to the West and from a recruiting standpoint I still had strong contacts in California."

And with that, Olson called Dempsey to say he'd come to Arizona. He was leaving a program that had a chance to win a national title for a program that was in disarray. It was challenge over (potential) championship, as the *New York Times* put it. "Some people thought I had lost my mind," Olson writes in his book.

Arizona fans were elated. On March 29, 1983, Olson signed his contract, eventually encouraging Arizona fans to get their season tickets immediately, since down the road it'd be too late. "I feel the potential is here at Arizona," Olson said in taking over a program that went 4–24 overall and 1–17 in the Pac-10 Conference. And with those words, his legacy at Arizona began.

"My hope here at Arizona back then was—knowing we couldn't recruit much locally and there was a lot to do—was to build a consistent program," Olson said, looking back. "I didn't think what has happened would happen. If we could just be fairly consistent and compete, maybe every once in a while have a special team we'd be OK. You thought that maybe it would be a middle-of-the-road conference team, looking at the other schools [with] an advantage over us." Yet in time, it was *Arizona's* advantage—because of Olson.

"In Lute's quarter of a century at UA, he developed a top-10 national basketball program that was consistently competitive," Dempsey said in the summer of 2014. "He was able to build a program with quality young people with integrity."

At the time of Olson's hire he was 48. Arizona's future looked bright—all because of its suave and debonair coach. In fact, Steve Kerr—years later and perhaps the only person who could ever chide Olson—said Olson looked the same a couple of decades later as he did in the mid-1980s. (By which, of course, Kerr jokingly meant he looked old then, too.)

Of course, that virtue helped in coaching. Former UA player Brock Brunkhorst had been so impressed with Olson—after serving a season with Lindsey—he said playing for Olson was like playing "for your grandfather." After all, the last thing you want to do is "disappoint your grandfather." Matt Muehlebach said playing for Olson was like playing for the "classic dad, and you never want to disappoint him."

So, Arizona players played hard, steady, and with fundamentals. "There was never a time I really thought Lute got frustrated with the situation," said former assistant Scott Thompson, who left Iowa to join Olson at UA. "There were times I saw him raise his eyebrows in almost a humorous chuckle in a we-have-a-lot-of-work-to-do kind of way." And they got after it. Every practice had a purpose.

"The thing about Coach Olson," UA star Sean Elliott said, "was that he would remember everything. *Everything.* We'd go in at halftime and he'd talk about plays and situations and they'd be exact. Coach is smart."

Said Muehlebach, "He valued fundamentals a ton. If you went to our practice, the first 45 minutes it was a practice out of the movie *Hoosiers*. But the next 45 would be like we're the [UNLV] Runnin' Rebels. The last four or five minutes it was go out and incorporate what you just learned and make it a game-like situation."

Olson became a coach famous for focusing on the details. "Lute was one of the first guys who would map out an entire season or practice," Muehlebach said. "Every minute was planned out. He's been one of the more efficient people I've met."

Visit The Naismith Hall Of Fame

Being an Arizona basketball fan means rubbing elbows with many of the best teams, players, and coaches in the country—and it's been that way for generations. Taking that one step further, being the best fans in the Pac-12 should also mean being the most knowledgeable fans in the Pac-12 and among the keenest in the country. That's why there is a lot more to do—and learn—at the Naismith Memorial Basketball Hall of Fame in Springfield, Massachusetts, than just to say hi to the plaque of Robert Luther Olson.

But since we are talking about Lute... He was inducted in 2002 with an all-star cast including Earvin "Magic" Johnson, the Harlem Globetrotters, Larry Brown, Drazen Petrovic, and women's coach Sandra Kay Yow.

Olson said he thought he was going to get into the Hall in 2001, when he led the Wildcats to the national championship game just a few months after the death of his wife, Bobbi. "[The Hall] took so much static from the media around the country—*how can you not include Coach when he's had five teams to the Final Four?*—and then it sort of hit me by surprise in 2002," Olson said. "I was really disappointed in 2001, because that was the year that Bobbi had passed and I felt that would have been the right time."

Still, it was an honor. Legendary coach Pete Newell introduced Olson in the 2002 induction ceremonies. Newell noted that Olson, in addition to his college success at Iowa and Arizona, had vast success in leading all-star teams overseas. One of the great accomplishments of Olson's career was directing the 1986 United States team to a surprise gold medal in the 1986 FIBA World Championships. Team USA has won only four of 16 World Championships through 2010, and Olson's championship was the only victory of that bunch to feature collegiate players.

For many years, Olson kept the gold medal on display in his office at McKale Center. "It's really a source of pride for anyone on that team or anyone on that coaching staff," Olson said in 2008. "At the time, it didn't seem like that big of a deal, but as it's gone on, why, it's a tremendous accomplishment."

The U.S. team featured Arizona's Sean Elliott and Steve Kerr (who suffered a knee injury in the semifinal game that would force him to miss the 1986–87 college season), as well as Navy seven-footer David Robinson, Syracuse forward Rony Seikaly, and North Carolina guard Kenny Smith, who scored 23 points in an 87–85 win over the Soviet Union in the championship game.

"That was the greatest Russian team they ever had," Newell said. "Lute took these young college kids over there and beat them. It's another testimony to how great a coach he was."

Olson was considered a favorite to coach Team USA in the 1992 Olympics, but the rules changed to allow professional players. With that, "the Dream Team" was born, and an NBA coach—Chuck Daly—was selected to lead Michael, Magic, Larry, and the rest. Though Olson was denied that Olympic opportunity, the 1997 national championship cemented his basketball legacy.

As it turned out, he couldn't be at the 2002 induction ceremonies because of a personal conflict: his son Steve's wedding in Italy. In absentia, Olson delivered a taped message thanking family and a multitude of coaches, players, assistants, and athletic directors before finishing with heartfelt words for Bobbi, who had been his wife of 47 years. "She is truly the Hall of Famer in our family," Olson said in the message. "I married Bobbi when she was 18, before she was old enough to know what she was getting into. Like she loved saying, I chased her until she couldn't run anymore, and she finally agreed to marry me....

"Bobbi was the real head coach, the No. 1 recruiter, and the team mom. Every player who has ever played for me knows these things to be true. Bobbi was my inspiration, my No. 1 supporter, my true love and my very best friend....

"I know she is looking down on this very special occasion, and I also know she is loving every single minute of it."

No surprise, then, that Lute became a household name in southern Arizona. In fact, he was bigger than life as far as basketball was concerned. Heck, many fans thought he could walk on water. Eventually, there were bobblehead dolls, Lute Lids (replicas of his hair), a *Tonight Show* appearance, and Nike junkets to coach overseas. Then there was the world championship in 1986. All of them the rewards of success.

In his second year, the Wildcats tied for third in the Pac-10 and made it to the NCAA Tournament. In his third year, Arizona won its first conference title.

"Lute was a success right from the beginning, but when things really took off was when he started beating the likes of the

Michigans and Iowas and Dukes and UNLVs," former UA coach Bruce Larson said in *Fire in the Desert.* "That was a whole new ballgame..."

It was all ramped up in 1988 when—then in his fifth season—UA went to its first Final Four. It was unheard-of territory for dusty Tucson. "That 1988 team, with all the talent we had in going to the Final Four, I personally believe that was the best team to come through there to this point," said former UA player Jud Buechler, a member of that team. "I feel [we were] even better than the one that won the national championship. Just look at the talent." Steve Kerr, Sean Elliott, Tom Tolbert, Buechler, Kenny Lofton, Craig McMillan and the rest. It was a joyride to a 35–3 record, Arizona's all-time best in the modern era. "More importantly," Buechler said, "it was the team that started the basketball craze at UA. From that point on it changed from being a football school to all of a sudden being a basketball school. I'm proud to be part of that team."

Credit Olson for building it. If Fred Snowden was the man who benefitted from McKale Center being built in the early 1970s, it was Olson who set the foundation for the program's success. He wanted to not just build a team, he'd say, but to build a program. And for years, Arizona was the team to beat in the Pac-10, taking over the throne from UCLA in the late 1980s through the 2000s. He led UA to 11 Pac-10 titles, four Final Fours, a national-runner-up finish (2001), and a national title, in 1997.

"Once we got the recruits like Sean Elliott and Steve Kerr and others we could do things like that," Olson said. "What we did was we got people excited about the Cats. People couldn't get tickets, and that helped in recruiting because we'd tell them they were never going to play in front of an empty seat in McKale Center. That's what they want to hear."

It was that potential that brought players such as Buechler to Arizona. And it was Olson's ability to turn players ordinary and superb into NBA picks. He had 31 go on to the pros during his tenure at Arizona and he coached 19 All-Americans during that span. He had 20 consecutive 20-win seasons, averaging just more than 25 wins a season. He is one of just three head coaches in NCAA history to have 29 or more 20-win seasons.

Richard Jefferson, in a tribute to the coach, reminded everyone that Olson went "to the Final Four the year I was born [1980]." How's that for perspective? Jefferson said Olson helped him grow into a man, making him accountable for all he did. Heck, one night in Las Vegas, Jefferson was even sent home after being caught messing around in a hotel hallway. "He speaks to you as a man and expects the same in return," Jefferson wrote. "It makes the growing-up process so much easier."

The same could be said for on the court, too. "He teaches you how to give up yourself so you are not so self-centered and he makes you understand that it's all about team," Jefferson wrote. "He makes that transition so easy. I think there are a lot of coaches that are very similar to him in the sense that they give an opportunity. Coach O gives you the tools to be successful. Whether or not you decide to use them is up to you."

Muehlebach described his time at UA as "the best four years of my life." Others have said the same. The magic and the memories—and, of course, the winning—helped all that. "He's the reason why I went to Arizona," said Buechler, who visited UCLA, California, Pepperdine, and Santa Barbara. "My last visit was UA. He's the reason why I went. I thought I'd be able to develop under him. I saw him as this father figure. For all of us, he's the one who took us in and developed us. The fundamentals I learned from him 100 percent paid off after playing for the University of Arizona."

Again, everything came down to fundamentals and good players. "It was great working with Coach O," said former assistant Phil Johnson, who left to coach at San Jose State and is now an assistant at the University of Texas at El Paso. "He expected us all to recruit great players that were good people and then get them better. Our teams were always very determined to win, and that's a reflection on Lute. One thing I really noticed when I first got to Arizona was how good the practices were the day after we lost a game. Coach O, the players, really everyone wasn't going to stand for losing!"

And that hard work was how the players got better. Of course, not every day or game was easy. Players who want to get better know that. "Lute was a great challenge! He pushed us every day to get better," said Matt Othick. "He would take your weaknesses and build them into strengths. He was a superior basketball coach. He was a winner who prepared you for a game better than anyone. When you walked on the floor you always felt like you were going to win."

In the end, his age—and health—created problems. In 2005 he was 69 and would have been—at the time—the oldest coach to guide a team to the Final Four. He was just moments away, a shot away after Illinois beat UA, 90–89, in overtime. Three years later, he abruptly announced his retirement in 2008 after a tumultuous year of health and eventual NCAA issues.

Olson feels he could have coached longer. "If I had not had the stroke where I was told by my doctor to get out of coaching and that kind of pressure," he said. "Before the stroke I figured I had a chance to coach into my seventies. My health had been good. I enjoyed working with the kids."

After coaching, Olson is still around and seemingly busier than ever, attending games and events to help UA and its alumni group. Invariably, the players continue to rave about him. If he's not at a wedding for one of his players (he was at Luke Walton's recently) or a fishing trip (with Craig McMillan and others) or a roast in his honor (Tom Tolbert was a recent guest speaker), he's around. Olson is seemingly everywhere.

"There are not enough words, paragraphs, or pages to tell you what Coach Olson means to me," said former player and current

Memphis coach Josh Pastner. "I wouldn't be where I am today if it were not for him." Simply put, his former players love him.

"That makes me feel great," Olson said. "I feel the same way toward them."

2 National Championship

Lute Olson figured it was Arizona giving the 47,000-plus fans in the RCA Dome their money's worth. Why not have overtime? Why not have them—and a national television audience—on the edge of their seats awaiting the 1997 NCAA champion? Yes, he was joking, but that's exactly what happened on March 31, 1997, when Arizona won its first—and only—NCAA title. Arizona did it with grit and determination, staving off defending champion Kentucky in overtime, 84–79.

"What I remember the most is just how tough our team was," said Miles Simon, the team's leader and Most Outstanding Player of the Final Four. "I remember Coach telling us in the huddle that the toughest team is going to win the game. He left it at that and let us take over as players in the overtime."

Arizona didn't score a basket in OT, but instead hit 10 free throws to get the win. "What overtime did was show our aggressiveness," Olson said. "We were going to take it to the basket. We were going to make them try to stop us." Kentucky couldn't. By the time Kentucky had hit its fifth point in OT the game was over. Arizona had done the improbable, becoming the first—and only team since—to beat three No. 1 seeds en route to the title. And all of them were blue bloods of the college basketball world.

Kansas? Gone in the Sweet 16. North Carolina? Bye-bye in the semifinals. And, then Kentucky, the program Olson had shunned a decade earlier when it came asking if he'd be its coach, was dispatched in the finals.

"They had to do it the hard way," Olson said. "No one expected them to be in the Final Four, but I felt they had gotten things together [late], so they could have taken on anybody." And they did—outlasting all comers.

Coach Lute Olson and the Arizona Wildcats celebrate their national championship victory over Kentucky.

Olson said what he noticed in overtime was Kentucky was spent physically in trying to keep up with smaller, quicker Arizona. And yes, he said the tougher team would win. "I knew who that [team] was," Olson said, "and I think they knew who that was, so this thing was as good as over."

Behind freshman guard Mike Bibby, Simon, Michael Dickerson, A.J. Bramlett, Bennett Davison, and the rest, UA played some of its best basketball of the season at the right time, defying logic for a team that lost its final two games of the regular season in the Bay Area. The team played well that weekend but still lost. Frustrated to be sure, that it couldn't win, that weekend gave UA hope that if it could play well for the next three weeks it would do well.

Of course, no one said it would be easy. Being down 10 points to slower, methodical South Alabama in the first round of the NCAA Tournament gave the Wildcats a huge scare. But UA went on a 22–4 run behind Jason Terry and Simon, including a 17–0 burst. "We showed a lot of heart," Simon said back then.

UA put an end to College of Charleston's 23-game winning streak with a 73–69 victory in round two. Simon had 20 points and Bibby had 18. Four Cats were in double figures.

Then the game of a lifetime came against No. 1 Kansas, a team that went into the matchup 34–1 overall. UA was a 10-point underdog according to oddsmakers, but that word alone—underdog—was what fueled Arizona players. There was no way UA was going to play into expectations. Olson remembered that Dickerson had asked, incredulously, "Us the underdogs?"

Still, Arizona would have to play well. Terry said UA would "have to play the perfect game." It nearly did, pulling off an 85–82 win behind Bibby's 21 points and Dickerson's 20. It had to survive a last-second three-point attempt by Raef LaFrentz to get the party started. Bibby was huge, playing beyond his years. He hit two free throws with UA up 83–82 with 18.1 seconds left. It set up LaFrentz's eventual miss.

"They said we had no chance," Bramlett said. "But we knew in our hearts that we could do it."

A week later UA defeated North Carolina for the second time in the 1997–98 season, setting up the meeting with Kentucky. "Everybody played their role," Simon said. "In today's game you see guys trying to do things they can't do. We were all willing to sacrifice for the betterment of the team and that's why we won."

He also said Olson just let the guys play. "We didn't run any plays. We had smart guys who knew how to play basketball. And we learned from Coach [Jim] Rosborough, Jessie Evans, Phil Johnson, and Coach Olson. The fundamentals we learned every day helped. I can see why it paid off in the game."

Olson joked that he wasn't sure if Arizona was going to make the tip-off. As was usually the case, the affable Jason Stewart, a religious type, said a prayer in the huddle before the game. "Once he gets going it's pretty hard to stop him," Olson joked. Then Arizona stopped Kentucky for the title.

Sixteen years later the team celebrated a reunion at the Fox Theatre in downtown Tucson. "It was great to see everyone," said Olson, who hadn't watched the game in its entirety until that night.

"Everybody obviously has a positive memory from winning the game," Simon said the night of the reunion. "The memories and emotions that were brought up in watching the game, and seeing my teammates, and how hard they were fighting and how each member of the coaching staff was pulling for each other...I think that's the memory that lasts longer than watching the game."

Tucson mayor Jonathan Rothschild did him one better, calling it "probably the greatest moment in Tucson sports history."

3 Sean Elliott: UA's Best

There's Sean Elliott and, well, nobody else when it comes to the best players who have suited up at the University of Arizona. Or, at least, there is a big gap between the No. 1 and No. 2. And No. 2? Well, that's up for debate. But when you help put a program—Arizona—on the map and are long considered Tucson's and UA's favorite son, No. 1 is hard to argue.

"He's the best all-around player we have ever had at Arizona, in my opinion," former Arizona coach Lute Olson said of Elliott. "He was a great passer, rebounder, penetrator, and he could hit the outside shot. About 60 percent of Anthony Cook's points came off an assist from Sean because Sean would draw the opponent's big guy to him. Sean would then find Anthony."

It was hardly luck in how Arizona found Sean in the early 1980s, the skinny kid with the knee brace. He attended what was then the first Lute Olson Basketball Camp, the summers before his sophomore and junior years at Cholla High School.

"Scott Thompson and I had this conversation and Scott said, 'We need to keep an eye on that kid. He could end up pretty good,'" Olson recalled. "Then he went to the five-star camp in Pittsburgh. I had suggested to him that once he got done with that camp he should get a copy of a good weight-training program. He did, once he got back. His mom thought it was such a good idea that she went through it with him. It was obvious that as he gained strength he was going to be something else."

Special would be the word. Elliott became UA's first—and only—player to lead the team in scoring for four consecutive years, finishing as the top scorer in school and Pac-10 Conference history. He ended his collegiate career with 2,555 points, shattering former

UCLA great Lew Alcindor's record. He was a two-time all-conference player of the year and a consensus All-American, winning the Wooden Award in 1989. And he still has an impact on the program.

"He was a terrific player and he was here for four years. When you look at the history of the four years, with the team winning and what he did individually, you can make the case he's the greatest player to ever play here," Arizona coach Sean Miller said.

"Then when you see the type of person he is, he and guys like Steve Kerr mean so much to where we are now because of the word identity. You think of Sean Elliott, you think Arizona. You see how well he's done since he left Arizona. It reflects well on our players and program."

Elliott was the first Arizona player to score 700 points in a season, doing it twice (1988, 1989). He's third in scoring average with 19.2 points per game and first in field goals (892) and free throws (623). He was clutch and consistent. All of that from a young local product who had just a handful of early offers, including UTEP and Arizona State.

"He was fantastic," said former Arizona teammate Tom Tolbert. "When we needed a basket, he was our go-to guy. He could create his own shot. He was the man and was as good as anyone out there. In my mind, we always had the best player on the court. When we were out there I'd think, *Man, I'm glad he's playing for us.*"

He was named a McDonald's All-American in his senior year, but wasn't able to play in the game after getting severely cut when his hand went through a glass window at home. "It was severe, but had he cut his hand in a different place, who knows [what would have happened]?" Olson said.

What would have happened had he not gone to Arizona? "I don't know, but we were not *not* going to get him," Olson said. "The only kid that really got out of [Tucson] was Fat Lever, when [Fred] Snowden was here."

Good-Bye, Lew

The tie came on a layup that gave Arizona a huge 77–44 lead over the visiting UCLA Bruins. Of course, it had to be the Bruins—the team that Lew Alcindor played for in the 1960s before going on to professional greatness (as, of course, Kareem Abdul-Jabbar).

With that layup, Arizona All-American Sean Elliott tied the Pac-10 record for career points: Alcindor's mark of 2,325.

The crowd counted down every point, and the scoreboard gave a countdown as Elliott closed in on the final 10. The record was his alone when he made a free throw. He made another basket—with 7:10 left in the blowout—and wasn't seen again in the game. His work was done as Arizona routed the Bruins 102–64. In fact, the score still stands as Arizona's biggest victory ever over the Bruins. At the time, it was also UCLA's all-time worst defeat.

"I had a fantasy that I would drive down the lane and stuff the ball [to clinch the record]," Elliott told reporters that day. No matter; a dream came true anyway. Tucson's favorite son had broken a prestigious record that had held strong for nearly two decades.

It took Elliott 123 games in four seasons. Alcindor needed 90 games (freshmen were not eligible to play during Alcindor's time). "I don't care if they put an asterisk by my name or not," Elliott said. "It's still the top one on the list."

And a painful one for the Bruins to watch. So painful were Elliott's points that UCLA's Pooh Richardson told Elliott to "stop shooting." Elliott couldn't. He needed 34 points to break the record and, well, finished with 35. "I've known Pooh for a while, and he's not a bad guy," Elliott said after the game. "I guess he didn't know what was going on. He said: 'Quit shooting!' And I said, 'But I have to!'"

And with it, he made a name for himself. The week of the game, a *Tucson Citizen* reporter reached Abdul-Jabbar to get his thoughts on the possibility the record could be broken. It was news to Abdul-Jabbar. "Who is Sean Elliott?" Alcindor said. On February 18, 1989, he found out.

Keeping Elliott at Arizona was another thing. After a fabulous junior year—one in which he led UA to its first Final Four appearance—Elliott contemplated jumping to the NBA. He was a finalist for the Wooden Award, and the night before the banquet Olson and Elliott went to a Los Angeles Lakers–Detroit Pistons game. "I got us seats right down basically under the basket for one reason:

to see how physical it was," Olson said. "You know how physical Detroit was back then. When we were ready to leave, he said, 'I'm not ready for this yet.' That sort of ended his thoughts about coming out. He realized he had to work on his body."

Elliott went on to win the Wooden Award a year later. A few weeks later, he had another accident. A month after his senior year in 1989, Elliott and Cook were test-driving a car in Tucson—a 1988 Mustang GT—when they failed to make a turn, eventually rolling the car on the side of the road. It reportedly came to a rest on its top. Both were wearing seat belts, preventing major injuries.

Two months later, he was the No. 3 pick in the NBA Draft, going to the San Antonio Spurs. Good things happen to good guys. And Elliott has long been considered a good guy with a big smile.

"Sean reminds me a lot of Tim Duncan," former Arizona and Spurs teammate Steve Kerr said in *Tales of the Arizona Hardwood.* "The two stand out to me because they are great people. They have a rare combination of unbelievable talent and humility. Most people who are that skilled tend to be flamboyant or self-possessed and a bit selfish. For Sean to be that humble and that good is unbelievable. To be college player of the year and be as accommodating and so soft-spoken yet fun is just awesome."

Tucson and the Arizona faithful will always feel that way about Elliott, who matriculated at nearby Cholla High, where they've retired his jersey. He entered school at 5'11", grew to 6'1", then 6'5", then 6'7". In 2000, the *Tucson Citizen* named him Tucson's best athlete of the 20th century. "I played [basketball] for fun," Elliott told the *Citizen.* "I loved to play. I never thought about growing up and becoming famous."

In August 1999, Elliott became even more inspiring when he became the first professional player in a major sport to have an organ transplant, receiving a kidney donated from his brother Noel. It came just three months after hitting the "Memorial Day

Miracle"—a 24-footer in the game's final seconds—that helped the Spurs win their first NBA title.

"Had he needed me to donate a kidney, I would have," Cook told the *Citizen* in 1999. "I'm sure all of Tucson would have helped. He put Tucson and UA on the map. You know, he's like their son."

Months later, Elliott was back on the court, helping the Spurs vie for the title again. He played in 71 more games—spanning two seasons—after the surgery. "It has been almost two years. I think people have forgotten about the transplant," Elliott told the *Orlando Sentinel* in 2001. "That's what I set out to accomplish, to become another player like everybody else...and to show people that you can be complete."

He retired as a player in 2001. Today he is the Spurs' radio color analyst, and also works as a college basketball analyst.

4 Sean Miller: UA's Savior

He's been called the right coach at the right time. Sean Miller has come onto the scene at the University of Arizona and done what Lute Olson did before him: succeed. "He was the perfect choice," said former Arizona State turned broadcaster Bill Frieder. "He recognized the culture of Arizona and has built on it. He's done a great job and has put it all together."

Today, Arizona is seeing the results of it all. Miller is 129–48 at Arizona and winner of two Pac-12 Conference titles. There have been the two Elite Eights—each one basket short of a Final Four berth. The most recent was in March 2014 in Anaheim. "It could have gone either way," Miller said of the team's 64–63 overtime loss to Wisconsin. "Obviously, it's disappointing when it doesn't go your way."

But everything else seemingly has since he came on at UA. Initially he had second thoughts after saying yes to the job. Eventually, he called it an "opportunity of a lifetime" to come to a place where winning a national title is a reality.

"We had a blueprint at Xavier that I felt really worked," Miller told the *Los Angeles Times.* "I wanted to bring that to a place like

Sean Miller has added a spark to Arizona basketball.

Arizona, where you had so many things that very few places have." Winning. Tradition. And, well, a national championship, won in 1997, a dozen years before.

"To be in charge of a new era of Arizona basketball and to build this program toward winning a national championship again is where my heart is," Miller said the day of his hiring. "I look forward to this new day in my family's life in Tucson."

Nothing has seemingly changed. He's already turned down a wooing from Maryland. And he has Arizona on solid ground after reaching the Sweet 16 in three of his five years at Arizona. All great runs to be sure.

"I wouldn't want anybody else in college basketball to be our coach," said UA athletic director Greg Byrne. "The process he implemented five years ago to get [us] to where we are today, where he's developed the team and coached the young men and how he's always focused on academics. He's impacted the lives of our student athletes in so many positive ways. He does a wonderful job."

And the players swear by him. He's tough. He's demanding. He makes players better. "He's obviously one of the greatest coaches in college basketball," junior guard T.J. McConnell said. "The sky is the limit for him. He'll continue to bring in the best recruits and be one of the top coaches in the country. I have no worries about him."

Why would anyone worry? "I think Sean Miller is one of the elite coaches in the game and it would not surprise me to see him win multiple national championships at Arizona," said former UA player Josh Pastner, now the head coach at the University of Memphis. "Or at least go to multiple Final Fours as Arizona's coach. He's that good. He's an elite guy as a recruiter."

Indeed, his recruiting classes have been superb, finishing in the top five in four consecutive years. Arizona should be in the hunt for a conference title, as well as a national title, every year.

"What he brings is a fire to win," said Bill Raftery, a Fox Sports college basketball analyst. "And it's a fire to win with style. Sean is a very competitive person and he coaches with that competitiveness very well."

Miller has led UA to record-setting performances, including 21 consecutive wins in 2013–14. The Wildcats were also the No. 1 team in the country for a school-record eight consecutive weeks.

"He's done a fantastic job," former Arizona coach Lute Olson said. "He's out seeing kids and key players [in recruiting]. It's fine to have assistants out there, but the kids want to see the head coach."

And they want to see the head coach and the program do well. Miller has done just that, and is poised for more as he begins season No. 6 with Arizona in 2014.

"It doesn't mean that next January things are going to be working out," Miller said. "With so much turnover in college basketball you really move in these one-week, one-month periods of time. When you do that it gets you to where you want to go a little easier."

When Miller, 45, arrived on Arizona's campus as the school's new head coach he likely dreamed of the success, the Final Four possibilities, and a national championship. Yet he also thought pragmatically. "I didn't know how it was going to work," he said. "A lot of people talk about having a three-year plan or five-year plan, but I was just hoping I wasn't going to be fired. I was hoping I'd be here in my fifth year or sixth year.

"There's bad luck in recruiting and not being able to recruit at the level you'd hope. I've been thankful I've been able to get both feet on the ground here. What I really hope is that we have a foundation that is really strong and that we are built for the future."

He's done that by going back to the past. He instituted the slogan "A Player's Program," which embraces the history of the program and invites former players to be part of the current success.

"Sean Miller has done something I thought was impossible," said former UA player Corey Williams, now a broadcaster. "I don't think anyone—and I say this with respect—could come in and have the success he's had, the success that Lute had. But he's made people forget about Lute Olson. But Sean has equaled Coach Olson's level."

Williams said he thought it would take at least 15 years before Arizona recovered from Olson's retirement. So much so Williams would talk with former players and wonder what would happen. "I thought we'd wander in the desert for 10 years before we found a coach, until Coach Olson was way in the distance," Williams said. "But [Miller has] been great, and I thank him for including us from the past. I never thought all this would happen."

It's never easy replacing a legend, but, in reality, Miller didn't do that. By the time of his arrival, UA already had gone through two seasons of interim head coaches with Kevin O'Neill and Russ Pennell/Mike Dunlap.

"You don't know how difficult it is to replace a legend," said Bill Walton, a college basketball analyst. But to see this crowd [at McKale Center], this loyalty, and the fans come here and do what they do is amazing. Lute built it [and] it's about sustainability. Lute did it for nearly 30 years. And now it's being done again. What Sean has done is absolutely remarkable, and in such a short time."

Former UA player George Rountree (1952–55), a frequent observer of UA in Tucson and on the road, said Miller is a "superior coach and a superior person. He's done a tremendous job."

Bob Elliott, second on the school's all-time scoring list, said, "I like what I see—and not just on the court but off of it. Sean's record not just here but at Xavier is what needs to happen: he's graduating players."

Bob Elliott also lauds Miller's "A Player's Program" philosophy because of what it emphasizes: "traditions and the program. He has said he wants the former players to have pride in our program. What he's doing right now is paving more asphalt on that road.

"Freddie [Snowden] paved some. Lute Olson has paved some. And now Sean is paving some. That's when and how you get a program that is nationally recognized."

Two deep runs in the NCAA Tournament and countless successes later, Byrne said: "[Miller] is one of the best inheritances anybody has ever made. Sean is the epitome of the modern basketball coach. He cares about the kids academically. The compliance people love working with him and his staff. He's relentless in recruiting and is a tremendous floor coach. And, on top of all that, he's a really good guy.

"Whatever Sean Miller would decide to do, he'd be very good at it," Byrne added. "He'd work hard at it." Today he works hard at guiding UA's program to future greatness, and its success seems assured.

5 NCAA Runners-up

The Wildcats entered the 2000–01 season as the No. 1 team in the country. Only once before in school history had that happened, in the 1997–98 season.

Arizona was loaded, a season removed from being the No. 1 seed in the NCAA Tournament, only to fall to Wisconsin in the second round. In 2000–01, UA was more prepared. And a healthy Loren Woods was back, although he had been declared ineligible for the season's first few games after taking money from a friend, something the NCAA deemed inappropriate.

But here was the starting lineup: sophomore Gilbert Arenas, sophomore Jason Gardner, junior Michael Wright, junior Richard Jefferson, sophomore Luke Walton, and senior Woods (or variations of it). Seniors Gene Edgerson and Justin Wessel came off the bench. "That was a very good team," Edgerson said. "There's no question we had a lot of talent."

Yet it was a tough road all season. First there was the suspension of Woods. Then came the death of Lute Olson's beloved wife of 47 years, Bobbi, on January 1, 2001. She passed away just a week after he had asked for time away to be with her. Arizona faithful knew something was very, very wrong the night after Arizona defeated Butler 72–60 in the first round of the Fiesta Bowl Classic. Olson was withdrawn and melancholy as he walked up the ramp to his car—a walk he had taken with his wife after games seemingly hundreds of times. A somber Olson said to a reporter, "Take care and happy holiday." Olson never—rarely ever—got emotional or sentimental. He did that night.

The rest of the season was unofficially dedicated to Bobbi. "We didn't want to let him down by losing," said Edgerson. "We wanted to play despite the situation. We didn't want to make it more stressful—especially when he was dealing with this horrible situation. We had his back. We played our butts off and got to the championship game. We lost, but we worked hard to get there."

Arizona won 20 of 23 during that stretch. A win in the title game would have secured Olson a place in history as the oldest coach in NCAA men's basketball history to win a title; he was 66 at the time. Arizona had already beaten two No. 1 seeds to get to the final, making it five consecutive wins over No. 1 opponents in its two trips to the championship over two seasons. UA could have equaled its record or knocking off three No. 1 teams en route to a title.

Against No. 1 Duke—in a matchup that was seemingly scripted from the beginning—Arizona won the opening tip and scored the first points behind Richard Jefferson. Arizona held the lead early.

CBS announcer Billy Packer sounded a bit surprised that UA was handling Duke so easily offensively. No other team had done that in the tournament. What's more, Arizona was doing it without a completely healthy Arenas (he was about 50 percent because of a shoulder injury). Likewise, Walton was suffering with a hand injury. "Gilbert was hurting and couldn't do much with that hurt clavicle," Olson said. "And Luke was injured and was limited."

Yet Arizona held Duke to 31 percent from the floor in the first 10 minutes. Duke didn't get a lead until 18–17 with 9:28 left in the half. Then the Blue Devils started to roll, going up 20–17. Still, no team had a lead to be proud of in the first 30 minutes.

With about six minutes left in the opening half, Packer said he felt the crowd was showing its displeasure because it felt Duke was getting all the calls—just as it had two days earlier in its comeback win against Maryland. The boos came streaming down with about four minutes left when Shane Battier blocked a Loren Woods shot and appeared to foul him. Nothing was called. Packer said the crowd booing "was a repercussion of the Duke program, where they've seen enough from the officials that give Duke the break. I've never seen this before in a basketball game."

His broadcasting partner, Jim Nantz, playing devil's advocate, said that maybe there were more Arizona fans in the building and they were showing their displeasure. "I'm not buying that one," Packer said. "It's Arizona-Duke and the neutrals are going one direction."

It sure seemed that way midway through the game and still very close. At midcourt, Gardner beat Jay Williams to a loose ball, and Williams all but fell over Gardner. It would have been Williams' third foul, but the only people in the building who didn't think it was a foul were the referees.

Olson said that play "turned the game around." Had Williams been called for his third foul, "I feel certain that would have made a tremendous difference in the outcome of the game." Williams, too, wasn't having a great game. He finished 5 for 15 and 16 points.

All that said, UA's Woods was spectacular in a matchup Duke couldn't meet. But he couldn't get the ball—or Arizona couldn't get him the ball—for a big five-minute stretch, enabling Duke to get out to a 61–52 lead with 8:30 left. Woods finished with a game-high 22 points and 11 rebounds.

Afterward, Arizona just couldn't recover. The Cats, which had shot at or above 50 percent in five consecutive NCAA games, was 28-for-71 from the floor, including a horrible 4-for-22 behind the three-point line. Arizona's dynamic duo of Gardner (2-for-11) and Arenas (4-for-17) were a combined 6-for-28 from the floor and 0-for-12 on three-pointers.

To this day, many Cats—including Olson—play the "what-if" game, wondering how a healthy Arenas would have done, and how a healthy Walton would have helped.

"I dislike Duke for many reasons, and 10 years after the fact I'm still not over it," Wessell told ESPN.com in 2011 on the 10-year anniversary of the meeting. "I dislike the Blue Devils because they robbed me of helping Lute Olson attain his well-deserved second national championship ring. They robbed my teammate, Loren Woods, from claiming redemption for what the NCAA unfairly did to him earlier in the season.

"They robbed John Ash, Eugene Edgerson, and myself of being the only three players in the storied history of Arizona basketball with two national championship rings. They robbed me of getting to stand at midcourt as a national champion and point to the heavens toward my high school coach, who had just passed away the week before."

Arizona had been tough and resilient all season. It just came up short on that day. It's still one of the toughest defeats Olson has ever been through. "All the emotions they had to go through, and they withstood them and did a great job to get to the final game," Olson said after the loss. "It's tough. Someone's got to lose it. Duke is deserving. We gave them a good run and couldn't get it done."

After the game—and while the media was doing its interviews—Olson did something he hadn't done in some time. He didn't leave the room before shaking the hands of Jefferson, Woods, Arenas, and Wright, saying thank you to each for his effort and for a great game. "We'd lost a basketball game, but as a coach I don't know that I'd ever been more proud of a team," Olson writes in his autobiography. "The team had been on an unexpected and difficult ride, too."

A week later, Wright, Jefferson, and Arenas all declared for the NBA Draft. Gardner did, as well, later, only to come back for the final two years of his collegiate career.

6 1988 Final Four Team

They are like Arizona basketball's firstborn—the 1988 men's basketball team. The first Wildcats team to ever get to a Final Four. Memories of great times and moments always come from Arizona making its way to Kansas City in late March for its chance at a national championship.

"It was like the Arizona fans and our team knew that it was going to be a special year," said former UA player Matt Muehlebach in a FoxSportsArizona.com story. "I remember Steve [Kerr] leading our team out for layups. At some point before the game started, I remember him pausing and sort of smiling and acknowledging the crowd, almost like a baseball player would doff his cap at the All-Star Game introductions. It was almost like he was saying, 'This is going to be a good year.'"

The magic all started on November 27, 1987, when UA traveled to Anchorage, Alaska, to play in the annual Great Alaska

Shootout. Arizona was all but a blip in the minds of college basketball's so-called experts. It entered the season ranked 17th in the Associated Press poll and 10th in the United Press International poll. Arizona beat Duquesne, Michigan, and then Syracuse for the tournament title. "That was a great team and one that gave us the national exposure," coach Lute Olson said. By the time the tournament was over, UA was No. 9 in the AP poll.

"People were looking at us to get beat," the team's star, Sean Elliott, told the *Washington Post*, "and prove that beating Michigan and Syracuse was just a fluke."

The love affair was official. After an emotion-filled trip to Olson's old school (Iowa), Arizona was No. 1 for the first time in its history. After the game, Olson admitted there were so many emotions in his return that he was afraid his team wouldn't be composed or ready. But it was, and it beat the Hawkeyes 66–59 on their home court. "I didn't fool them for a second," Olson told the media after the game. "I think they knew maybe this was a game their old coach wanted to win more than some others."

Arizona proceeded to win five more games and ended 1987 as the No. 1 team in the polls. Then on January 2, 1988, Arizona went into New Mexico and lost 61–59 in the Pit. The Wildcats struggled all night. Kerr went 3-for-10 from the three-point line. Elliott had 27 points, but it wasn't enough to get Arizona the win. UA had four shots in the final 42 seconds but missed every attempt.

Arizona quickly moved on. It won its next eight and returned to No. 1, only to lose to Stanford and Todd Lichti. Stanford, behind coach Mike Montgomery, seemingly always gave UA trouble. In fact, UA lost the four previous years to the Cardinal, in 1985, '86, '87, and '88.

But that Stanford loss seemed to fuel Arizona as it reeled off 15 consecutive wins. In fact, only one team came close during the streak: it was famed UCLA, coached by Walt Hazzard. Sean Elliott came to the rescue with a brilliant last-second shot to send the

Watch the "Wild About the Cats" Video

In the early months of 1988, nothing in Tucson was as popular as the Arizona Wildcats basketball team...unless it was the little rap ditty about the Arizona Wildcats basketball team.

The infectious song, "Wild About the Cats," can never be forgotten by anybody who lived in Tucson during that time. It was, according to a newspaper account from back in the day, the most requested song for at least two weeks on popular KRQ-FM, the station that helped produce the song and its accompanying video.

The song largely disappeared from public view for many years, but an audio recording popped up on the Internet several years ago, and the video finally made its way to YouTube. A search for "Wild About the Cats" will do the trick.

More than 25 years later, the nostalgia value is off the charts—and the game highlights in the video are treasures. The music and the lyrics don't hold up as well, although it's very much in the style of the time, reminiscent of the Chicago Bears' famous "Super Bowl Shuffle" from a few years earlier.

Coach Lute Olson, in his book, writes, "While a critic commented, 'It's not exactly a masterpiece; or, for that matter, a minorpiece,' the city loved it."

Most of all, it showed just how much fun these guys were having on their way to the Final Four.

The song begins:

W-I-L-D Cats
W-I-L-D Wildcats
W-I-L-D Cats
We're wild about the Cats

KRQ's star DJ Mike Elliot brought in guard Harvey Mason Jr., the son of famous jazz drummer Harvey Mason Sr., to the station on a couple of occasions and suggested collaborating on a song about the team.

"About that time, there was a lot of Super Bowl shuffling going on," said Mason, who would go on to win multiple Grammy awards. "It was his idea, and I knew I would do it. He wrote most of the rap lyrics for the guys; I did the music and the chorus."

The song begins with vocals from a few of KRQ's on-air talent, and then we hear from the Wildcats. Jud Buechler. Sean Elliott. Steve Kerr. Tom Tolbert. Matt Muehlebach. Sean Rooks. Kenny Lofton. Craig McMillan. Joe Turner. Craig Bergman. Mason.

The prominent players got the best—and the cheesiest—speaking parts. After a set-up line, the player would rap the final words, like this:

When Craig McMillan is in the game, he makes the offense flow.
I better find the open man, and get the ball down low.

Or this:

Elliott's here, it's time to play.
They want me in the NBA.

Or this:

Give Kerr the ball, give Kerr a hand.
I'll drill it in from three-point laaa-aaand.

The song also functioned as a public-service announcement, with a couple of anti-drug references. *"Ask anyone and you will find / We don't do drugs, they wreck your mind."*

One regret is that the team didn't get Coach Olson into the studio. But the best part might have come later, during the celebration of the team at Arizona Stadium after the Final Four loss to Oklahoma.

"We had the parade and they played the song," Mason said. "We all did our part, and when it came to Coach's part, he started to do this crazy little dance. It was so fun. It was a day I'll never forget. It was like Lute Olson's version of the robot. Unbelievable. It's something that I'll never forget."

game into overtime. Arizona won in the extra period and earned its second Pac-10 title under Olson.

UA's average margin of victory in Pac-10 games that season was an astounding 24 points. "We really dominated opponents," Olson said. That streak continued through the NCAA Tournament when it beat Cornell by 40 (90–50), Seton Hall by 29 (84–55), Iowa by 20 (99–79), and North Carolina by 18 (70–52).

"That was the game [when] North Carolina coach Dean Smith said, 'Well, we came closer than anybody else because they only beat us by 18,'" Olson recalled. "That's how dominant that team was."

It was also rewarded. It was the first time—at least on the record—a team was allowed to catch up to Olson and mess up his hair. Sure, Bennett Davison did it on camera after UA won the national title in 1997, but it was 1988 that did it in the locker room. "The whole team came after me," Olson writes in his book. "It was, as everything had been that entire season, a team effort. If that's what they wanted to do, they had earned that right."

That Arizona squad had what few Arizona teams have had since: a major killer instinct. Elliott told the *Orange County Register* at the time, "We're not interested in playing close games." Years later, Kerr called the team "iconic." Tolbert said, "We had everything."

When it's all said and done, it's often said the 1988 team may have been Arizona's all-time best team. It was clearly one of the most talented. "It could have been. We had a great record of 35–3, and that would be pretty hard to make a case for anyone else," Olson said. "They walked through the schedule."

Unfortunately, Arizona's joyride ended with an 86–78 loss to Oklahoma, not helped by Kerr, who went a miserable un-Kerrlike 2-for-13 from the floor. "I think about that game all the time," said Kerr. "In fact, I'm thinking about the game right now."

"It doesn't seem that long ago," Olson said. "You coach team after team after team, so it goes quickly. You get done with a season and then the next one comes."

One thing is certain about the 1988 team—everyone has stayed very close friends. Most close teams do. "That's what's nice to see, because they are all still close friends," Olson said. "It was always a closely knit group. You knew at the time this was a special group because of the chemistry."

7 1994 Final Four: Stoudamire, Reeves Shine

In Reggie Geary's mind, Arizona's second Final Four run started about 10 months earlier, when UA went on a trip to Australia shortly after losing to Santa Clara in the 1993 NCAA Tournament. Gone were forward Chris Mills and center Ed Stokes. No longer did Arizona have its Tucson Skyline from years past. It was going to be "small ball," with a three-guard lineup—a lineup more out of necessity than anything else.

"Coach decided to put me in the starting lineup to see what it would look like, sliding me up from sixth man," Geary said. "Coach knew he had two explosive guards in Khalid [Reeves] and Damon [Stoudamire] so he wanted to see how my skill set would balance the team out."

Although he wasn't part of the team, Miles Simon said it showed just what an innovator Olson was in being one of the first to use a three-guard lineup. If UA hadn't been known as "Point Guard U" by then, it soon became so.

"[Olson] was ahead of his time as a coach," Simon said. "We didn't run any plays. We just had smart basketball players that knew how to play right away. The fundamentals we learned in practice every day—I can remember them now and see why they paid off in the game."

They certainly did in Australia, as UA prepared for what would be a glorious ride to the Final Four in Charlotte. "What I saw in that 1994 team at Arizona is what I just saw in UConn in 2014," said Corey Williams, now a sports broadcaster and a member of that 1994 UA team. "Guard play is key to any college basketball program. The guards are the extension of the coach, and if you don't have good guards and have the ability to run the coach's stuff, then it won't work."

And in 1994 it seemingly worked...a lot. UA went 9–1 in Australia behind its three-guard lineup. "And we did it against mostly professional teams [from Australia]," Geary said. "I think Coach O's vision after the trip had everyone on board, believing in the three-guard lineup. And the best part was, no one in the country knew what we had or how we were changing the game."

Arizona was so under the radar that it was picked to finish third in the Pac-10. After all, it was coming off its second consecutive first-round NCAA loss. But it helped to have standouts Reeves, Stoudamire, and a couple of undersized big men in Joseph Blair and Ray Owes. Arizona played fast and few teams could keep up. Arizona won its first eight games, then fell to No. 5 Kentucky on a last-second shot in Maui.

"After Kentucky, the doubt was gone," Olson said of playing tough teams. Despite the loss, that game gave UA hope—and inspiration.

"Those two are both NBA lottery picks," then Kentucky coach Rick Pitino said of Reeves and Stoudamire, "and I'm an NBA guy."

UA knew it could play with anybody behind the duo. They were quick. "That allowed us to do things defensively that we hadn't been able to do," Olson said. "This team could really get after people, pressure the ball, disrupt offense. They played defense better than any defense we had."

And offensively—yikes!—it was tough to stop UA's backcourt. Reeves and Stoudamire combined to average 42 points a game. As the late Al McGuire put it, "These guys are unstoppable one-on-one. Reeves can take anybody to the basket, and Stoudamire makes Arizona impossible to press."

So teams didn't—if they knew better. "No one could stay in front of Damon; no one could stay in front of Khalid," Williams recalled. "They created so much havoc that it made guys like us shine. That team was wide open."

Guys like Dylan Rigdon, Williams, and Joe McLean would be ready and waiting to hit shots. "We'd just wait for Damon to do his thing and either Joseph Blair would get a dunk or I'd get a wide-open three," Williams said. "The luxury of playing like that? You can't even put into words."

Still, not all was perfect. UA was just 6–3 in the conference in the first week in February, two games behind UCLA. After a loss to Washington, things didn't look great. It was then Olson issued a challenge to his team: they'd have to "run the table and get some help." UA did its part—until it fell to Arizona State in the regular-season finale. Still, UA held on and won the conference race.

Then the Wildcats exorcised the demons of previous first-round losses. UA beat Loyola Maryland 81–55. "I told [Olson] that first-round jinx was over," Stoudamire said, "and that we wouldn't have to answer those questions anymore."

Then came a big win against Virginia (71–58) and an even bigger win against Louisville (82–70), in which all five starters scored in double figures.

Arizona proceeded to hand No. 1 seed Missouri a 92–72 loss, and with that it was on its way to the Final Four in Charlotte to face Arkansas, the state university of former Arkansas governor and then-president Bill Clinton. When told Clinton was pulling for Arkansas, Blair was asked, "Are you a Democrat or Republican?" His response was simple: "Neither. I'm a basketball player."

In the end, Arkansas was too much for Arizona. The Razorbacks harassed Stoudamire, who went only 2-for-13. Likewise, Reeves missed all nine of his three-point attempts.

"For some reason, recognition for this team has been minimal until the 20-year anniversary," said Geary years later. "I hope this team is remembered for their teamwork and the passion we demonstrated every time we took the floor, for the great scoring combination of Damon and Khalid, and for Coach introducing the three-guard offense. In the end, I think it's one of the greats."

8 Steeeeeeeeeve Kerrrrrrrr

Steve Kerr is nowhere to be found on the school's all-time top 10 scoring list. (He's at No. 19.) He is, however, somewhere in the top three of Arizona's all-time greats.

If there was a player who was one of Arizona's favorite sons it's Kerr, the work-his-butt-off player who was so self-made that he became a five-time NBA champion. He could easily be placed on the school's Mount Rushmore of significant basketball figures along with Sean Elliott, Miles Simon, and Lute Olson.

Today, he's an NBA coach, recently named the head coach of the Golden State Warriors. He signed a five-year, $25 million contract. In his entire NBA career—unbelievable as it is to consider—he made $16 million.

"After he got the job he called and said, 'It's all unbelievable,'" said Olson, who had a front-row seat at Kerr's Warriors press conference. "It was 'I can't believe this is happening.... To have the career I had, to become a general manager of the Phoenix Suns, to become this broadcaster and now this.' He said he couldn't believe it."

How does this happen for a player who was lightly (if at all) recruited? For one thing, he worked hard toward becoming one of college basketball's all-time best shooters as part of one of Arizona's most memorable teams. "It has to do with the timing, and it being so new to our fans when Coach turned it around," Kerr said of his fame as a UA player. "I guess I'm part of the turnaround and helped symbolize the beginning of the program. Everyone was so excited about the program and it was so brand new. Sean was the star, and I got a lot of notoriety, too."

Undeniably Kerr, at 6'3", was a star, too. Late UA announcer Roger Sedlmayr made the phrase "Steeeeeeeeeve Kerrrrrrrr" as recognizable (if not more so) as "Luuuuutte." Even now, every time Kerr gets announced at a game or a function related to Arizona, he gets that type of call from the fans.

So how did the chant start? Sedlmayr first announced his name in such a way after three straight baskets against Arizona State "and it seemed all I was saying was Steve Kerr, but after a while I elongated it," he once said. "A game or two later the band caught on. A year later it was not only the band but it was everyone else."

That night against ASU, Kerr hit five of seven shots and the legend began. The game also came on the heels of his father being assassinated at the American Embassy in Beirut in mid-January 1984. That night, Arizona brought him in as a son.

To say Arizona fans love Kerr would be an understatement. But what many don't know is that his arrival at Arizona almost never happened. In fact, it was by accident that he ended up at UA at all. Olson, in his first months as Wildcats coach and in search of players, went to see Tom Lewis, a recruit he had been after as Iowa coach. On a Saturday morning, Olson had been scheduled to see Lewis play. But it was Kerr who caught his eye.

"I thought to myself, *The kid has a good feel for the game*," Olson said. "At that time, he shot the ball really low. He wasn't going to get that shot off in our league. After the game, I talked to the AAU coach who had him and said, 'Tell me a little bit about the Kerr kid.' And he said, 'Well, first of all, he has already graduated from high school and he's looking for a place where he can walk on.'"

Olson stayed another day to catch more of Kerr and later asked his high school coach more about the skinny kid with the unorthodox shot. "He said he was the best unrecognized player who has ever come through [the school], along with a kid named Kiki Vandeweghe [who eventually went to UCLA], who wasn't being recruited."

Olson arranged for an open gym so he could see Kerr play against better players. There Olson sat, along with wife, Bobbi, and, well, nobody else. "We watched for about an hour and a half and waved to him on the way out," Olson said. "On the way to the car, I said to Bobbi, 'What did you think?' And she said, 'You've got to be kidding me.'" It was one of the very few times that Bobbi was wrong.

A few months later Kerr was a Wildcat, getting a late call to come to Arizona. By that time, Kerr had accepted a scholarship to Cal State–Fullerton, but he hadn't signed. He made the decision having never visited the campus. Kerr said his most difficult thing to do at the time was to call the coaches there to tell them he had changed his mind. "I felt bad because I was reneging on the commitment, but it was obvious I made the right decision [in the end]," Kerr said. "But it was one of the hardest things I had to do."

He showed up a few months later and went on to do nothing less than have the career of a lifetime, become one of the school's favorite sons, and see his jersey retired. "When Steve had his jersey put up, he said, 'I would like to thank Mrs. O for her support, for always believing in me,'" Olson said with a smirk.

Kerr was unassuming for a Division I basketball player. He was skinny and undeveloped. Yet the first time his new teammates saw him they knew he was special. Harvey Mason said much of the tone of the team was set by Kerr, a strong leader, not just in basketball but in life. "That's a guy who does things the right way," Mason said. "You come in as an 18-year-old kid and you meet Lute Olson and think this man is amazing and expects so much. And then you have everything backed up from a guy like Steve, who is one of the best players. You learn a lesson from Coach Olson and then it's enforced by Steve."

Steve Kerr was a standout on some very good Cats teams before finding success in the NBA alongside Michael Jordan and the Chicago Bulls.

As Mason said, Kerr set the standard for his teammates for life. "We all expected a lot from each other, and I don't know about the other guys but I wanted to make my teammates proud," Mason said. "A lot of my motivation of what I do and what I've done is to make them proud, that I've done some good work."

9 Damon Stoudamire: Mighty Mouse

Damon Stoudamire will long be remembered for being one of the best all-time basketball players in Arizona history. There's never been a doubt about that. His teams finished with a 101–24 record in his four years at Arizona and the Wildcats made it to the Final Four in his junior year. But what was his legacy?

"I don't know what it is, to tell you the truth," said Stoudamire, the 5'10" guard who made UA fashionable in the backcourt alongside Khalid Reeves. "From a team standpoint I didn't play on any of the great teams. Decent ones though. I thought we may have underachieved. We didn't get out of the [NCAA Tournament] first round three out of four years. Yes, we got to the Final Four and not many have here. But on paper..."

As an individual, on paper, he was as good as any Arizona player in the last 20 years. He had the desire to win. By the end of his career, "Mighty Mouse" finished with 1,849 points (then third and now sixth) and 663 assists (then second, now third) on the school's all-time rolls.

He was a three-time All–Pac-10 Conference player, sharing conference player of the year honors with Ed O'Bannon in 1995, becoming only the third UA player to be named conference player of the year. "I'm happy with it," Stoudamire said at the time. "As long as no one thinks it's a sympathy vote or anything like that. I think I had just as good a year as Ed and he had as good a year as me. I guess this was the right way to handle it."

Not bad for an undersized guard who looked to attend Louisville before deciding on Arizona, which finally offered him a scholarship after he received his qualifying test score. "He called me once he got that test score," Olson said, and the coach was thankful he did. When Olson recruited Stoudamire he remembers seeing "a bug-on-the-water type" in his freshman year of high school.

Of all places, Olson first saw him work out at Long Beach State, where Olson had coached more than 10 years earlier. "He was quick, could shoot, and could penetrate," Olson said. "There was never any doubt when I was following him through his sophomore and junior years that he wouldn't be a great player for us. His size didn't really bother me." And Olson was right. Stoudamire turned into the school's second consensus All-American (Arizona now has six).

"No one could press us during the time he was here because he would take the ball right through," Olson said. He did it many times, but the most memorable were his performances at Stanford, when UA went into overtime to win 89–83, and his fearless prediction of beating Oregon on the road when Arizona desperately needed it.

"I told Damon after he did that it's good to have confidence in your team, but I'm not sure you'd want to [make predictions]," recalled Olson. "You didn't want to give [the opponent] extra incentive. But Damon backed it up."

And Olson backed him when it mattered. After beating Oregon—in a hotly contested game—Olson was headed to Portland to meet with Nike officials. While driving up, he listened to a local Portland sports-talk show and heard the host criticizing Stoudamire. Olson promptly called in and gave the broadcaster his thoughts. "How can he speak about a guy he knew nothing about?"

Catch a Game in Eugene

Arizona's natural rival is Arizona State, a team it has dominated for the last three decades. UCLA is the more even-suited rivalry, and indeed every game is seemingly an adventure and more.

But it's playing the University of Oregon that often stirs the juices. To this day going to Eugene may be the best trip of the season. That, too, is seemingly always a fight for Arizona. Whether it's a season in which Damon Stoudamire guarantees a win, like he did in 1995, or when Arizona faced the likes of Luke Jackson, Freddie Jones, and Luke Ridnour and the games were always action-packed, the excitement and craziness was always there. These days they play the game at Matthew Knight Arena.

Back in the day, they played in Mac Court, where the building seemed to sway with every high-intensity basket. If you didn't see a game in Mac Court you missed out. It rocked.

"I walked into Mac Court in 1993 and thought it was the Boston Garden," said Corey Williams. "We laughed at how old it was. Then the students started coming and they were sitting right behind us. We could hear every word. Suddenly it wasn't funny anymore."

That was the night Stoudamire guaranteed the win and got it as UA won 97–89. He pointed to the crowd and the crowd snarled back. Oregon's student section was always ready. Whether it was the tall, blonde cheerleaders in the shocking yellow outfits or the high-flying Ducks ready to put up a fight, the Oregon faithful was good to go.

Richard Paige, Arizona's former sports-information man for men's basketball, remembered his first trip to Mac Court. The contest was the first road game for the Wildcats since Coach Olson's return from a leave of absence following the passing of his wife, Bobbi. It was February 1, 2001. UA had won six in a row and jumped back into the top 10 of the AP poll. Meanwhile, Oregon was on the rise, led by Fred Jones, Bryan Bracey, and Anthony Lever, and it was the first year when the Ducks were reaching their potential under Ernie Kent.

There is a protocol to traveling on the team bus. Coaches sit up front, support staff fills the middle, and the players occupy the back. The team—as is usually the case—was silent on the bus trip there. "The Pit Crew was fired up for this game," Paige said. "Back in those days, the students used to gather out front of Mac Court, conveniently right in front of the spot where the visiting team unloaded. The students would work themselves into a frenzy as the bus approached, and when it stopped they would scream as loud as possible. Those along the curb might even reach out and try and rock the bus from side to side a little, just to let us know they were there."

Olson was typically the first one off the bus—but not that time. That time it was Paige. "I stood up and waited in the aisle for the rest of the coaching staff to follow Lute off the bus," Paige said. "For some reason, he took a bit longer to gather his things in his seat. While doing so, he caught my eye and nodded, signaling that it was OK for me to head out.

"I stepped forward and the bus driver threw open the door to a loud chorus of 'BOOOO!!!,' from the horde of fans. With my first step onto the sidewalk, I was greeted with the following:

'Fuck you, Lute!' shouted one fan.

'Hey, that's not Lute,' said another.

'Well, fuck him, too!' said a third.

"And with that, the crowd roared its approval," Paige said. "I walked quickly into the building with my head down, not wanting the Pit Crew to see how hard I was working to keep from smiling."

Arizona lost the game 79–67, but eventually reached the NCAA title game two months and a day later.

Olson said. "Damon is a great kid. This guy had no idea what he was talking about. I just had to tell him. It was the right thing."

Much has been written of the differences between UA guards and roommates Stoudamire and Reeves. One's neat, the other's messy. Felix Unger and Oscar Madison is what some called them. But how was it for Stoudamire, the neat one? "He keeps his stuff on his side and I keep my stuff on my side," Stoudamire said at the time. "Don't get me wrong, Khalid will pick up once in a while. It just depends on who we got coming over. When he wants to be neat, he can be neat."

Then again, there was help from Denise Reeves, Khalid's mother, who moved to Tucson when the basketball season started. "It's great to have Mama Reeves here," Stoudamire said then. "She washes his clothes now. She does all the stuff he really didn't want to do."

After a 13-year career in the NBA, Stoudamire started his coaching career, spending time at Rice and then as a Memphis assistant under former UA player Josh Pastner. He's now at Arizona as an assistant under Sean Miller.

"I'm happy to be back," said Stoudamire. "It's going to be a great situation. Walking through the halls made me numb. I've got butterflies but for different reasons—not as a player but as a coach."

Miller said Stoudamire is a welcome addition. "Obviously, Damon was a great player and a difference-maker in our program's history, and his pro career speaks even louder with the success he's had," Miller said. "But from my perspective it's about building the best program at the University of Arizona, and if you're looking to hire a coach there are a lot of qualities you look for that have nothing to do with how good a player you were. Some of the great players weren't good coaches, some of the best coaches in the game weren't very good players."

Stoudamire has proven to be both.

Shortly after the 2014 season, Stoudamire's name popped up for the Oregon State job, but after initial talks (nothing serious) with Beavers officials Stoudamire is still a Wildcat. He acknowledges that he does want to be a head coach someday. "That's the goal," he said. "That's why I'm doing this. I love dealing with kids, and I'd love to see how it would be to be a head coach."

10 Simon Says Championship

They are perhaps the most famous three words in Arizona basketball history: "Simon says championship." It's a forever snapshot: Miles Simon kneeling on the court inside the RCA Dome, cradling the basketball as the final seconds tick off the clock in UA's 84–79 overtime victory against Kentucky to win the 1997 NCAA title.

After CBS announcer Jim Nantz delivered the suspiciously scripted cornball line, "a milestone victory for Arizona," analyst Billy Packer did it better, followed simply by playing off Simon's name with "Simon says championship."

The 1997 championship was a superb team accomplishment—achieved by mature-beyond-his-years freshman point guard Mike Bibby, leading scorer Michael Dickerson, defensive ace Bennett Davison, underrated center A.J. Bramlett, and super sixth man Jason Terry, among others—but the season ended the way it did because Miles Simon was unstoppable when it mattered the most. "A lot of people felt he was really cocky and all that," said coach Lute Olson. "But he just had a lot of confidence, and that was important to us that we had somebody like that."

Dickerson and Bibby were quiet stars, so everybody looked to Simon, a 6'3" guard whose mantra during the tournament was, "We're not scared." And then he went out and played like he was ready to beat everybody.

He scored 20 or more points in four NCAA Tournament games, and he had 17 in the Sweet 16 victory over top-seeded Kansas. Then Simon had 30 points, six rebounds, and four assists in the win over Providence to get to the Final Four. He had 24 points, five rebounds, and five assists against No. 1 seed North Carolina. He finished with 30 points, including 14-of-17 free throws, in the championship game. For his efforts, Simon was selected the Most Outstanding Player of the Final Four.

"I tell you, once he hit that tournament, there was just nobody better," said assistant coach Jim Rosborough, who worked with the perimeter players. "He was focused. He was on a mission. Maybe even he would say that was when he kind of came out of his shell and grew up. He stepped up. There's no question at all." Given the stakes, his effort against Kentucky stands as the greatest individual performance in Arizona basketball history. And don't forget his defensive contributions. He was the primary defender on Ron

Mercer, who had averaged 18.1 points and 15 shots per game that season. Simon helped hold Mercer to 13 points on just nine shots.

Kentucky, meanwhile, was intent on not getting beat from the perimeter, which is how Arizona had dispatched the Tar Heels two days earlier, hitting 11-of-29 three-pointers. UK's plan worked... in part. Arizona attempted only 13 shots from behind the arc (making six), but Simon took advantage of the in-your-face defensive pressure, using a quick first step to drive into the lane, where he contorted to put up an array of floaters...or else he got fouled and made Kentucky pay from the line.

It was a storybook ending to a season that began with, of all things, Simon on an 11-game academic suspension. "He was just on a roll and doing some stuff that we hadn't even worked on in practice—all those up-and-under moves," Rosborough said. "It was just something that was in him. Miles was as good as anybody I've seen in that three-week time period [spanning the NCAA Tournament]. He wasn't that good all year, but he meant everything to us."

Simon landed on the cover of *Sports Illustrated* with the headline Cool Cat, and his stock was never hotter. But he decided to bypass the NBA Draft and come back for his senior season, often saying he was enchanted with the thought of winning back-to-back titles. The 1997–98 season ended in disappointment, though, as Utah upset the Wildcats in the West region final.

Simon, who is 12th on UA's career scoring list (1,644 points) and 10th in assists (455), was the 42nd overall pick, going to Orlando in 1998. He played in only five games after that season's lockout, which cut short the practice time he arguably needed to develop. Simon, who fell into the "tweener" category at the guard position, played overseas for a few years and then in the CBA before knee injuries ended his competitive playing days.

A former star at Mater Dei High School in Santa Ana, California—he was the first player to be named CIF Player of the

Year twice—he joined the Arizona coaching staff in 2005. His tenure ended in 2008, after which he became an AAU coach and launched a promising career as a TV analyst.

While all Arizona fans will always have the memory of "Simon says championship," he holds a more tangible reminder (other than the ring). In the spring of 2014, he gave the website NiceKicks.com a tour of his sneaker collection he keeps at his Southern California home. At the end of the video, he goes into the house and pulls down a shoe box from a closet shelf. On the lid are the words Final Four. Opening the box he reveals a net from the 1997 regional final. Underneath that is the pair of black Nike Air Max Up-Tempos he wore in the national championship game.

"One of the best basketball shoes that I've ever worn," he said. "I'm still saving them. Don't know if I will ever get rid of them or they just might decompose by themselves. But pretty sweet. And shoes that really mean a lot to me."

Pretty sweet, indeed.

11 Arizona vs. Duke

Arizona has only played Duke nine times in basketball, including a meeting way back in 1961, but it seems like so many more than that.

Duke never seems far from the minds of Arizona fans. It's the whole "East Coast bias" thing. It's how former coach Lute Olson likes to refer to Dick Vitale as "Dookie Vitale" because of the analyst's tendency to fawn over the Blue Devils. It was how Olson started and sparked the debate of why Salim Stoudamire was actually such a better shooter than Duke's more-hyped J.J. Redick. It was the debate, way back when, over whether Sean Elliott or Danny Ferry should be the college player of the year (an honor they shared in 1989). It's how every Arizona-Duke game seems to be *an event.*

Indeed, for teams that haven't had a regularly scheduled game since 1991, they sure do seem to intersect quite a bit. Here are the eight games the teams have played since 1987:

Tucson, December 30, 1987—Arizona 91, Duke 85

These were the days when the Fiesta Bowl basketball tournament was a big-name, four-team holiday event at McKale Center. When Duke and Arizona met in the 1987 championship game, the Wildcats were 11–0 and enjoying the first No. 1 ranking in school history for a second consecutive week. Duke was 6–0 and ranked ninth.

Sean Elliott scored 31 points, and Tom Tolbert added 19, to lead Arizona. Danny Ferry and Kevin Strickland each scored 25 points for Duke. The Blue Devils tried to rally, hitting three three-pointers in the final 46 seconds, but UA held on, making 11 of its final 12 free throw attempts.

Quote: "I think it's hard to accept after 10 or 15 years of eastern teams dominating. People have a hard time believing a Pac-10 team could be No. 1 in the country."—Arizona center Anthony Cook, in the *Sacramento Bee*

East Rutherford, NJ, February 26, 1989—Arizona 77, Duke 75

Sean Elliott was a star again in another epic matchup against Danny Ferry. Elliott scored 24 points, including a three-pointer over Ferry with 53 seconds remaining that broke a 70–70 tie at the Meadowlands. Duke freshman Christian Laettner had a chance to tie the game with one second to go, but he missed the front end of a one-and-one.

Ferry had 29 points, 12 rebounds, five assists, five blocked shots, and two steals in the game. Arizona, which led by 19 points in the first half, improved to 22–3 on the season and moved to No. 1 in the polls the following day. (Side note: President Richard Nixon, a Duke law school graduate, attended his first Blue Devils basketball game and talked to the team in the locker room afterward.)

Quote: "This is the kind of game you win in the Final Four, or in the championship game."—Sean Elliott, in the *New York Times*

Durham, NC, February 25, 1990—Duke 78, Arizona 76

Arizona held a 45–23 rebounding edge, but the Wildcats had a tough time against Duke's aggressive man-to-man defense, committing 22 turnovers. Duke sealed the game with a pair of steals after the Wildcats closed to within 73–72 late in the game. Phil Henderson led third-ranked Duke with 28 points. Arizona was at the tail end of an eight-day, 7,000-mile road trip that began with a loss against powerful UNLV.

Quote: "I kept waiting for them to get tired. Those guys must have taken their vitamins."—Duke center Alaa Abdelnaby, in *USA TODAY*

Tucson, February 24, 1991—Arizona 103, Duke 96 (2OT)

The Wildcats won their 61st consecutive home game, getting a spinning layup from Sean Rooks to tie the game at 78 at the end of regulation and a game-tying 10-foot jumper from Chris Mills with 11 seconds left in the first overtime. Matt Muehlebach scored seven points in the second overtime to help lift Arizona to victory. Brian Williams had 24 points and 11 rebounds for Arizona but was one of six players who fouled out. The game featured 91 free throws—as well as 11 lead changes and 14 ties—in one of the greatest games ever at McKale.

Quote: "I'd sure like to meet the ghost of McKale. He's definitely got a jinx on somebody."—Brian Williams, to the Associated Press

Lahaina, HI, November 26, 1997—Duke 95, Arizona 87

It was the first loss for the defending national champion Wildcats, who fell to the Blue Devils in the title game of the Maui Invitational. William Avery, a freshman guard, had 21 points to lead Duke, while Miles Simon scored 25 points for Arizona. Although the final score was close, Duke dominated from the start, forcing 11 first-half turnovers and leading by 24 after the break. Arizona's wish to go undefeated in its attempt to repeat as NCAA champions was thwarted.

Quote: "Their defense wasn't tough. We made it tough on ourselves."—UA guard Jason Terry, in the *Tucson Citizen*

Minneapolis, April 2, 2001—Duke 82, Arizona 72

Arizona fans will always wonder what would have happened in the national championship game if Gilbert Arenas hadn't been suffering from a shoulder injury (and if Luke Walton hadn't suffered a broken right thumb less than a week earlier). Arenas shot 4-of-17 from the field and point guard Jason Gardner made only 2-of-11 attempts. Shane Battier led Duke with 18 points, 11 rebounds, and six assists, while Mike Dunleavy supplied the dagger with five three-pointers, including a trio in succession in the second half.

Quote: "I think the main thing with our guys is I think they played hard under difficult circumstances. The effort has been there. The togetherness has been there. Everything that they could do, I think has been done."—Lute Olson, in the *New York Post*

Anaheim, CA, March 24, 2011—Arizona 93, Duke 77

Derrick Williams turned in one of the greatest halves of basketball in school history—he had 25 points, including hitting 5-of-6 from three-point range—but the Cats still trailed top-seeded Duke 44–38 at halftime of this Sweet 16 game. Then everybody else showed up for Arizona, which unleashed a 19–2 run to take control, hounding Duke on defense and dunking as if the Blue

Devils were an intramural team. Williams finished with 32 points and 13 rebounds.

Quote: "We had a saying going into the game: 'Attack or be attacked.' Which one is it, because there is no in-between."—Sean Miller, on his postgame radio show

There's no love lost between Arizona and Duke, as players Luke Walton and Jason Williams demonstrate during the teams' 2001 NCAA championship matchup.

New York City, November 29, 2013—Arizona 72, Duke 66
Fourth-ranked Arizona used its 2013–14 hallmarks—balance and defense—to defeat Duke and take home the championship of the NIT Season Tip-Off at Madison Square Garden. Guard Nick Johnson scored 13 of his team-high 15 points after halftime to lead the Wildcats, which made life difficult on Duke freshman star Jabari Parker, who scored 19 points but was just 7-of-21 from the field and missed all five of his attempts from three-point range. Five players scored in double figures for Arizona.

Quote: "We're an all-around team. Really you could see it in the box score."—Nick Johnson, in the postgame press conference

12 Khalid Reeves: When On, Watch Out

Sean Elliott may hands-down be the best player to ever wear an Arizona uniform, but when Khalid Reeves was on few were better. That includes Elliott. After all, no player in the history of the program scored more points than Reeves in one season, at 848. Additionally, his average points per game that season—24.8—still stands as an Arizona record.

But it all depended on the day. Some days Reeves, the New York City kid who made his way to the desert, just didn't have it. Sometimes basketball seemingly wasn't all that important.

"He was a great talent," former teammate Matt Othick said. "He had some similarities to Brian Williams...he definitely had other interests other than just basketball. He could have been as good as he wanted to be. He was unstoppable one-on-one."

He proved it on December 30, 1993, when Michigan's Fab Four (Chris Webber had already advanced to the NBA) rolled into town to participate in the annual Fiesta Bowl Classic. It was the title game, and no one was going to stop Reeves, UA's enigmatic shooting guard.

He went 13-for-14 and 11-for-12 from the free throw line to finish with 40 points in a 119–95 win (and it felt even more lopsided). It was the first 40-point night for any UA player since Al Fleming went for 41 in 1976—although Reeves had flirted with the number four times that season. He had four of UA's six 30-point games in that 1993–94 season, his senior year.

"I don't know if you'll see a better performance than this," Olson said at the time. "We certainly saw some great performances out of Sean Elliott here, but to say that anyone had a better game than this one would be difficult." Reeves, as they say, was in a zone.

When asked who was the best player, many Wildcats of that time said...Khalid Reeves. "Khalid had more talent in his finger than we have working two eight-hour days," said Corey Williams. "He'd have 40 points, 16 rebounds in practice. We'd get to the locker room and Lid would already be showered and out of there. He never broke a sweat. He'd just dominate everyone and had the look of not even trying. At the end of the day, I think that's why his career [in the NBA] wasn't what it could have been."

That seems to be the final analysis, even from good friends and his coach. When Damon Stoudamire arrived at UA, his first impression was "the dude is really good. He had a natural talent and ability. You knew he'd make it. He was blessed with a talent that God gave him."

Together they turned Arizona into what is now known as Point Guard U—if you're a guard and you want to be known, the University of Arizona is the place.

"He was the best player and most talented," Stoudamire said. "The thing about Khalid was that he was a introvert, but he was a real good guy in his own way. But the rest of the world never saw that. He had a great personality, but I got to see it because I was around him. He was misunderstood just because he seemed he was unapproachable. But he just had a comfort zone and just comfortable around the people he was around."

The fact that Arizona got Reeves to come to Arizona at all was a surprise because Olson rarely—if ever—recruited in the East. He thought it was "a waste of time because distance is always a problem." But one day Christ the King's then-coach Bobby Oliva called Olson to say that Reeves wanted to visit. Olson was skeptical. "I figured he'd go somewhere else, but Oliva said he wanted to play in the West."

Indeed, UNLV, UCLA, Georgia Tech, and Arizona were the candidates. Reeves visited with his mom, Denise. He liked it in Tucson, but UA had another guard coming in the next week and Olson told Reeves that it was the team's policy to take the first player who commits. "He called back and said, 'I want to commit,' Olson remembered.

After a rocky first semester, Reeves had a career to die for. He finished third all-time in scoring with 1,925 points, finishing with a 15-points-per-game average.

After six years in the NBA—each year on a different team—he's now an assistant coach with his former high school at Christ the King in Queens, New York. "This is where I want to be," Reeves told the *New York Post*. "I just love teaching the kids how to play and being around the kids and my old school. It's a great atmosphere to play basketball."

13 Fred Snowden

Arizona basketball legend Bob Elliott, who followed Fred Snowden from Ann Arbor, Michigan, to Tucson 40 years ago, has mentioned this line many times about Snowden's impact on the Wildcat program today: "If there's not a Fred Snowden, there's probably not a Lute Olson." And without a Lute Olson, there's certainly not a Sean Miller. Elliott's words carry weight considering Arizona was not a nationally recognized program in the modern era before Snowden's arrival in Tucson in 1972.

The late Dave Strack, Arizona's former athletic director, hired Snowden from Johnny Orr's staff at Michigan in 1972 to become the Wildcats' head coach. He happened to be the first African American head coach for a Division I program.

"Tucson became a basketball town and Arizona became a basketball school when Dave Strack hired Freddie Snowden to lead the program," said Elliott, the third Michigan product Snowden recruited to Arizona after Detroit's Eric Money and Coniel Norman. "You have to remember they were averaging only a couple hundred fans at Bear Down Gym before Freddie was hired. They moved across the street to McKale Center midway through the [1972–73] season. They sold out the place without any plans of a season-ticket program. Without Dave Strack that does not happen. There's no Fred Snowden, no Eric Money, or Coniel Norman.... The program would not be the same."

Snowden's first recruiting class, known as the Kiddie Korps, featured five freshman starters, including Norman and Money. They became the talk of Tucson and the West Coast. When McKale Center opened midway through Snowden's first season, Arizona basketball became an immediate hot ticket. "Fred was the catalyst," former assistant coach Jerry Holmes told the *Tucson Citizen* in a 2009 interview. "The Fred Snowden regime in that time started the tradition of Arizona basketball, without question."

Not only did Snowden attract top young talent immediately following his hire, his up-tempo, high-scoring style of play captivated the community. Money and Norman and fellow Kiddie Korps members Jim Rappis, Al Fleming, and John Irving gave Snowden a

Dave Strack

Nobody means more to Arizona's transition to a nationally competitive athletic department than Dave Strack. Strack became Arizona's athletic director in January 1972 after three years as business manager and associate athletic director at Michigan, where he is legendary. He coached Michigan's basketball team from 1960 to 1968 and led the Wolverines to three consecutive Big Ten titles and two consecutive Final Fours.

He coached Michigan to national runner-up in 1965, when the Wolverines lost the title game to UCLA. Strack compiled a 113–89 overall record at Michigan. His 113 career victories place fourth on Michigan's all-time list.

Strack was certainly accustomed to the big time by the time he arrived in Tucson. That experience helped him take Arizona's program to new heights. He opened McKale Center in 1973, expanded Arizona Stadium in 1975, modernized Kindall/Sancet Stadium in 1975, and administered the Wildcats' move from the WAC to the Pac-10.

"I'll take some credit for moving Arizona out of the doldrums," Strack said with a chuckle in a 2013 interview with the *Arizona Daily Star*. "We were at Bear Down Gym when I got here. That's where my office was, too. It was bad when I got here, very bad. Basketball was sort of a stepchild when I got here. It's not that way any longer."

His tenure at Arizona included the hiring of the first African American head coach of a major university, basketball coach Fred Snowden. Snowden revived Arizona's basketball program, taking the Wildcats as far as the Elite Eight in 1976.

One of Strack's last hires was Ben Lindsey from Grand Canyon University as the basketball head coach. Cedric Dempsey, who replaced Strack as Arizona's AD in 1983, fired Lindsey after one season in which the Wildcats went 4–24 overall and 1–17 in the Pac-10. Dempsey went on to hire Lute Olson away from Iowa, and Olson built Arizona into a national powerhouse.

Strack, the AD when Arizona entered the Pac-10 in 1978, also dipped into Michigan's esteemed football program for coaches under Bo Schembechler. He hired Wolverines football assistants Jim Young and Larry Smith to handle the task of making Arizona competitive heading into the 1980s. Young and Smith were a combined 79–41–3 as the Wildcats' head coach.

Strack resigned as Arizona's AD in 1982, two years after a scandal involving the football program's use of an athletic slush fund for improper payments to coaches, alumni, and recruits. The infractions occurred under Tony Mason, another former Michigan assistant who Strack hired to replace Young when he left in 1976 to take the top job at Purdue. Strack remained at Arizona as a professor of education after his resignation.

As a basketball player, Strack was the team captain and MVP at Shortridge High (IN) before arriving at Michigan. He became a three-time letter winner for the Wolverines and captained the 1945–46 team. He was inducted into the Indiana Basketball Hall of Fame in 1992 and the Michigan Hall of Honor in 1984. For the Wolverines, he recruited the likes of players Cazzie Russell, Bill Buntin, and coach Rudy Tomjanovich. Russell was the first of two national players of the year in Michigan history. Strack passed away at age 90 in 2014.

16–10 record in his first season, a 10-game improvement from the previous season under coach Bruce Larson. The Wildcats finished tied for second place in the Western Athletic Conference, averaging 81.2 points a game. (In the year before Snowden's arrival, Arizona averaged only 66.5 points.)

"When I came to Arizona, I wanted to fill McKale Center with an exciting brand of up-tempo, pressure basketball," Snowden said in a 1990 interview with *Cat Tracks* magazine. "We felt that we would get the fans to come out and it worked."

Arizona improved year by year with records of 19–7, 22–7, and 24–9 in Snowden's first seasons. That 1975–76 team, which featured Elliott at center and was led by Kiddie Korps holdovers Fleming and Rappis, went to the NCAA West Regional final but lost to UCLA.

Snowden's second and last NCAA Tournament appearance came in 1977 with a loss in the first round to Southern Illinois. It was essentially the coach's last hurrah with Arizona. After the Wildcats joined the Pac-10 in 1978, Arizona struggled with recruiting and competing at a high level.

Snowden's Midwestern recruiting ties were no longer, and he took the bold stance of trying to recruit kids from Los Angeles away from UCLA and USC. The strategy did not entirely work. Snowden also lost transfers, including future Olympian Leon Wood, who played one season (1979–80).

"I think Freddie felt that if the UCLA programs can be built on the L.A. kids, so could his," Elliott said in the *Arizona Wildcats Handbook*. "He felt like he could fight fire with fire." It never happened.

In his last three seasons, Snowden was 34–47, prompting him to resign under pressure and take a job within the athletic department in 1982. Snowden instead left Arizona and entered the private sector, running his own consulting firm. He later joined Baskin-Robbins as vice president for urban affairs. He began working for Food 4 Less Supermarkets, Inc., in 1990 as vice president of urban affairs. He was named executive director of the Food 4 Less Foundation in 1992.

Two years later, Snowden died of a heart attack in Washington, DC, while attending the unveiling of President Clinton's empowerment zones legislation, which includes South Central Los Angeles. He was 57.

Still, his legacy of putting Arizona basketball on the national map is intact. "I remember talking to Lute when he obtained the job here," Elliott told the *Arizona Daily Wildcat* in 2003. "It's easier to rekindle a flame that's been lit than to try to take over a program that has never had the fire lit.

"All you need to do is look 120 miles to the north on I–10. [Arizona State]—despite the success they've had, despite the players they've had—their best year of attendance is 9,000 per game in a 14,500-seat arena. That's the best they've ever done. Lute took the path that Freddy had paved and added to it, but he didn't have to start with a dirt road."

14 Cedric Dempsey

Arizona's men's basketball program was in shambles that winter of 1982–83. Cedric Dempsey knew it. Heck, who didn't?

Ben Lindsey had been brought in to replace the famed Fred Snowden the season before and was bungling everything. Off-the-court issues were a problem as well, obviously, as UA limped to the end of the season with a 4–24 record, the worst in school history. Arizona needed a change and Dempsey—"one of the most influential leaders in intercollegiate athletics history," as current UA AD Greg Byrne described him—was the man to do it.

"I was on the front page of the paper a few times the first few weeks [after] I took the job," Dempsey said with a smile. "It was firing Lindsey, McKale Center's priority seating, hiring Lute [Olson] and going on probation on football. The first week on the job I had to be in front of the NCAA."

Such was life for Dempsey, who returned to UA in 1982–83 after stints at the University of the Pacific, San Diego State, and Houston. But he will be long remembered for being the guy who convinced Olson to come to Arizona. It happened one cold night in Kansas City, after Iowa had just lost to Georgetown in the Sweet 16. And as Olson was headed to speak to the media about the loss, Dempsey approached Olson and said, "We'd like to have a chance to talk to you about our job. Would you be interested?"

Dempsey already had permission to speak to Olson through Iowa AD Bump Elliott. The question took Olson by surprise in that he was preparing for postgame questions, so he suggested talking the next day.

And that's where it all began.

"He was the No. 1 guy, no question," Dempsey said. "One of the problems was, because of Arizona law back then, we could only offer him a one-year contract. And I had just let someone go after nine months."

The next morning Lute and Bobbi and the entire family met with Cedric and it felt like *they* were interviewing *him*. Soon after Lute and Bobbi boarded a private plane to Tucson to talk. "Well, it was cold in Iowa City," Lute writes in his book. "A few days in a nice warm city seemed pretty appealing to me."

Arizona wanted to keep the job possibility secret so it put Lute and Bobbi at the Westward Look Resort on the outside of town. It turned out it wasn't such a secret. A reporter from the UA school paper found out Olson was coming in. Furthermore, the Westward Look was owned by an Iowan, and many Iowans stayed there. Olson bumped into a few the following morning. Later in the afternoon, Olson said it wasn't so much of an interview but Arizona convincing him that he should take the job. And after touring Tucson and looking for places to live, Lute and Bobbi decided UA was the place.

Then came the tough part. "My biggest concern was when he agreed to come and he wanted to go back home and tell his players," Dempsey said. "I've seen that before and that's always the most [concerning] part. I thought Lute was ready to move and I think he saw the potential at Arizona that we see today. It's a great lifestyle. The timing had to be just right."

Just a couple of years earlier, Olson had turned down a job at USC. He had also been courted by Stanford and Washington but told them he wasn't interested. Dempsey did have a plan B: his name was Gene Bartow, the former UCLA coach who had replaced legendary John Wooden.

"On the Sunday that Lute took the job, I still wasn't sure at that point he'd take it," Dempsey said. "Bartow was unpacking in his room. I went to him and told him where we were [in negotiations] and we offered the job to Lute and that he was going to take it. 'You know as well as I that doesn't always hold out. I'll respect you if you want to go but you and your wife are welcome to stay for a week,'" Dempsey told him.

Olson went home and told his players, and yes, there were tears. "'Right now, I think it's the best thing for Bobbi and me to get out west, 'cause that's where our family is,'" he told his players. "I assured them that Bump would bring in an outstanding coach. 'You guys are going to be really good. You're going to have a great season.'"

And with that, Dempsey was successful in bringing Olson to the desert.

He was also instrumental in taking what was then a middle-of-the-road athletic department into what is now one of the top 10 to 15 programs in the country. And in basketball, it's arguably in the top five. He inherited a program that was $450,000 in the red and eventually turned it around to the point where there's been a surplus every year since 1985. The budget during his tenure was no more than $20 million and is now $66 million. "To this day, Arizona has been able to stay in the black, which is contrary to most schools," Dempsey noted.

He hired Dick Tomey in 1987 after the departure of Larry Smith and has seen the softball team win eight national titles. The golf teams, baseball team, and swimming programs have all won national titles since then. It was 11 years of success for Dempsey, who left UA in November 1993 to become the third executive director of the NCAA. He had previously been the NCAA men's selection committee chairman, in 1989.

"It was very difficult to leave, and I debated about it," Dempsey said. "At the same time, I was concerned where the profession was going. When the opportunity came [to join the NCAA] I thought I had to do it. I was pleased with what I had accomplished at Arizona. I'm pleased to see that there are still a number of staff there, a number of coaches."

While at Arizona, Dempsey, now retired, was diagnosed with non-Hodgkins lymphoma. He battled it three times and after 10 years defeated it. "I'd go into chemotherapy for six months and be fine," he said. "And for six years [I] went back and forth. I lost my hair but I never let it bother me. I just figured that if things were going to happen, well, things were going to happen."

As for his best time at Arizona? "Every day, just going to work," he said.

He made what the job is today. "The impact he made as director of athletics at Arizona, Houston, and Pacific were tremendous, and we are still receiving those benefits today at Arizona," Byrne said. "Because of the leadership he showed in those roles, he made such a strong name for himself nationally that led to him being named the president of the NCAA, where he was a stable force during a time of tremendous transition. He has touched the lives of countless student athletes, coaches, fans, and administrators."

15 Fred Enke Sr.

The man known for telling his Notre Dame team to "Win one for the Gipper" also won one for Arizona. Knute Rockne, the famed Fighting Irish coach, recommended Fred Enke Sr. for the Arizona coaching job at a time when the Wildcats were searching in 1926 for stability after having four coaches in a five-year stretch.

One of those four was J.F. "Pop" McKale, who stopped coaching basketball in 1921 to concentrate on his athletic director position. He was also the football coach and was returning to coach the baseball team.

Rockne was impressed by Enke, a former All–Big Ten standout in football and basketball at Minnesota, while Enke was assisting at a football clinic at Notre Dame. Enke coached as an assistant at South Dakota State in 1922 before Louisville hired him in 1923 to be the athletic director and coach the football, basketball, and baseball teams.

He was only two years into his demanding position at Louisville when McKale came calling in 1925. "I took the train out to Tucson and [graduate manager of athletics] Slony [Louis Slonaker] and McKale met me, took me around the campus, and then out to Wetmore Pool. The pool was a big thing in Tucson those days," Enke was quoted as saying in the book *They Fought Like Wildcats* by Abe Chanin. "Viewing the campus was a shock to me because there was no gymnasium. Here I was to be the basketball coach, see, and there was just that little Herring Hall. I decided to take the challenge. I wired my wife that we were going to move to Tucson, that I'd taken the job as basketball coach and assistant in football at a salary of $3,000."

Enke's basketball coaching career at Arizona extended from 1925 to 1961. In all, he compiled a record of 509–324 at Arizona. When he left the game, he was one of only five coaches to have eclipsed the 500-win mark at that time. Including his two-year tenure at Louisville, his career record was 523–344 in 38 seasons.

Enke also served as an assistant football coach through 1962, except for one year, when he served as the football team's head coach in 1931 after McKale gave up coaching but remained the athletic director and baseball coach.

Enke won 11 Border Conference titles with the basketball team and coached the Wildcats to the National Invitation Tournament at Madison Square Garden in 1946 and 1950 and the school's first NCAA Tournament appearance in 1951.

"Fred Enke gave Tucson a reason to express its pride," former U.S. Congressman Morris K. Udall, a basketball standout under

Fred Enke Jr.

Fred W. Enke Jr. was always at the head of his class. He was a first-team all-state selection at Tucson High School in football (1941 and 1942), basketball (1943), and baseball (1943). The Badgers won state titles in all three sports with Enke Jr. as the leader.

Enke Jr., a navy pilot during World War II, prepared with his unit to raid Japan before the war came to an end on September 2, 1945. Two weeks later, he enrolled at Arizona at age 21. He immediately lettered in all three sports, including basketball, which was coached by his legendary father.

Enke Jr. was Arizona's first major-college All-American, earning third-team Associated Press honors in 1947 when his 1,941 total yards—1,406 passing, 535 running—led the nation. As a quarterback/halfback, his total that season included 364 yards in a late-season game against Kansas. His father also coached him in football, as an assistant coach with the Wildcats for Mike Casteel.

He is on a short list of the Wildcats' best all-around athletes, described in Abe Chanin's 1979 book *They Fought Like Wildcats* as the school's last great three-sport star.

He hit .345 as the captain of the baseball team in 1948. Pop McKale, who coached Arizona's baseball team at the time, was quoted in a newspaper report as saying that Enke was the best pro prospect in the Southwest.

"As a kid coming out of high school, you think of going away to school," Enke Jr. told Chanin. "But for me, it was going into military service. And after three years in navy aviation I got over wanting to go away from home.

"Oh, there was some criticism when I was starting guard for my dad on the basketball team, but I knew that playing for my dad would mean that I would have to tough it out or quit."

In the same year in which Enke Jr. was a third-team All-American in football, he was an All–Border Conference selection in basketball.

Following his college career, Enke headed to the NFL, where he played a combined seven seasons with the Lions (1948–51), Eagles (1952), and Colts (1953–54). He tallied 4,169 yards passing and 640 yards rushing during his career.

Enke had two years of football eligibility remaining when he became the 47th pick of the 1948 draft. His good friend on the basketball team at Arizona, Morris K. Udall, negotiated a contract for Enke with the Detroit Lions; Udall was a law student at Arizona at the time.

Enke started 10 games as a rookie for the Lions, completing 100 of 221 passes for 1,328 yards, which were good passing numbers in the 10-team league at that time. He also earned All-Pro honors in that rookie season.

During the off-seasons in the NFL, Enke completed his bachelor's degree in education and earned a master's degree in administrative education at Arizona. Meanwhile, he coached Arizona's freshman baseball team and volunteered his time mentoring children at the local YMCA.

Near the end of his time with the Lions in 1951, he thought about following in his dad's footsteps, possibly becoming a coach. He contemplated pursuing the head football coaching job at Arizona after Bob Winslow was fired that year. He stuck with the NFL instead.

After he retired from the pro game in 1954, he became a prominent cotton farmer in Casa Grande, Arizona. The Enke farm that he owned is now the University of Arizona Maricopa Agricultural Center, a 2,100-acre research farm within the College of Agriculture & Life Sciences.

In 1976, Enke Jr. was inducted into the first class of the Arizona Sports Hall of Fame. His name is on display at the Ring of Honor at Arizona Stadium.

Enke Jr. passed away at age 89 at his Casa Grande home in 2014, with his wife of 62 years, Marjorie, by his side. His four children, Debbie, Diana, Denise, and Fred (III) were also there along with some of his grandchildren and great-grandchildren.

"[My father] was a great athlete and an outstanding father to the four of us," his son told InMaricopa.com. "I never heard him say a bad word about anybody."

Enke, told the *Tucson Citizen* when his former coach passed away in 1985. "When he first came in, UA hadn't had much luck in football. Basketball was a ho-hum thing, at best. That man took Arizona to the NCAAs, to the National Invitation Tournament, and to national prominence."

Enke's son Fred W. Enke Jr. was a three-sport star at Arizona from 1943 to 1948. The younger Enke passed away at 89 in 2014. "It was a lot of fun," Enke Jr. said in the book *Tales from the Arizona Wildcats Locker Room*. "It was when we gained prominence. It wasn't strange. I'd flown in the navy so you live dangerously there, too. But it was fun."

Enke Sr. was a player's coach. He was the type of coach who never micromanaged and who expected his players to have fundamentals by the time they stepped foot in Bear Down Gym.

"He got along with everyone," one of his players, Bob Honea, said in *Tales from the Arizona Wildcats Locker Room.* "He was my fatherly image. If he would have said 'boo,' I would have taken off for the cotton patch. He was just a good guy who watched after us."

Enke Sr., who lived until he was 88 in 1985, was the school's winningest coach until Lute Olson broke his record.

16 Bob Elliott: Big Bird Rises

Bob Elliott is arguably one of the most underrated and underappreciated former Arizona Wildcats of all time. After all, how does the second all-time scorer (2,125 points), who was fourth in scoring average (18.7), second in field goals (808) and rebounding average (9.5), and the first to score more than 675 points in a season not get his due?

It's hard to say, but consider this: Elliott is not on a list of Arizona players named to the Pac-10 or Pac-12 Halls of Honor. "That's not up to me. I don't make that decision," said Elliott, UA's big man in the mid-1970s and a Tucsonan who has become one of the city's biggest (and tallest) businessmen. "If it's something you don't control or make a decision on, you don't worry about it. You can't dwell on it."

So, he won't. But "Big Bird" Bob Elliott, or "Parajito Grande" as they know him in Nogales, Mexico, was part of Arizona's best recruiting class ever to that point. Herman Harris, Jerome Gladney,

Big Bird rises—this time against Rick Washington of UCLA in 1976 NCAA Tournament play.

Len Gordy, Gary Harrison, Jay Geldmacher, Bob Aleksa, and Kent Markle all joined him in the Class of 1973–74.

Elliott had received more than 300 letters from colleges wanting him. It came down to his home-state school (Michigan) and Arizona. It may have appeared that Michigan had the upper hand, since Elliott's father worked at Michigan's football stadium. Both of Elliott's parents were Michigan alums.

But Elliott made his recruiting trip to Tucson on a fall day, and it was sunny and warm while it had been rainy and near freezing in Michigan. Additionally, Arizona had Fred Snowden, who was legendary in Michigan from his time there. Elliott knew he wanted to play for Snowden. And Snowden knew he needed a player like Elliott—so much so that he put up with one thing he may not have for anyone else: a cat. Former UA assistant coach Jerry Holmes talked about visiting the Elliotts in their home, where they had a cat.

"[It] was a huge cat," Holmes said in *Tucson: A Basketball Town*, "just looming around. I am allergic to cats. This huge cat jumps on my lap. I would have hung out with that cat if that was what we had to do to get Bob to commit to Arizona."

Elliott did. All six feet and seven inches of him. (It should be noted here the UA athletic department listed UA's center at 6'10", but Elliott admitted, "I was not then nor have I ever been six feet 10 inches tall...but nobody knew the difference with eight inches of Afro on my head.")

But his official height didn't really matter, in part because taller centers had as hard a time stopping him as smaller centers. By the end of his college career, he finished with 2,125 points, a school record that had held up for 12 seasons—until Sean Elliott came around. Bob became the school's second All-American (Roger Johnson was the first) in 1975–76 and the school's first first-team All-American, as well as a Helms Foundation winner.

Still, with all the success and all the victories and deep run into the NCAA Tournament, Elliott says his legacy is this: he was part of a team and program that was the first to reach the Elite Eight in 1976 (losing to UCLA) and "brought in enough money and goodwill to build that [UA] library that is sitting there. That's [the] 1976 team's claim to fame," Elliott said.

In 1976, the library wasn't eligible for bond money for its construction. But because UA received extra money for participating in the NCAA Tournament and going so deep in it, those proceeds helped the library to get built. "The Arizona board of regents were very happy with the additional positive publicity for the state of

Arizona and were more than supportive toward the library project," Elliott writes in *Tucson: A Basketball Town*. "The new library was completed across from McKale Center and is still serving students today."

17 Pop McKale: If It Weren't for Him

He wasn't Arizona's first coach—that was Orin Kates back in 1904–05—but James Fred "Pop" McKale may well have been UA's first and foremost basketball coach. So much is owed to the man whose name graces the building UA plays in these days, the McKale Center.

McKale began coaching Wildcats basketball in 1914–15, and the team promptly went undefeated, 9–0. He followed it with a 5–0 mark. Then 10–2. He started his career 21–0 before losing. In his eight years as coach, "Pop" never had a losing season, finishing 49–12, for an 80.3 win percentage. No Arizona coach with more than three years' tenure has a better winning percentage.

Yet, basketball was McKale's *least* favorite sport. He was a football and baseball guy, and coached those teams as well. Yet it's said that without McKale's efforts and interest in sports, Arizona athletics wouldn't have been what it was in the 1920s—and indeed, throughout his tenure as athletic director, which stretched to 1957.

"Many who knew J.F. McKale will remember him as 'Mac' or 'Pop,'" said Arizona regent James Dunseath, speaking at the dedication of the UA McKale Memorial Center. "To most of us who played for him, he will always be 'Coach' or 'Mr. McKale.' Today, as we put his name on the building we are most proud of, we all remember him as 'the Grand Old Man of Arizona Sports.'"

McKale moved to Tucson from Michigan in 1911, when he first became Tucson High's baseball coach. Because he was so successful at Tucson High, UA students petitioned university president A.H. Wilde for McKale to be named the coach for all its athletic teams. He eventually became that guy, in addition to founding the Epsilon Alpha chapter Sigma Nu fraternity at UA.

In the mid-1920s he had a player who eventually became famous—John "Button" Salmon, who after the first game of the 1926 season suffered severe injuries from an automobile accident. McKale visited Salmon every day in the hospital where upon Salmon's last message was "tell the team to bear down." It's been UA's mantra since 1926.

18 John P. Schaefer

University presidents normally do not get inducted into sports halls of fame, but in John P. Schaefer's case at Arizona, it makes sense. Schaefer, now president emeritus of Arizona, served as university president from 1971 to 1982, and played a major role in moving the Wildcats from the Western Athletic Conference to what was then the Pac-8.

Presidents of the six other WAC schools were outraged when Arizona and ASU announced January 6, 1977, that they would leave the WAC for the Pac-8 (and the lucrative Los Angeles market with USC and UCLA) effective as of the 1978–79 season. The WAC presidents sent a telegram to the Arizona Board of Regents indicating that they expected Arizona and ASU to honor their football scheduling contracts with their schools through 1981.

Schaefer disagreed. "We feel it is in the best interest of the WAC to look for new members," he told the Associated Press. "The increased membership would alleviate the scheduling problems caused by the withdrawal of the Arizona universities and enable the WAC to complete their schedule much sooner." The WAC presidents relented and sought other members. In three consecutive years, starting in 1978, the WAC added San Diego State, Hawaii, and Air Force.

Schaefer also overcame the objections of ASU and its football coach Frank Kush. A 2002 *Arizona Republic* article stated: "For any ASU fan that savors the victories and moments associated with playing the powers of the West Coast, go ahead and say it: 'Thank you, U of A.' Namely former University of Arizona president John Schaefer. Against the will of ASU fans and coach Frank Kush, Schaefer spearheaded the idea that a couple of WAC schools in cactus country could play with the big boys."

The *Tucson Citizen* reported in 2005 that Schaefer raised the notion of Arizona and ASU joining the Pac-8 with Jack Hubbard, president of the University of Southern California, on a flight in 1976. "We sat next to each other on a plane en route to Taiwan," Schaefer recalled to the *Citizen*. "I brought it up, but he said he was about to bring it up himself. He agreed it would be a good fit.

"I wanted to bring more national recognition to the university. ASU wasn't hip on the idea, but within six months the deal was sealed. It's been great for both schools. The financial and public exposure benefits are immeasurable."

ASU was hesitant to leave the WAC because the Sun Devils were coming off an undefeated football season in 1975. ASU was riding a 13-game winning streak and talking national championship. In 1976, ASU was slated to host UCLA, the defending Rose

Bowl champion and would-be conference-mate, in the season opener. After the Bruins defeated ASU 28–10, Sun Devils supporters became more leery of moving from the comforts of the WAC.

On September 16, 1976, a week after ASU's loss to UCLA, the *Arizona Republic* wrote, "The Sun Devil Club and the Sun Angel Foundation both released statements to the Phoenix Press Box Association urging ASU to stay in the Western Athletic Conference." A letter to the editor asked, "Isn't it better to be first in the WAC, than last in the Pac?" ASU athletic director Dr. Fred Miller told the *Republic*, "I think at this time we are better off staying where we are."

Five days later in the newspaper, an Arizona official was quoted as saying, "I can't understand it. Don't they want to grow?"

President Schaefer added to the *Arizona Daily Star*: "The possibility of affiliation with the Pac-8 continues to look attractive to the University of Arizona. I personally look forward to meeting with the presidents of that conference to explore further the pros and cons of membership in the Pac-8."

An October 9, 1976, article in the *Arizona Daily Star* claimed that Arizona had the approval of at least one Pac-8 president—UCLA chancellor Charles Young—to make the move to the conference without ASU.

Ultimately, ASU budged, realizing the kind of impact moving to the Pacific-8 Conference would have for its academic image. The Arizona Board of Regents, at the behest of Schaefer, primarily, immediately approved the bids of Arizona and ASU on November 28, 1976. The schools started to compete in the conference less than two years later.

19 Jason Terry

Jason Terry finished 12th on the school's all-time scoring list with 1,461 points, and had 493 assists and a school-record 245 steals. He was the *Sports Illustrated*, CBS/Chevrolet, and *Basketball Times* college basketball player of the year in 1999.

All esteemed accomplishments, but 15 years later he did what he had set out to do when he first stepped on UA's campus: become a college graduate. In May 2014, Terry earned his degree in social behavior and human understanding. "Man 15yrs but through hard work, dedication, family support, and GODs blessing I am a College graduate," Terry tweeted out in mid-May after earning his degree.

He added later on *The Doug Gottlieb Show*, "It's a tremendous accomplishment for myself and for my family. I'm not the first graduate out of my family, but it was a promise that I made to my mother once I accepted a scholarship to the University of Arizona.

"It took me 19 years, but I finally completed the task and was able to do so in front of my four younger daughters, which set a mark and a precedent for them—and for me—to say, 'Hey, look: you graduate from high school, you have another step. If your dad can do it, you can do it also. When you're done with high school, I'd love for you to go to college and accomplish the same thing.'"

He accomplished plenty as an individual at UA, but the player who became famous for his high socks, blue shoes, and affable ways was instrumental in helping win the NCAA title.

But when Arizona lost to Utah in 1998, he gave up his blue shoes for good, giving them to a young kid in Anaheim after UA lost in the Elite Eight. "I never want to play in those again," he said after the loss.

Terry, a 6'2" guard, became the perfect sixth man. Unselfish. Hardworking. Role and glue guy. "That's my role: come in and provide a spark," he said back in 1997. That was also his role in 1998.

But it was a moment in December 1996, just a couple of days after Miles Simon returned from academic ineligibility, that Terry made the most unselfish move by a player. "When Miles became eligible, we didn't start him the first couple of games. And Jason Terry came in the office and asked if we could talk about the situation," coach Lute Olson recalled. "He said, 'We've got to get Miles back in the starting lineup, Coach.' I said, 'Yeah, but are you going to sit Bibby down? He's a freshman and his confidence will be totally destroyed.' Michael Dickerson? You couldn't do that. So, I said, 'Yeah, I agree with you, but who are we going to sit down?' And J.T. said, 'Me. I love coming off the bench and I think I can give the team a lift.'"

Olson remembered being impressed by the young man's poise and selflessness. "There aren't many kids who would do that, I tell you."

And so Terry became the sixth man—but with a starter's heart. "There's no question that J.T. is a competitor," Olson said. "[His toughness] is not really the same as Miles', it's just different. But he's got that inner drive. There's no doubt it's there. He comes off as a jokester, but there's no question he gets the job done."

Indeed, his jokes were plentiful. Ever friendly and fun and sometimes off-color, Terry had some zingers. When some of the UA players attended the Australian premiere of *Jurassic Park: The Lost World*, J.T. jokingly came up with this bon mot while eating a chocolate-covered ice cream bar: "Man, whoever thought something this white could be so good?"

Or consider the time, while in Spokane, Washington, when Terry saw a plane parked next to UA's plane. All he could see was the GRO on the side of the plane. "Look at that," Terry said,

"Negro Airlines. I bet the service is bad but the food has to be really good." (The plane actually belonged to Allegro Airlines.) Yes, everyone laughed.

There were also serious times, too. It became gravely serious at the end of his career when he got tangled into an NCAA investigation after his mother, Andrea Cheatham, wrote a letter to the Pac-10 Conference, Arizona, and the NCAA. She felt her son's relationship with agent Larry Fox was not appropriate and that Fox "had spent considerable time, money, and favors [on Terry], laying the groundwork for an indebted relationship." It was felt, additionally, that Cheatham wrote the letter because she specifically wanted someone else to represent her son. Her name was Ndidi Opia, a Bay Area attorney. Cheatham denied those allegations.

Meanwhile Terry, for more than a year, denied that he had taken money against NCAA regulations. Then came the investigation, and he ultimately admitted to taking more than $11,000 in money and benefits before and during his senior year. The violations made Terry, after the fact, ineligible for his entire senior year.

Arizona had to forfeit its first-round, 61–60 NCAA Tournament loss to Oklahoma and paid back more than $45,000, the total proceeds it received for participating in the 1999 NCAA Tournament. "To say he feels badly is an understatement," Olson said in 2000. "There's no question about his feelings in terms of what he's done to himself, primarily, but also the position that he placed the basketball program in."

Upon admission of the transgression, Terry became ineligible to be considered for the school's sports hall of fame and to have his jersey number retired. (However, he does qualify in that he was named college basketball's player of the year.) "Never say never," said then–UA athletic director Jim Livengood when asked about Terry's prospects of entering the Ring of Honor and hall of fame.

Terry has come and gone numerous times since his glory days at UA in 1999, when he averaged 21.9 points per game and was named a first-team All-American and Pac-10 player of the year. He led the league in scoring, assists (5.5), and steals (2.8), and became the only player in UA history to finish his career with more than 1,000 points and 200 steals.

And to think it all started on his recruiting trip to Tucson where the "weather got me"—as did his host, Damon Stoudamire. "I just stayed on his couch all night," Terry said. "Most recruits go out, but I didn't even go out. I didn't go to any parties but [instead] watched them go to the 1994 Final Four. I thought, *One day we're going to win it.*"

20 Nick Johnson: The Prime Recruit

It was Sean Miller's first day on the job at Arizona, and he had somewhere to be, someone to recruit. He hopped in the car and made the first of what would be many drives up Interstate 10, stopping at Gilbert Highland High in the Phoenix area. His target? A combo guard named Nick Johnson.

"[Miller] made it a point to make himself known," said Johnson, who went on to play for powerhouse Findlay Prep near Las Vegas to end his high school career. "From that day on, he and [the] coaching staff really made it a point to be a big part of my life. I chose to come to Arizona because I thought they believed in me the most."

Much of Miller's first recruiting class with the Wildcats fell into his lap—Derrick Williams, Solomon Hill, and MoMo Jones switched from USC, and the staff had previously recruited Kevin Parrom when it was at Xavier. But after that class, Miller had to go about earning his own recruiting chops. Especially in the West, and

Johnson was the elite recruit who started a tidal wave of momentum for the young Arizona coach.

"Almost from the very second I became Arizona's head coach, he and I have been connected," Miller said of Johnson. "He was our top priority in recruiting."

Johnson was a three-year delight at Arizona, his time culminating with the 2014 Pac-12 Player of the Year award, multiple first-team All-America mentions, and a team appearance in the Elite Eight. From start to finish in Johnson's junior season, Miller praised the team's chemistry—and he pointed to Johnson as being the glue guy.

For instance, it was Johnson's idea to find housing before the season for several of the guys. Seven players ended up in a duplex near campus, which helped improve upon the camaraderie from the previous season. And that togetherness resulted in a team-first attitude on the court.

"A lot of the things that you see on the court started a long time ago with us," Miller said during the NCAA Tournament. "It started a long time ago with Nick wanting to be on a special team this year. He's certainly the leader."

Johnson averaged 16.3 points, 4.1 rebounds, and 2.8 assists as a junior, working hard to expand his offensive game with a variety of floaters and midrange shots. And that doesn't take into account his value as a leader, or the fact that he was arguably the best perimeter defender in the league, able to guard three positions as well as play three positions on offense.

"It's hard to learn three positions, let alone do it effectively," Miller said. Johnson was more than effective. He could be super flashy. That blessed leaping ability he inherited from his father—"Jumping Joey" Johnson, owner of a 52-inch vertical jump—filled a highlight reel at Arizona that might as well be entitled "Saint Nick." First up in that show could be the championship game of the Diamond Head Classic in Honolulu on Christmas Day 2012.

Johnson exploded from behind to swat a layup attempt from Chase Tapley in the final seconds to preserve a 68–67 victory over San Diego State. As Johnson would say late in his UA career, "I don't have a 47-inch vert for nothing."

Johnson, a three-year starter, was in line for an all-out assault on many Arizona career records had he decided to stay one more season. As it is, he's still forever standing in elite company, joining Sean Elliott, Chris Mills, Damon Stoudamire, Mike Bibby, Jason Terry, and Derrick Williams as UA players who earned the Pac-12 Player of the Year Award.

While Johnson might not have reached Mount Rushmore status with the Wildcats—and the final few seconds against Wisconsin in the 2014 West Region final were an unfortunate ending—he'll be forever linked to the early feel-good years of the Miller era.

"I can't stress it enough," Johnson said while announcing he was turning pro, "it's been a great experience at Arizona."

21 Pete Williams: The Cornerstone

When it comes down to it, there are the icons of the Arizona program through the years: Sean Elliott, Steve Kerr, Bob Elliott, Damon Stoudamire, Mike Bibby, and so many more. But there's one guy who should be given plenty of kudos in catalyzing the program's entire success. He's Pete Williams, often the guy many claim to be the cornerstone of what the program is all about—or at least how it started.

Williams was a rock in Lute Olson's first two seasons, leading the team in points per game (14.5), rebounds (9.9), and field goal percentage (60.4) in his first season, 1983–84. A season later, he was first in rebounds (8.5) and field goal percentage (60.7), numbers that are more impressive when considering he went against the likes of 6'10" Detlef Schrempf and seven-footer Christian Welp.

Remember that Williams was 6'7", and a wispy player at 190 pounds. He always held his own, though. He was the Pac-10's best rebounder back then. And arguably the team's best player.

"I know everyone likes to talk about Steve Kerr and Sean Elliott...they are the ones who made Arizona a national program," Olson said. "But the reason that guys like Sean and Craig McMillan would consider [playing for] us was because of the job Pete did in terms of turning the program around."

Williams appreciated the coach's words, and in *Tales from the Arizona Locker Room*, he said he didn't want to shortchange anyone who started with him or came afterward. As for his own legacy, he said he'll consider himself "one of the key building blocks along with several others...and I'm happy with that. It would be nice to relish in all the success that came after that but I have no problem in being one of the guys who got it all started."

He was indeed a key building block, and was perhaps the reason why Olson became known for who he was in only his second year in the program. Olson suspended Williams and Morgan Taylor after they were out late in Seattle after losing to Washington. At the time, Arizona was closing in on what would have been the school's first Pac-10 title. Arizona was scheduled to get to UCLA next, but the pair was not going to play. Williams remembers Olson was so upset in his senior leader that "he couldn't even look at me. And that just showed me how disappointed he was in me." But rules were rules, and Olson was steadfast in his standards, star player or not.

It was one of Williams' biggest regrets from his time at UA. "I use that example to this day in saying no one person is bigger than the program," Williams said. To this day, he understands exactly the coach's reasoning and applauds it. "That's a coach who has integrity, not only for himself but the whole status of his program," Williams said. "You can't help but respect that. That just showed no one is bigger than the program and I'm not going to compromise my integrity for it."

Arizona lost to UCLA 58–54 without Williams and Taylor, falling to third in the conference.

"I remember I got blitzed in the *Star*, as you'd expect, and a lot of fans were really upset with me," Olson said. "They said, 'Hey, we have a chance to win the Pac-10 title, and that's never going to happen again.'"

But after the game, when UA returned home, Olson received a handwritten letter from Odiemae Elliott, prospect Sean Elliott's mom, appreciating what Olson did on that trip. "She said, 'You're exactly the type of coach I want Sean to play for,'" Olson said. Elliott had already committed, but it was further reassurance that he had done the right thing.

22 Illinois Collapse

As Lute Olson said, it was going from the highest of highs to the deepest of lows. That's how the team's stay in Rosemont, Illinois, could be described in March 2005.

On a Friday, Arizona was enjoying a last-second victory over Oklahoma State. It was a victory that propelled the Wildcats to their seventh Elite Eight and had Olson on the verge of becoming—at the time—the oldest coach to reach the Final Four. He was 70.

"We never doubted we could win that game," Olson writes in his book *Lute! The Seasons of My Life*. Indeed, Arizona looked like it was well on its way to another Final Four appearance. For 36 minutes, the Illini couldn't stop Channing Frye and Arizona. The Wildcats were up by seven, eight, and eventually 14.

Olson & Co. were four minutes from making it happen against then-No. 1 Illinois. Those four minutes might as well have been a lifetime.

"Maybe the guys thought they could sit on [the lead]," Olson writes. "I wanted us to be a little more aggressive." Instead, UA became skittish. Olson added it didn't help that the crowd of 18,000 fans (mostly from Illinois) were loud and that the referees stopped calling the game like they had been. "I just felt the officials put their whistles away," Olson said.

And down the stretch, Illinois played unbelievably well. One three-pointer led to another, and by the time UA looked up it led by just eight with three minutes left. "You could feel the momentum shift," Olson said. "You could see the look on Illinois' faces that *maybe, just maybe*...They began picking up their intensity."

One big shot came after another, and the gap continued to close. "Believe me, in that situation you can feel the game start to slip away," Olson writes. "You do everything you can to stop it, short of going out on the court and tackling somebody. We needed to make one play. We needed one stop.... We needed one play and we were going to the Final Four."

Instead, the game went into overtime as UA took a last feeble shot in regulation that could have won it. Olson tried to rally his guys by telling them the same thing he told them in 1997: "It's going to come down to who the tougher team is. Both teams exerted a lot of energy. We just have to be tougher than they are."

Arizona was and then it wasn't.

When Arizona inbounded the ball with 11.8 seconds left, it took too long to get into the offense—not good when every second mattered. Mustafa Shakur got the ball but passed it off to Hassan Adams (who had been terrific to that point). To Adams' surprise,

Mustafa Shakur and the rest of the Arizona Wildcats fell just short to Illinois in 2005.

he was guarded by Deron Williams, who had previously been on Salim Stoudamire all game. Illinois had guessed right. Little wonder, since Salim had had a miserable night. Stoudamire was a decoy; it was Adams who was supposed to take the ball to the basket and make a play. If he didn't, maybe he would get fouled and get to the free throw line. Instead, he couldn't get to the basket, eventually throwing up a misguided shot that bounced badly off the rim. UA lost 90–89. It was the first group of seniors in the Olson era that fell short of the Final Four.

"Hassan was playing spectacular and he was supposed to get to the basket," said Jawann McCellan, a freshman at the time. "He was supposed to go one-on-one or create opportunities for other people. If they didn't stop him he'd make the play. But if not, [he was to] give it to Salim on his strong side."

In the end, Olson, after consoling a group of stunned men in the locker room by telling them he was very proud of what they did all season and in that game, spoke to the media about what a great game it was to watch if one didn't have a stake in it—an ESPN Instant Classic. "For 36 minutes we played the best game we had played all season," Olson said. "We played very well, but to Illinois' credit they came back."

Years later, Olson admits that he's never watched the game tape. Neither have a number of the key participants for UA. "You can't change the outcome," he said.

McClellan agreed: "It gives me bad feelings. We were right there."

23 Jason Gardner: Arizona's Mr. Iron Man

In an unusual twist of fate, Arizona's Jason Gardner played more minutes with the Wildcats than any other player, yet he did not play one minute in the NBA.

The point guard had contemplated leaving for the NBA early after his sophomore year in 2001. In fact, he told ESPN.com he was leaning toward going pro during pre-draft workouts. "You've got to do what's best for you," Gardner was quoted as saying. "I really don't think that going back [to Arizona] is the answer. I don't."

In the end, Gardner resisted the temptation to go to the NBA and completed a storied four-year career with Arizona. He is Arizona's Iron Man, having played a school-record 4,825 minutes. He averaged a record 35.5 minutes per game during his 136-game UA career. And he became the third-leading scorer in Arizona history, with 1,984 points.

With his Naismith Player of the Year Award following his senior season in 2003, Gardner became the fourth player to have his jersey number (No. 22) retired at McKale Center. His jersey hangs alongside those of Sean Elliott, Steve Kerr, and Mike Bibby.

Gardner is also the only Wildcat to rank in the top five in career scoring, steals, and assists. Gardner, Elliott, and Damon Stoudamire are the only three-time All–Pac-10 selections in Arizona history.

Yet despite all of the accolades, he is Arizona's only first-team All-American who went undrafted.

His height (5'10") was undoubtedly a factor with some scouts. Some also questioned whether Gardner could get his shot off and be consistent with it at the next level. As a senior, he shot 39.2 percent from the field and only 33.2 percent from three-point range, numbers that made scouts wary of his pro potential.

"We played at a high level at Arizona, and I played against a lot of those point guards coming out, so you always wonder, *Why not me?*" Gardner said in a 2011 interview with the *Arizona Republic*. "When you grow up as a kid, you think, *Oh, I'm going to play in the NBA*, so when it doesn't happen, it's a little bit of a shock, but you got to get back up. At the end of the day you have to find a way to get over it. I ended up having a great career in Europe, playing with a lot of good people, learning a lot more about basketball."

Gardner's eight-year career overseas included successful stops in Slovenia, Belgium, Israel, and Germany. He was named the MVP of the German basketball Bundesliga in 2008–09.

"My family got to see a lot of different places throughout Europe," Gardner told the *Arizona Republic* when asked about his experience overseas. "My daughter got to see the London Bridge and the Eiffel Tower, and when she sees those things now, she's like, 'Daddy, we've been there.' At one time, I was like, 'It's OK playing here,' but now when my daughter says things like that, it makes me appreciate it more."

Gardner turned to his lifelong desire to coach in 2011, becoming an assistant at Loyola of Chicago. After two years there, he joined the staff of former Arizona player and assistant Josh Pastner at Memphis. After only three years of directly learning the coaching profession under Porter Moser at Loyola and Pastner at Memphis, Gardner became a head coach in his hometown of Indianapolis. He was hired by Indiana University–Purdue University Indianapolis (IUPUI) in April 2014.

"I think it's a great fit for Jason," said Lute Olson, his former coach at UA. "He's going to do well there. He's well-liked in Indianapolis and he didn't rush into a big job right away."

Considering how he has proven himself at Arizona and overseas with his work ethic, Gardner's coaching career should prove fruitful. "Look at the guy," Pastner told the *Indianapolis Star*. "He's 5'10", and the guy got his jersey retired at his high school (North Central in Indianapolis). He got his jersey retired at Arizona. He's sharp. He has a high basketball IQ. He's hard-working. He's always been around winning. He knows how to win. He's a winner."

24 Eric Money

Although he played at Arizona 40 years ago, Eric Money left a lasting mark on the Wildcats program.

Money and former Detroit Kettering High School teammate Coniel Norman followed former Michigan assistant coach Fred

Snowden to Tucson in 1972–73, the first year the NCAA allowed freshmen to play.

According to the book *Tucson: A Basketball Town*, written by Money and former teammate Bob Elliott, Snowden referred to Money as "Franchise." Money was a play-making point guard who could score and set up his teammates against the elite in college basketball.

Money, a six-foot guard, was the leader of the Kiddie Korps, the all-freshman lineup in Snowden's first year that included Norman, Jim Rappis, Al Fleming, and John Irving. Street & Smith's basketball magazine rated the class No. 1 in the nation at the time.

And they earned it. Money and Norman each set the Arizona freshman scoring record in 1973–74. Money had 37 points in his college debut against Cal State Bakersfield on November 29, 1973. Norman topped that with 38 points three months later. And each had 37 points in an additional game in their freshman season.

"I think the stats show that Coniel and I were one of the best backcourts, if not the best backcourt, the program has produced," Money said in a 2010 interview with TucsonCitizen.com.

The backcourt duo made headlines after their sophomore seasons by declaring hardship for the NBA Draft. Money was drafted in the second round by hometown team Detroit, the 33rd pick overall. Norman dropped to the third round, 37th overall, taken by Philadelphia.

In the NBA, Money averaged 12.2 points over six seasons. His best pro season was in 1977–78 with Detroit, when he averaged 18.6 points and 4.7 assists per game. Just two years later, he was out of the NBA and selling cars in Tucson. He attempted a comeback with the San Diego Clippers in 1981–82 but did not find a roster spot. And with that, his basketball playing days were over.

Money mentions in *Tucson: A Basketball Town* that his decision to turn pro early was out of necessity for financial reasons, especially if he were to become injured. "The options were slimmer at that time," Money writes. "The rules on hardship were different. You couldn't test the waters like you can today. It was a tough call, loyalty to the team versus going pro and helping your family.

"The constant possibility of injuries shortening your career takes some of your options away. If I'm going to get hurt, I'm going to get paid for it."

Before his playing days were over, Money was one of a few NBA players who appeared in the 1979 movie *The Fish That Saved Pittsburgh* starring Julius "Dr. J" Erving. As fate would have it, future Arizona basketball coach Sean Miller was also in that movie, appearing as a trick ballhandling kid.

Money was also an NBA oddity: he scored 23 points for the Nets and four for the 76ers in the same game (sort of) in 1978–79. He opened the game at Philadelphia as a starter for the Nets and, more than four months and a four-player trade later, he ended it as a reserve with Erving and the 76ers.

The Nets had filed a protest after the November 8, 1978, game ended 137–133 in Philadelphia's favor in double overtime. Former NBA commissioner Larry O'Brien upheld the Nets' protest to replay the game because its coach Kevin Loughery was assessed three technical fouls instead of two and an ejection. The game resumed March 23, 1979, with 5:50 left in the third quarter and Philadelphia leading 84–81. The 76ers won 123–117. "I think Doc said something to me like, 'At least this time you're on the winning side,'" Money told the *Los Angeles Times*.

Money went on to become a junior high school physical education teacher and assistant high school coach at View Park Prep in the Crenshaw District of Los Angeles.

25 Hadie Redd: UA's First African American Player

He wore No. 3 and No. 23, but he might as well have been No. 1. Hadie Redd was that big back then, when he became the first African American basketball player at the University of Arizona in 1951.

"He had a huge impact," said former teammate George Rountree.

There were cultural changes at Arizona, at the tail end of Fred A. Enke's glory days as a coach. Rountree said Redd was probably the second-best player he's ever played with (Roger Johnson being the best). Clearly, Redd was the best offensive player. He was also described as affable, kind, and compassionate.

"He was a very talented basketball player and someone who could jump out of gym and could easily dunk. He was a heck of an offensive player," Rountree said. "He was a talented person, but someone who took a huge amount of abuse [in the 1950s] in Texas. Huge amount."

Never more so than when Arizona went to Lubbock, Texas, for a basketball trip in 1954. Redd, in a story that was reprinted in the *Tucson Weekly* in 1997, recalled when Enke called him over to give him some news.

"Oh, God! I thought I had done something wrong," Redd recalled before a trip to Texas. "One thing was he didn't want us to dunk the ball. He'd always tell us to use the backboard. I thought maybe he'd seen us doing some clowning. I walked over to him, and he had his head down."

Redd recalled Enke putting his hand on his shoulder, sensing it was a major concern.

"I don't know how to put this to you," Redd recalled Enke telling him. "Please believe me that I tried everything I could. We're going to Lubbock, Texas, and I've tried everything to find a hotel to accommodate the whole team. The answer is always the same: No! But I want you to go, the team wants you to go, and basketball wants you to go. It would be good for the state, too. I want you to think about that."

Of course, Redd was going to go. How could he not?

I can't let someone else do this. I'm here. I have to take the challenge. I just have to do it, Redd thought.

He told Enke, "Let's go. I'm ready."

He told his father he had decided to go to Texas and his father applauded the decision. But there was one thing he couldn't do: tell his mom. Why?

"If you did," his father told him, "Arizona would be minus one basketball player, and that would be you."

He didn't tell his mom until after the trip. Good thing, too, since the trip wasn't easy. When the team arrived at the hotel in Lubbock, the doorman placed a hand on Redd's chest and said, "You can't come in."

The players banded together and said they didn't want to play the game, but Redd insisted—after all, that's what they were there for.

He stayed with an African American family. The patriarch, Dr. Miner, had a small hospital and that's where Hadie stayed. "He made me as comfortable as he could," Redd said.

Still, it was difficult. It was a lonely feeling seeing the bus go one way and him going the other. There were no meals with the team, little communication. It all but brought tears to his eyes. At the hospital, the TV wouldn't work, and neither did the radio.

"You're saying to yourself, *What have I done?*" he said. "Out of all the teaching that my mother and father gave me, my teachers, my coaches, the whole lot...the olive branch. None of that's working."

He felt as if he were being treated like someone from another world. It wasn't easy. That was more than understandable, Rountree said.

Texas Tech played in a small gym and maybe 700–800 fans showed up, Rountree remembered. "We walked up to warm up and they said, 'You black bastard, go back to Tucson. We don't want you here!'" Rountree said. "That was the exact verbiage. I will remember it as long as I live. Hadie was frightened and it shook him."

"We never really talked about that stuff," Rountree said years later of Redd's troubles. "I thought Fred Enke treated him very nice. But I'm not sure he knew how to deal with it. It was very difficult for Hadie to deal with."

Eventually, Redd became an All–Border Conference second-team player in his junior and senior years. He led the team in scoring each of those years, finishing with 784 points in his career.

A former policeman and detective in the San Francisco area, he passed away in March 2011 at the age of 77.

26 Tom Tolbert

For the lack of a better term, Lute Olson called Tom Tolbert "a free spirit" and, well, "unique."

He was actually trying to be nice, because Tolbert was the source of Olson's angst for most of the mid-1980s. The hair Olson had on his head was all that was left after pulling most of it out because of Tolbert's antics off and on the court.

Still, having Tolbert was lucky for Olson and unlucky for UNLV coach Jerry Tarkanian, who also recruited the bulky forward from Cerritos Junior College via UC Irvine. That's where he was before junior college, and where his coach told him he wasn't good enough to play at even that level. "If I [had gone] to Vegas," Tolbert was quoted in Olson's book, "I could see myself there 10 years later, being a pit boss."

Sure, Olson admitted that there were times he had wished Tolbert had chosen UNLV; there would have been less stress. Olson has long said Tolbert always played on a court that was slanted, that Tolbert seemingly was always on the offensive end because defense was foreign to him.

"No matter what I tried, I couldn't get him to hustle," Olson writes in his book. "So we battled often, and sometimes loudly. Tolbert could take it. And sometimes he'd give it back. Tolbert took everything we could give him."

Tolbert gave back, too. Like one time (of many) when the team had to run around the campus mall and around McKale Center, about 1.5 miles. The team was told to take a run after practice. Along the route is a water fountain on the mall about 1½ feet deep. Everyone ran it...except for Tolbert, who ducked away from the team and jumped in. He waited for everyone to come around a second time, and that's when he joined them on the way back to McKale Center. Olson was never the wiser.

"I pulled it off. He didn't know about it until about five years ago when I told him about it," Tolbert said. "He had no idea. Absolutely I pulled it off."

When a manager came by to check to see that everyone was running, he saw Tolbert in the fountain. He asked him what he was doing, but Tolbert simply put his finger to lips and said, "'Shhh, don't tell anyone.' He kept walking."

In a nutshell, that was Tolbert: a do-as-I-please type who got the job done, but always on his own terms. He became famous for his under-the-basket, reverse layup against North Carolina that helped Arizona get to its first Final Four. He was a big man who could score, and who perfectly complemented Anthony Cook and Sean Elliott.

"It's hard to describe your legacy, but I think I just helped the team get to its first Final Four," said Tolbert, now a well-known radio sports talk show host in San Francisco. "And for that I'm pretty proud."

But it was one play, captured in photo, with him looking up to nail the shot at 70–52 against North Carolina, that was easily his best moment and his best game.

The Tar Heels simply couldn't stop Elliott (24 points) and Tolbert (21) in the second half. "I didn't play well in the first half, and that's when Lute sat me on the bench and asked me, 'Do you want to go to Kansas City?' I said yes," Tolbert recalled. "And he said, 'Prove it.' I had 18 points and five rebounds in the second half."

And it was Tolbert's circus shot that helped. He said he had "screwed around like that in practice a lot." As it said on the score sheet: "Prayer goes in."

Boy did it ever. Arizona had been down 42–40 early in the second half. Tolbert went 7-for-11, scoring 12 points in Arizona's 19–6 run to put the game away. The spurt started with that reverse layup. Tolbert faked J.R. Reid off his feet, jumped into him, and threw the ball one-handed back over his own head. It turned into a three-point play. "I put a little English on the shot and saw the trajectory. Yes, it was odd but I knew it had a good chance of going in," he said. "I saw it go in. It was a pretty sweet moment."

A week later, UA was in the Final Four.

"That squad was the team that helped lay the ground work for future Final Fours and a national championship. Lute had that thing going anyway and Sean coming in was huge," Tolbert remembered.

"It was a great time. When you get to the NBA, you get paid to do it—and it's a lot of fun, but your teammates have wives and kids. It's a job. In college it's about school and hanging out with your teammates and playing basketball.... You don't realize how good it is until you leave. You're never able to be part of a team like that again, being in Tucson.

"Playing with Sean, he was fantastic—best player on our team. When we needed a bucket he was our go-to guy. He was the one guy on the team who could create his shot. He was the man. He was as good as anyone who ever played there. Went on to have a real good NBA career. When we played I always felt we had the best player on the court. [If] we needed something, Sean could get it for us.

"[He] could do it all.... [When we'd] get into a jam it's good to just say, 'Do your thing big boy.'"

Tolbert may be effusive about Elliott's legacy at Arizona, but his own is just as assured.

27 The Udalls: Politics and Basketball

Arizona basketball history features a prominent father-and-son combination with Fred A. Enke Sr. and Fred W. Enke Jr.

Likewise, Matt Brase played for his grandfather Lute Olson at Arizona from 2003 to 2005.

Cousins Damon and Salim Stoudamire were quite a pair of guards for the Wildcats program, but they never shared the same court with Arizona.

As far as brothers are concerned, the top combination is Morris K. "Mo" Udall and Stewart Udall, who played in the 1940s. (Their cousin Calvin Udall also played with the Wildcats, although he was never a teammate of either of them.)

What made the bond between Mo and Stewart and the Arizona program even more special is that each served for the military during World War II before returning to Arizona to play for Enke Sr. Years later, they became significant political figures in the United States.

Stewart played for Arizona from 1938 to 1940, then returned for the 1946–47 season after the war ended. Mo played in the 1941–42 season and returned from military service to finish his Arizona career from 1946 to 1948.

Stewart, a guard, was an All–Border Conference second-team selection in 1939–40 then had a six-year hiatus from basketball. "That [absence from basketball] was unusual," Stewart Udall said

Secretary of the Interior Stewart Udall and U.S. Representative and brother Mo Udall gather with University of Arizona staff for an NCAA meeting in 1966. From left are UA athletic director Dick Clausen, Secretary Udall, Representative Udall, and faculty athletic representative Thomas Hall.

in *Tales from the Arizona Wildcats Locker Room*. "But some athletes say once you develop a skill that you don't lose it."

Stewart Udall returned as a 26-year-old elder statesman of the team in his only season with Mo, who was 24. That 1946–47 team won the Border Conference title and finished 21–3 overall.

Knowing that Arizona was built for success, with players like Enke Jr., George Genung, and Linc Richmond, Stewart Udall and teammate Marvin Borodkin approached athletic director "Pop" McKale before that season to ask for a series against Wyoming (then a basketball powerhouse). The Cowboys went to the NCAA Tournament annually during that era and won the title in 1943.

"McKale didn't want it," Stewart Udall said. "I figured if we played Wyoming it would put us on the map to the big time."

Stewart and Borodkin went over McKale's head to school president Alfred Atkinson, but Atkinson quickly shot down the idea because the well-respected McKale had already made a decision. Still, that kind of aggressive lobbying was a harbinger of the path ahead for Stewart Udall, who earned his law degree at Arizona in 1949 and later was elected to the U.S. House of Representatives. He served as the nation's Secretary of the Interior under presidents John F. Kennedy and Lyndon B. Johnson.

Mo Udall chose to pursue a career in politics after becoming one of the first Arizona players to be drafted by an NBA team in 1948, when he was selected by the Denver Nuggets. Mo Udall became Arizona's first pro player, during the 1948–49 season with the Nuggets. In the off-season, he returned to Arizona to finish his law degree.

Mo Udall led the Wildcats with 13.2 points a game in his senior season and was selected to the All–Border Conference team as a forward. He achieved this success despite having only one eye (he lost his right eye at age six when a friend accidentally poked him with a pocketknife while they were attempting to cut a string).

He used a glass eye, which did not prevent him from joining the military during the war—only because he tricked the medical examiner by covering his glass eye each time he was told to alternate during the exam.

Tales from the Arizona Wildcats Locker Room describes the time when Mo Udall came under scrutiny following a game at New Mexico. An Albuquerque sportswriter mentioned that Mo Udall was a liar, saying, "No one shoots like that with one eye." To the sportswriter's surprise, Udall removed the eye from its socket, and said, "Mister, I haven't been able to see much out of this one, so you try it."

That kind of dry wit defined Mo Udall throughout his Arizona career and esteemed political career. He graduated in 1949 from Arizona's law school and served as a U.S. congressman from 1961 to 1991. He unsuccessfully ran for president in 1976.

28 Aaron Gordon Seeks Perfection

For Sean Miller, the time spent coaching Aaron Gordon was, well, way too short. How could it not be when coaching one of basketball's prodigies? "It feels like you're just getting started," Miller said. "Then you wave good-bye."

On April 15, 2014, Gordon, called a "program changer" before he signed with Arizona a year earlier, announced that he was leaving Arizona. Despite his love for Arizona "from top to bottom" he decided to leave after one short-but-sweet season.

He compared himself to Scottie Griffin. Who? The combination of Scottie Pippen and Blake Griffin, of course. Time will tell.

In his first year at Arizona, he looked the part of a potential pro and a wet-behind-the-ears freshman. So many ups and downs—which resulted in more highlights to count because of the hops on the ups—that Gordon figured it was time to pursue the dream he's had since the first grade.

It was no shock that Gordon, a 6'9" forward from San Jose, California, would jump. All season he had been called a one-and-done player. He was Arizona's first since Jerryd Bayless did it in 2008.

Gordon had long been considered a lottery pick, and his stock may have increased even more when he was named USA Basketball's male athlete of the year—this despite questions about his offensive game on the perimeter. In his lone season at Arizona, he averaged 12.4 points, 8.0 rebounds, and one block per game, and shot 49.5 percent from the floor. He also shot a shockingly low 42.2 free-throw percentage.

"Contrary to popular belief, I learned a lot," Gordon said of playing for Miller. "I can't sum it down but I understand the game of basketball better than I did the year before. I learned how to play the game better."

He came in with huge expectations, one of the better recruits to play at Arizona and arguably the best under Miller. "Everybody is going to have expectations but I don't worry about people's opinions," Gordon said. "It's kind of a daily thing where pressure goes up and down. I relax myself by saying 'all you need to do is win.' That's what I came in saying and that's what I'm going to stick to."

It wasn't always easy, even though Arizona made it look simple most of the time in 2013–14 in racing to a 21–0 record and eventually 33–5. All season Gordon—Arizona's human highlight reel, complete with high-flying dunks—sought perfection and improvement.

He acknowledges, however, perfection is an elusive quality. "As a freshman it's hard not to have ups and downs, but I tried to be as consistent as possible," he said.

In high school he took interest in a class called "Façade of Perfection." It looked at the "fake life" of youth through the lens of advertising.

"It's just not true. It damages people's minds because nobody is perfect," he said. "Perfect is an abstract thing. Trying to be perfect is abstract. No one is perfect."

Through the season he said he had taken "baby steps" in his improvement after not knowing what to expect. In the end, nothing changed. He was determined to be the best player he could be and is now looking for a sound and solid career in the NBA after being the fourth overall pick by Orlando.

"I'm a perfectionist," he said. "What interested me in that class is that you're never going to be perfect no matter how many shots you take and no matter how long you're going to be in the gym you're just not."

29 Kenny Lofton

Pop quiz: only two players have ever played in the Final Four and in a World Series. Who are they? Answer: Kenny Lofton and Tim Stoddard.

How it happened for Lofton, Arizona's quick and athletically gifted point guard, was a bit by chance. Lucky for him—and yes, aided by his God-given talent—baseball was available to him. But it was basketball that got him noticed while living in a Gary, Indiana, apartment with his partially blind grandmother.

When he recruited Lofton in the mid–1980s, coach Lute Olson thought of him as a "tough kid." What Lofton had, according to Olson, was confidence and quickness. He could also score and play a little point guard and pester his way into being a tough defender.

"Kenny's game was speed," Olson writes in his autobiography. "I knew the way they played basketball in that area: the kids run up and down the court as fast as they can and when the horn goes off, they look up at the scoreboard to see who won. He didn't have a natural feel for the game; he played at one speed—full-out. I thought with some coaching we could contain his skills with our offense. So Kenny accepted our scholarship offer."

In an interview with Deadspin.com, Lofton said his college choices weren't many—just Purdue, Louisville, or Arizona. "I just wanted to have an opportunity to play basketball and go to school, and [Arizona] had nice, warm weather, so I couldn't beat that." Still, Arizona was a surprise. The guy who couldn't get a whiff from nearby Michigan or places closer to home had found one in Tucson.

Lofton said he "had found a place that sure wasn't known much for its basketball. I'd tell people back at home I play for Arizona, and everyone would say, 'Yeah, that's where there's plenty of sun, lots of old people, college kids lying out all over the place getting tanned, and...don't they have pretty good baseball out there, too?"'

Eventually Lofton became the team's sixth man. He was a key player in Arizona's run to the Final Four in 1988, as Steve Kerr's backup and the team's resident thief. He played in 129 games, starting 54—most of them his sophomore year when Kerr was out with a knee injury. He finished his career with 329 assists, 200 steals, and an average 4.8 points per game.

It became obvious to the coach after Lofton's sophomore year that the NBA wasn't in the cards for the player. He wasn't going to be a point guard and he wasn't a good enough shooter, Olson writes in his book.

"He really took offense with that," Olson said in a 2014 interview about those words. "He feels that if I had given him the green light like I had given Steve Kerr the green light, [then maybe] he would have played in the NBA."

But serendipity played a factor in Lofton becoming a household name. It came from baseball, via softball. Each season before basketball began, the Wildcats played in a team-building softball game—and Lofton had a knack for making every play, covering the field from foul line to foul line.

On offense, if and when he made contact, he'd find a way to beat out the throw or get on base. At the end of Lofton's sophomore season, Olson met with baseball coach Jerry Kindall to recommend they take a look at him. Lofton went for a tryout and, well, wasn't all that impressive. "He's got a lot to learn," Kindall said. "He doesn't get the bat around curveballs."

"But if he gets it on the ground, you can't throw him out either," Olson countered, according to his book.

Before his senior basketball season, he joined the UA baseball team as primarily a defensive replacement and a pinch runner. Plenty of scouts attended UA baseball games and local scout Clark Crist saw Lofton. Apparently he liked what he saw, because the next summer the Houston Astros made Lofton their pick in round 17.

It wasn't a surprise to Lofton's good friend Harvey Mason. He remembered one day when UA was in Anchorage, Alaska, for a tournament, and the team was having a snowball fight during their free time. "Basically, it was Kenny versus the rest of us because he had such a ridiculous arm," Mason told Deadspin.com. "He was throwing snowballs like 100 miles per hour, just knocking guys off their feet. Afterward, we said to him, 'Man, you should play baseball.'"

It only took a few months for that to be realized.

Still, Lofton didn't want to give up his dreams of becoming a pro basketball player. In interviews with ESPN's now-defunct *Up*

Close, Lofton said, "I've always said that basketball at Arizona taught you that there are a lot of things you cannot control. That taught me a lot. That you want certain situations to be a certain way but it couldn't [be] and that you had to deal with it and accept it."

When asked if he was happy about UA's national title, he said he was for the team, but as far as Olson was concerned, "Lute Olson is a different kind of guy. Like people say, he wants to make sure his hair is straight. But he's a good teacher of the game. And that's what I liked about him. But he showed favorites, and that's what I didn't like."

The two have a very good relationship today, Olson said, but the coach holds firm: realistically, Lofton wasn't an NBA type. "Kenny didn't have the size, although he had all the athleticism in the world," Olson said.

Olson said Mason, one of Lofton's best friends, reminds him, "'How many millions did you make in baseball?' He did very well, but deep down he still feels the same way, but…Harvey has been telling him that for years."

These days Lofton owns a television production company. And, he's made cameos in a number of television shows, too.

Oh, and he became a six-time MLB All-Star and a four-time Gold Glove Award winner in 17 major league seasons. When he retired from baseball, he was 15th on the all-time stolen base list with 622.

30 Mike Bibby: The Ultimate Point Guard

Mike Bibby isn't sure what his legacy at Arizona is—nor does it really matter to him. "That's for other people to decide," he said.

Others have done just that, and the college basketball history books don't lie: Bibby became the first freshman point guard to help lead a team to the NCAA men's basketball title. Yet Bibby deflected any talk about himself, doing what he knows best: dishing the assist.

He called it "the right situation at the right time. We all complemented each other. All the pieces of the puzzle were there." If so, he was a key piece, like the corner piece that starts it all.

He called Arizona's run to the title "a once-in-a-lifetime chance, and to do it with Coach Olson to get him his first title was a big deal. It was a big deal for the school and for Tucson."

He was Kid Cool, the unflappable one. That was Bibby, Arizona's 6'1" point guard, who dribbled the ball like there was a string attached to it.

"He was a tremendous competitor," Olson said. "He was just like Jason Terry in a sense that when big shots had to be made, boy, he could hit [them]. Mike was good."

And Arizona was thankful to have the kid from Phoenix who committed his junior year, choosing UA over Duke and UCLA. The appeal of being closer to home and playing for Olson won him over. He also became close to assistant coaches Jessie Evans and Phil Johnson.

"I always thought it was a good fit for me because I could go home when I wanted to and still not be at home," Bibby said. "And then there was [the legacy of] Point Guard U. I just thought it was good for me."

It was good for everybody, except for UA's opponents, even if his time was short. In his two-year stint with UA he was 55–14. He was named the Pac-10 Conference's freshman of the year and a year later was the conference's player of the year.

He felt good from the start. Consider day one, game one, against North Carolina. Arizona traveled to Springfield, Massachusetts, and beat the Tar Heels. Bibby had 22 points in 33 minutes in his debut. "I came in not knowing what to expect and I had a pretty good game," he said, looking back. "But I also put everything into it. There was no playing around or messing around when I got to Arizona."

If he did mess around he never showed it. He was as stiff (personality-wise) as a saguaro in his freshman season. He rarely spoke to the media, and when he did it was short, hardly stop-the-presses information. "That's kind of how I am," he said. "I'm pretty quiet until I get to know the individual and get to feel comfortable where I am at."

He felt comfortable right away with Josh Pastner, who was part of the same class as Bibby. They became fast friends, and seemingly there wasn't a day when they weren't working on their games, shot after shot after shot.

"I was in the gym with Josh every night and day," Bibby said. "And if we weren't at the gym we were at an elementary school shooting. I put a lot into it, a lot of work into my game. Josh got me over that hump and got me to the top level."

He reached the top level, indeed. He's one of only four players to have his jersey retired (joining Sean Elliott, Steve Kerr, and Jason Gardner) and is one of only five consensus All-Americans in UA's history. He also received the third-most votes on the John R. Wooden Award ballot.

In his two years at UA, he made the remarkable look ordinary. And when he was really good, he made the ordinary look remarkable. Figure in his performances in the tournament, when he played well beyond his years, hitting key free throws against No. 1 Kansas in the Sweet 16 and key shots against North Carolina in the semifinal game. He could have easily been named the tournament's most outstanding player; instead Miles Simon was named the guy. Yet, he, too, was worthy.

"A lot of credit should go to Miles because he was such a good leader," Olson said. "But typical of most freshmen, Mike didn't want to step on anybody's toes."

After UA won the title, Olson said that Bibby was a huge reason why.

"You don't see that he gets nervous," Olson said. "I think he has a settling effect on his teammates. If you have a good point guard who handles stressful situations well, it's kind of like having a coach who does the same thing on the sideline."

Arizona's run to the title in 1998 seemingly looked good—and it would have been the first time a team went back-to-back in NCAA titles since the Duke teams of the early 1990s. But Utah derailed Arizona on March 21 with a 76–51 defeat.

"That was so disappointing," Bibby said. "I expected us to go all the way. Or at least get [to the championship game]. Utah played us tough and our shots weren't going in that night. It was tough, but things go that way."

It did, too, on one of Bibby's more spectacular days, when No. 6 Arizona went to play No. 4 Stanford at Maples Pavilion. Arizona's then–basketball sports information director Brett Hansen said it was the single most impressive performance he's seen in person: 26 points, 10 assists, and one turnover...in 37 minutes.

"It was a good game," Bibby said. "What I do remember? Them killing me for having my son's tattoo Michael on me. I guess I just wanted to have a good game."

It wasn't as if Bibby didn't handle himself well in seemingly pressure-packed times. Fans at every venue—excluding McKale Center, of course—gave him grief for being the son of then USC coach Henry Bibby. The two were estranged at the time.

"It was nothing, but I guess people used it as entertainment," Bibby said. "It was fine. It was stressful but it was fine. It happened."

31 Gilbert Arenas: The Goofball

To say Gilbert Arenas was one of the more perplexing players to ever suit up for Arizona would be an understatement. To say he was one of the more talented players would be accurate. To say he was one of the more underrated would also be true.

He didn't call himself "Agent Zero" for nothing. He wore No. 0 because, according to Arenas, people always said he "wouldn't amount to nothing."

How wrong they were. And how strange his journey has been.

His arrival at Arizona is legendary. On the recruiting trail—even though Arenas wasn't all that sought after (DePaul and Kansas State were in the mix)—Arizona coach Lute Olson ended up in Arenas' apartment in North Hollywood to discuss the possibility of a basketball scholarship.

"Coach Olson had his hand on the table and started to tap the national championship ring on the glass and you couldn't help but notice it," said then assistant Rodney Tention, the key recruiter for Arenas. "Gilbert was like, *Shit, how can you go wrong?*"

One problem: Arenas had promised his father that he'd visit DePaul because he had family back in the Chicago area. He fulfilled that pledge, and shortly after the visit committed to Arizona.

Tention asked Arenas at what point he decided to commit. "Once he put that ring on the table," Tention recounted the player saying. "At that point it was a done deal."

"There were just too many phone calls, and it was getting to me," Arenas told the *Tucson Citizen* in the fall of 1998. "The phone was ringing every other minute."

And why not? The kid was a great player, averaging 29.8 points, 9.1 rebounds, and 6.1 assists per game as a junior at Grant

High in North Hollywood, California. Yet Arenas, a 6'3" guard, was overlooked by many in recruiting, and slipped through the cracks for many schools that could have used the talented guard. Additionally, according to Tention, Arenas wasn't highly recruited because he had missed about half of the summer AAU schedule because of school commitments.

To convince Olson he needed to look at Arenas, Tention showed the coach a tape of the player scoring 44 points against Los Angeles Crenshaw. "Coach said, 'We gotta recruit him,'" Tention remembered. "That's how it started."

Eventually, the "goofball" and so-called "charmer" would have an impact on Arizona, good and—well, it depends on how you look at it—bad. Arenas' talent chased away (scared away?) the likes of Ruben Douglas, who transferred to New Mexico. It also chased away Luke Recker, who couldn't see much playing with Arenas in front of him.

Instead, he flourished for Arizona alongside Jason Gardner, Richard Jefferson, Luke Walton, Loren Woods, and the rest. He averaged 15.4 points as a freshman, helping lead Arizona to a No. 1 seed in the West.

Then, Arenas turned into the sometimes funny, sometimes aloof, sometimes affable player many remember. He sure was popular (depending on whom you talk to). But his antics grew old, particularly with upperclassman Gene Edgerson, whom Arenas loved to tease and irritate.

"He was just immature," Edgerson said. Tention agreed, pointing out that Arenas was still 17 when UA was midway through its schedule in the 1999–2000 season. "He was just being a kid, basically," Tention said. "He'd be squirting mustard on a wall [or something] and I'd tell him he's not in high school anymore."

But the hijinks rarely stopped. The best story, unsurprisingly, involves Edgerson. Arenas often let out the air in Edgerson's car tires. Finally, Edgerson had had enough and before practice took a heavy nuts-and-bolts implement to practice. Arenas got wind of it and hid from Edgerson in McKale Center. Edgerson was on the floor looking for his nemesis; Arenas was in the stands hiding.

"It was little stupid stuff like that," Tention said.

As practice was about to start, Olson walked onto the court and noticed Arenas missing. He asked assistant coach Jim Rosborough where the player was. Roz told him there was a problem with Arenas and Edgerson. "Take care of it," Olson was said to have uttered. Roz did.

Tention was often there to help too. "I'd go on the road and come back and hear stories about Gilbert, and Coach would tell me to take care of it," Tention said. "I'd say, all right, I've got it."

The one constant in the entire Arenas-Olson relationship was Arenas' seemingly respect or fear of Olson. Tention recalled Arenas having a poor game against Washington, "and Coach jumped all over him. And Gilbert didn't talk to him or look at him."

"Coach said, 'OK, fine, if you're going to act like a baby I'm going to treat you like one," Tention recalled.

Eventually, Arenas, the Robin to Jason Gardner's Batman, had a fantastic career, albeit a short one. Still, UA coaches weren't sure Arenas would leave early for the NBA after his sophomore season; in fact, most thought he'd stay. "We heard he was thinking about leaving but we thought he'd stay," Tention said. "Somebody got to him. Or they got to his dad and he decided to go."

Two months later—despite reports Arenas could go in the first round of the NBA Draft—Arenas was picked in the second round by Golden State. (There are no guaranteed contracts in the second round.)

"He called me during the draft and [we were] on campus watching [it]," Tention said. "He hadn't gotten a call yet. He was really upset. He asked what he was going to do." As they were talking, Tention heard Arenas' named called. He told Arenas to hold on and then Gilbert heard his name. They quickly ended the conversation. "He didn't expect (to be a second rounder)," Tention said. "It was crushing to him."

Eventually, he proved to be more than good enough—becoming an NBA All-Star and a star of major proportions. But he also had a fall equivalent to his rise. In 2009, he was charged with a felony for pulling a gun on former Washington Wizards teammate Javaris Crittendon. Arenas eventually spent 30 days in a halfway house and was suspended 50 games without pay by David Stern, then the NBA commissioner. The three-time NBA All-Star was out of the league three years later, attempting to make a return a couple of times and most recently playing professionally in China.

32 McKale Center

It's 428 feet long, 339 feet wide, and 77 feet from floor to ceiling. And Arizona's McKale Center is the place where many opponents come in seeing red and leave blue. Literally.

For more than 40 years Arizona has been a house of horrors for opponents and a comfort zone for those in an Arizona uniform. No other school in the West in the last 30 years has won more games on its home court than Arizona.

"Playing in McKale was like magic," said former UA player Corey Williams, who played in the mid-1990s. "You were quicker, jumped higher, and shot better. The crowd carries you and your opponent is helpless. Winning is never in doubt."

At least it felt that way. Heck, it *was* that way more than 84 percent of the time. In the last 25 years, Arizona has gone undefeated at home in 11 seasons. Overall, it's 538–102.

"One of my first great memories of Arizona basketball was coming onto the floor as a freshman and seeing a sold-out crowd for the Red-Blue Game—and things just got better from there," said former UA player Matt Muehlebach, the only player to go through four years never losing in McKale Center. "I always thought we had a very smart crowd. They understood when it was a big game or an important time in the game. Those fans can feel good knowing they are a big part of a lot of those wins."

The building was home to a 71-game winning streak, 10th-best in NCAA history. And Arizona has been beyond good at home. UA is the only school to have two home-court winning streaks in the top 10 in Division I men's basketball.

More than seven million fans have attended Arizona basketball games since its opening. It all started on February 1, 1973—Fred Snowden was the coach—when Arizona christened the building with an 87–69 victory over Wyoming. Two days later it picked up win No. 2 vs. Colorado State.

Winning became natural in McKale Memorial Center, named for the late J.F. "Pop" McKale, Arizona's former athletic director and coach from 1914 to 1957. Arizona won its first 67 of 70 games there, setting the trend early and continuing through the 2014 season, one of the undefeated seasons.

"There was a smell in McKale, and to this day you can go into that elevator next to the ticket office and that smell has been there since I was a freshman in college," former Arizona great Bob Elliott said. "There are certain smells and they will say where you are at. I can close my eyes and smell it, and I know that elevator is going to take me to the locker room."

Elliott was part of only one defeat in McKale Center. "The crowd was always crazy," he said. "It could get so loud it was deafening, to the point you couldn't understand what was being said by the crowd; it was just noise. There was a point where it would hurt your ears."

Only once since it's been built has McKale seen a losing record. And that came in Arizona's darkest season, when it went 4–24 under coach Ben Lindsey. UA went 4–10 on the home court. But since then the Magic in McKale has long been there. Great games and great memories.

Who would have thought its construction would be considered a "fiasco," as author James Cooper and architect Lew Place said.

Place said that because budgets were so tight back in the late 1960s, when McKale Center's idea was first conceived, it took three years for construction to start because it took so long to complete the architectural drawings. And by the time they were ready to break ground, the cost had doubled to $8 million.

It almost came to a point where UA was considering enclosing UA Stadium instead, which would have cost $2 million. Place argued that when McKale was designed it was for a multipurpose use, including the drama department. Originally, it was designed to hold large pageants. (Before money was approved through the U.S. government it had to be multipurpose.) As it turned out, the drama labs were to make up only two rooms.

Originally, the dressing rooms for the locker rooms were a rose pink. Snowden quickly quashed that, and had the color changed to a blue gray.

Another odd fact was UA officials put in a vinyl floor...a 3M Tartan floor. "They realized that it was so hard and they were getting leg problems, things like shin splints from running on it," said longtime Arizona official Dick Bartsch.

Eventually, UA rented a floor from the community center and later purchased a portable floor. And it only had two baskets. Later on, Olson requested more baskets to make the building more practice-friendly. Eventually, it boasted six baskets.

Retractable seating eventually came in, as did the permanent floor. And over the years, it has served as a worthy home to UA basketball.

33 1998 Team: No Repeat Championship

In 1998, Arizona had a chance to become the first team to repeat as men's college basketball champions since 1991–92, when Duke did it. It appeared that Arizona, with all five starters back from the 1997 team, was capable. It played well for most of the season and in the NCAA Tournament, soundly beating teams en route to the Elite Eight in Anaheim, California.

But Anaheim has proven to be one of the worst—if not the worst—venues for Arizona. It seemed they could never get a break, much less a win. It didn't get either that March afternoon in 1998 when it faced Rick Majerus & Co. Top-ranked Arizona fell to No. 3 seed Utah 76–51 in the West Region, falling short of the right to advance to the Final Four in San Antonio.

One of the reasons was that UA's guards just couldn't hit shots, playing like it hadn't all season. Even Arizona's press couldn't stop Utah. Then again, the Utes had Andre Miller (a future NBA star) in the backcourt. Miller had a triple double with 18 points, 13 assists, and 14 rebounds. Mike Bibby, Miles Simon, and Michael Dickerson were no match for Miller—at least on this day.

"The worst possible situation for us is if all three don't shoot it well," Arizona head coach Lute Olson said then. Olson added recently, "You have a couple of guys who have off games and, well, you know. The difference in 1997 compared to 1998 [is that] whenever we needed a big bucket they hit it. It was a case of that not happening that time." Dickerson, Simon, and Bibby went a combined 6-for-36 for the game. Bibby was 3-for-15, Simon 1-for-9, and Dickerson 2-for-12.

Utah also controlled the rebounds, 49–34. Arizona shot 28.3 percent from the floor (17-of-60), and 18.2 percent from beyond the three-point line. Utah's triangle-and-two defense had something to do with that. The day before the game, Majerus said he had something up his sleeve, but wasn't ready to say what it was. The critics were skeptical. No team had held UA to fewer than 70 points during the season and only four times had they been held to fewer than 80 points.

"I felt after watching their game [against Maryland in the Sweet 16] and looking at the tape that we had to visit an old friend, the triangle-and-two," Majerus said after the game. "I felt if we could take Bibby out of the game, that was the key. These guys went out and executed perfectly."

Said Bibby after the game, "[Utah] played a great game. They beat us good. We knew it was going to be a tough game. They beat us every way possible."

It's still one of the worst games Olson has had to watch and/or coach through. "It was a huge disappointment," Olson said. "I knew we'd be good and I thought we were obviously a better team than the 1997 team because we had a year's experience. It was disappointing because it was one of those teams that could have won the national championship, just like the 1988 team."

Indeed, the season seemed ripe for a repeat champion. Arizona returned everyone and was confident. There was talk of possibly going undefeated—but that all ended with an early-season loss to Duke in the Maui Classic championship game.

Two games later UA lost again, this time to Kansas in a thriller in Chicago for the Great Eight. The Jayhawks avenged the previous season's upset. UA lost again four games later in a long road game to Florida State, and early on UA was 7–3 before reeling off 19 consecutive wins.

Of those 19 consecutive wins, 16 came against Pac-10 Conference opponents, giving UA a chance to become the first Pac-10 school to go undefeated in conference history. But USC played its best game of the season under Henry Bibby (yes, Mike Bibby's dad) and got a fortunate bounce on an Adam Spanich bucket.

With 2.8 seconds left, Spanich threw up a three-pointer that hit the back of the rim, hit with a thump/thud and fell in. "I didn't know if it would go in," Spanich told L.A. reporters. "I just shot it. But I was like, 'Oh no,' and then I saw it go in. Then I didn't see anything for like 10 minutes."

It was the biggest win for USC in nearly 30 years—and a win that Henry Bibby said "saved the season." It was USC's eighth win overall.

"That was tough, making us 17–1 [in conference]," Olson said. "To be fair, that 1998 team had a large target on its back. That was the case all season. You know, being Arizona, you're going to get everyone's best shot, but this made it even more tempting for teams we played."

34 Bobbi Olson

She was probably the most elegant woman in any room she entered. She also had a sharp sense of humor, a quick wit, and a soothing, calming voice. Her timing was always spot-on.

It's arguable that Roberta Olson—Bobbi to all those who knew her—was as important to the Arizona program as her husband, Lute, in their time together. Consider that when Kentucky wooed Olson to become its coach in the mid-1980s school officials failed to do one thing when they met with Olson for negotiations: they didn't include Bobbi in the meetings.

"I knew they had made the mistake in doing that and knew he wouldn't go," said Cedric Dempsey, Arizona's AD at the time. And unsurprisingly, Olson decided Kentucky wasn't the place for him. He shunned the blue-and-white Wildcats for the red-and-blue Wildcats.

For 47 years, Bobbi was Lute's constant companion. The two married in 1953. When Olson won the NCAA title in 1997 and he was still conducting interviews deep into the night, Bobbi waited

Bobbi Olson was an integral part of the Arizona basketball program.

against a wall in the RCA Dome and replied to his "I'll be right there" with a quick, "I've waited 40 years. I can wait a few more minutes."

"She was the team mom," Kerr said. "She was great. She was the softer side of Lute."

As Bruce Fraser said, Bobbi was all about the "wink and the smile."

"She was awesome," said Luke Walton. "I remember her being one of the reasons why I signed. She had that way about her, that comforting feel about her. She was the one, when Coach Olson was furious with us, she'd tell us that she had our back, that there were no worries. Every time she was around everyone felt better."

Olson said that when she was on road trips she always sat in the first seat on the bus and would remind the players to keep their heads up after a loss. And to her husband she said, "You have one hour to get over this and I don't want to hear anything more about it." When she spoke, Lute listened.

And, of course, there were those famously delicious apple cinnamon pancakes. Corey Williams said it was the pancakes—and the presentation—that won him over. Other recruits, too, he said. He called it "putting the best foot forward" when it came to showing what Arizona offered.

Being from the Midwest—Batavia, Illinois, to be exact—Williams didn't know what to expect when Olson invited the recruits up to the house for breakfast. "We're expecting to see butlers and maids bringing us food and that we'd have a restaurant-style, catered affair. Hey, it's Lute Olson," Williams said. "We get there and there are a few plates and Bobbi is in the kitchen with her apron on and she's making pancakes one at time.... To this day, I don't know what it was, but she made a syrup with butter already in it. Heated, man!

"It was the best breakfast you've ever had. If you're a kid thinking this is what [the program] is about, you're thinking, *It's a real family atmosphere.* As a parent you feel safe being around these people. It was a down-home experience. Some schools go at you with big and fancy, and they came with intimate and personal."

That was Bobbi, who did all she could to make everything better for the players, for everyone. "She always had that way about her," Olson said. "Whether it was about the high school kids or the college kids, she was always good with them. She was very close to the players."

Invariably, when players came into the program they struggled. Bobbi was there to soften the blow. Richard Jefferson recalled times when conversations became life-changers.

Sadly, life changed for everyone in the Arizona family on January 1, 2001, when, after a 2½-year battle with ovarian cancer, Bobbi passed away. She was 65 years old.

"When she fell ill you could see that it was one of the great marriages I've been able to see," said Arizona radio voice Brian Jeffries. "The effect it had on Lute was very apparent and I understand completely. It was a very tough time."

Jefferson was a junior the year she passed. "Mrs. Olson meant so much to all of us," Jefferson said at her public ceremony, which was held in front of thousands and broadcast live on four television stations in the Tucson area. "She knew what to say and when to say it," he continued.

"We come in as boys, we really do. Some of us are here for four, five years, and we leave here as men—and that's because of Coach Olson and Mrs. Olson."

On the day of the memorial UA announced that it was renaming Lute Olson Court the Lute & Bobbi Olson Court.

Her passing came 30 months after first being diagnosed with Stage 3 ovarian cancer while on vacation in Hungary. In the spring of 1999, at a basketball banquet, it was announced she was cancer-free. The crowd roared and the energy in the room was unbelievable. But just months later it had returned, and she entered into the hospital in early December 2000. Lute was seemingly always by her side, deciding to not travel with the team to Connecticut to face the Huskies on a road trip. It was then he took a leave of absence, putting longtime assistant Jim Rosborough in charge. Three weeks later, Bobbi passed away.

"Bobbi faced her illness with great courage," Olson said at that time. "Her love of family remained her priority and even in her last moments she continued taking care of and comforting all of us as only a wife and mother can do. She died today, 01/01/01—No. 1 wife, No. 1 mother, No. 1 grandmother—always No. 1."

35 Coniel Norman

Unemployed and feeling disconnected, Coniel Norman, a former prolific scorer for Arizona, needed some balance in 2010. His almost three decades away from normalcy, living the street life far from his hometown of Detroit, going from one low-paying job to the next, had taken its toll.

"It got to a point where I was not sure I would ever come home to Detroit and see my family again," said Norman, a former NBA player. "I pretty much thought that was it."

Norman spoke to sportswriter Javier Morales about his story. Depression forced him to seek help at a Los Angeles hospital in February 2010. He never thought about giving up on his life; he simply needed reassurance of his place on earth.

"It was a tough time for me," Norman said. "With the recession, I couldn't find a job. I needed some help, so that's why I went [to the hospital]." Norman was without money and insurance. The hospital asked him for names of his immediate family. They were able to locate one of his sisters, who alerted another sister, Renee Norman of Detroit, about his whereabouts.

Renee's daughter, Cassie Norman, had reached out to media in the summer of 2009 for help in locating her uncle, whom she feared was homeless. She had never had the chance to meet her uncle. Norman said he been disconnected from Detroit and his family for more than 27 years.

"When my sister called me, I knew then that it was time to come home, and they came out there right away and got me," Norman said. "I feel truly blessed that we're back together again."

After declaring hardship after his sophomore season at Arizona, Norman, a lean 6'3" guard, played for three seasons in the NBA (1974–76 with the Philadelphia 76ers and then briefly in 1978–79 with the San Diego Clippers). He also served in the army for four years, beginning in 1980, after his NBA career was over.

Despite his affiliation with the NBA and the military, Norman struggled financially for the better part of two decades in Los Angeles. Norman, the Western Athletic Conference Freshman of the Year and Player of the Year in 1972–73, never made more than $30,000 in a season in the NBA.

He was released as a rookie in training camp after he was selected in the third round of the 1974 draft by Philadelphia. He ultimately rejoined the 76ers three months into the season, earning close to the league minimum of $15,000. After he was released the following season, he failed to make the Washington Bullets in 1977. He toiled in a Detroit recreational league before the Clippers gave him a chance in 1978 (the minimum salary in the NBA had jumped to $30,000).

"After the Clippers let me go, I decided to join the army because I thought that would be for the best," said Norman, whose defense and ballhandling skills were reportedly short of NBA caliber—although he let reporters know back then that he was confident in all facets of his game.

"I was stationed in Germany and I lived there for almost eight years before coming back. I spent only a couple of weeks in Detroit before going out to live in Los Angeles at the suggestion of a friend. I lived there until coming back to Detroit."

Despite never making his mark in the NBA, Norman said he does not regret leaving school early. "I wouldn't say that I made a mistake," he said. "At that time, I thought it was the best thing for me to do."

Norman's military background afforded him the opportunity to be housed at Piquette Square, a $23 million apartment complex for homeless veterans in Detroit. He has since moved back to California.

Norman, nicknamed "Popcorn" since his high school days because of his ability to pop the ball in the hoop from anywhere on the court, broke Ernie McCray's season scoring record with 576 points as an Arizona freshman in the 1972–73 season. Norman topped his own record with 618 points in the following season before bolting to the NBA. Eight Wildcats have scored more since, led by Khalid Reeves whose 848 points in 1993–94 are the benchmark. Jerryd Bayless holds the freshman scoring record with 592 points in 2008.

Norman did not have the benefit of the three-point line or a shot clock, which were introduced to the college game in the mid-1980s. When asked what his scoring output would have been had the two been in play. "Something like 31 or 32 points a game," Norman laughed.

He continues to hold Arizona's career scoring average record of 23.9 points a game. The highest average since is Sean Elliott's 19.2 mark from 1986–89.

36 Ernie McCray: Record Breaker

Ernie McCray called to his wife in the other room. He thought she might want to catch what was happening on TV. It was February 10, 2008, and Arizona freshman guard Jerryd Bayless had just scored 26 points in the first half against Arizona State. McCray figured his name was about to get mentioned—a lot. "You have to watch," McCray told his wife. "My record is going to be broken."

Nope, not that day. Bayless finished with 39 points. McCray's UA scoring record of 46 points endures.

McCray is and has been many things. Arizona's second African American basketball player. A player who averaged a double-double during his college career. An educator. Activist. Blogger. Poet. Keen observer of the human condition. If you called him an aging hippie to his face, he might give you a hug.

His scoring record certainly doesn't define him, but he does get a kick out of the fact that we're still talking about what happened on February 6, 1960. He scored a staggering 46 points in a win against Cal State, Los Angeles.

"I scored every kind of way you could score," said McCray, who was a lean 6'6" for some of the final teams coached by Fred Enke Sr. "I had some inside stuff, but I would have to guess I had maybe three or four of what today would have been three-point shots. I was all over the place. I was just running free and guys were getting me the ball. I was truly in the zone. It was just that kind of night where the ball would pretty much bounce off your head and serve as a tip-in."

Until then, it had been a miserable day. The proudest moment of his basketball life was preceded by moments that don't make him particularly proud. "I was married all through college and was going through some wicked kind of stuff. On this day, I had pretty much had it with that kind of stuff," McCray said. "So I was hanging out with some friends early in the day, and we did a little drinking. I was a little tipsy, and going into the gym, I remember thinking, *Oh my goodness, I'm just going to embarrass myself and my mother.* She was a big basketball fan.

"I mean, I wasn't stumbling, but I was feeling it. All of my energy was on keeping it together, and I think I put myself in a zone just to keep from embarrassing myself and my school and my family."

McCray was raised in Tucson, attending the segregated Dunbar School. Growing up, he was not always welcome in restaurants and forced to swim in the one "colored pool" unless it was on a day when the pools for whites would later be drained. "How's that for a message?" McCray said.

He went on to become a star player at Tucson High. He doesn't remember exactly how he got onto the Kansas Jayhawks' radar in the mid-1950s, only that he was. "But they made no bones about the fact that your job there is to get the ball to Wilt [Chamberlain]," McCray said. "I'm a team player, but I didn't like the thought of, that is basically it—just be one of four other guys. If you're a good ballplayer, you have somewhat of an attitude."

McCray's hometown university finally discovered "Easy Ernie" after his senior season. "As far as Arizona was concerned, they weren't that interested in me," he remembered. "The idea of having black basketball players was still so new to everybody."

UA freshman coach Allan Stanton saw McCray play at the YMCA. "He said, 'Has Enke come talked to you?'" McCray said. "I said no, and he said, 'Well, let me give him a call.' The next day I had a scholarship."

McCray averaged 17.8 points and 10.8 rebounds per game in his UA career. His rebounding average is second-best in school history, trailing only Joe Skaisgir. "I had an opposite swag," McCray said of his playing style, using a modern term. "I developed a style where I wanted to make what I was doing look so easy that I'm just going to smooth my way through this and you're going to run ragged trying to deal with me.

"That's who I puffed myself up as, but I was never into the trash-talking culture. I didn't have the coordination to talk shit and play at the same time."

McCray was selected in the 17th round by the Cincinnati Royals in 1960, but never played in the NBA. Looking back now at his Arizona days, he always figured somebody on Fred Snowden's high-flying teams—Bob Elliott, Coniel Norman, Eric Money—would have broken his scoring record. Yet it was Damon Stoudamire who came closest, with 45 points against Stanford on January 14, 1995.

"I wouldn't mind somebody else enjoying that record," McCray said. Then he added: "But I'm also liking it."

37 Richard Jefferson

Richard Jefferson's lasting Arizona legacy ended up having nothing to do with his springy legs, thunderous dunks, and crazy athleticism that left jaws on the floor when he played to the Wildcats crowd. Instead, his legacy became about two things: defense and generosity. Classify them both under unselfishness.

Like most high school stars, Jefferson was never asked to play a lot of defense growing up, but in his junior season at Arizona he combined his greyhound athleticism with the ferocity of a pit bull to become one of the most noted lockdown defenders of the Lute Olson era. Led by Jefferson and seven-foot shot blocker Loren

Woods, the 2000–01 team held opponents to just 39.7 percent shooting—the second-best defensive mark of Olson's tenure—as the Cats marched all the way to the national championship game.

In the regional final, Jefferson, a 6'7" wing, held Illinois guard Frankie Williams—the Big Ten Player of the Year—to 3-of-15 and nine points. In the Final Four, Jefferson hounded Michigan State's Jason Richardson into a 2-of–11 shooting night. Richardson finished with six points, nine below his average.

"Once kids realize they get praise for doing the dirty work, they don't mind doing it as much," Arizona assistant Jay John said in the *Seattle Times* during the Final Four. "He just said, 'I'm going to try what you guys say. I'm going to defend and play hard.'"

Jefferson parlayed that defensive ability into an opportunity to leave for the NBA following his junior season, after averaging 11.2 points and 5.0 rebounds during his Arizona career. He was selected 13th overall by Houston, which traded his draft rights to New Jersey. That launched an ongoing 13-year NBA career in which Jefferson has earned nearly $107 million.

Which brings us to the second thing about Jefferson's legacy. That would be his willingness to part with some of those piles of gold, giving $3.5 million to the Arizona athletic department in August 2007 toward the $14 million needed for the construction of a dedicated basketball facility adjacent to McKale Center. The donation, which was believed at the time to be the largest ever given by a current athlete to his alma mater, earned Jefferson naming rights.

The Richard Jefferson Gymnasium, completed in late 2008, has been a boon for coach Sean Miller, both in terms of recruiting and player development, giving his players (and the famous alums who come to visit) a full-time home.

"For the most part, my main reason was to just give back to the school," Jefferson said when announcing the gift. "My teammates with the New Jersey Nets, they probably get tired of me talking about Arizona so much. My second main reason was so they wouldn't ask Gilbert [Arenas]."

Talking further about naming rights, Jefferson joked, "We're going to call it the 'Not Gilbert Arena.'"

Those playful jibes at his ex-teammate came after Arenas wrote on his blog: "Me and Richard, for some reason, always end up having a bragging session when we're around each other and try to out-do one another. For some reason, he thinks he's better than me. He can't fathom that he's only the third best player from Arizona, and I'm No. 1. He just hates that I'm No. 1."

Jefferson was known at Arizona for his fun-loving personality, and he became best friends with classmate Luke Walton. They took their official visits together and committed together. "Luke had that old Cad convertible," coach Lute Olson said. "You could see those two guys out there, and I'm sure they were hits with all the coeds."

The friendship would later get Jefferson in trouble with the NCAA, which suspended him one game during the 1999–2000 season because he had accepted tickets from Luke's famous father, Bill, to the NBA Finals as well as return travel to Tucson. Jefferson had to donate $281 to a charity as restitution for the travel.

Jefferson was a part of Olson's selective and effective recruiting of Phoenix-area prospects—a group that included Mike Bibby, Channing Frye, and Jerryd Bayless. Jefferson, from Phoenix Moon Valley High, blew up as a major prospect the summer before his senior year, but Olson had already been hot on his trail.

In a *Sports Illustrated* story from August 1997 chronicling Jefferson's rise as part of a larger angle on summer recruiting, writer Seth Davis noted that Olson called to remind Jefferson of Arizona's early interest.

"I think Lute's getting a little paranoid," Jefferson said with a grin.

Jefferson was obviously worth the effort. "He was a winner," Olson said. "He was accustomed to winning. He was a great three-man because we could run certain plays where he'd run down and do things. We'd run the backdoor cut, and he'd hit shots. He could just jump over anyone."

And nobody has yet topped his financial contribution. "Without Coach Olson, none of this would be possible," Jefferson said in December 2008 at the dedication to the gym that bears his name. "He helped me become a man and to be very successful not only here but also in life."

38 Roger Johnson: The Guy Could Play

There was no hesitation or question in Bruce Larson's voice when he spoke about Roger Johnson, who became the Wildcats' first All-American basketball player, in 1951.

"He could play today," Larson said. "That's the kind of player he was. He wasn't a good shooter, but he could run and jump. He had the kind of skills the great players of today have."

He was the first UA player to score more than 1,000 points in three seasons and was an All–Border Conference selection for three years. He finished with 1,046 points, second all-time when he finished. Yet despite his eye-popping numbers, he never led UA in scoring in any season.

"He was [also] a good baseball player," Larson said. A very good one. After being named to the Helms Foundation All-America team in basketball—as a third-team member—he was named a second-team All-American in baseball just months later. He played center field.

Before his Arizona basketball career began as a sophomore in 1949, Johnson was praised in an Associated Press report to "have the makings of one of Arizona's all-time greats.... He has height, speed, basketball savvy, a good shot and lots of fight," the report reads.

"In baseball, Roger could cover the outfield like nobody else," former Tucson High teammate Brad Tolson told Greg Hansen of the *Arizona Daily Star*. "In basketball, he could take off at the foul line and get all the way to the basket. You couldn't dunk then, but, oh my, he could do things the other guys couldn't dream of."

Larson remembered that talent. "Of the guys I coached—at least those of my era—he's one of the few," Larson said, "who I can recall could make Arizona's team today."

In one of Arizona's best seasons in its history, a 24–6 campaign in 1950–51, Johnson stood above the rest. He led Arizona to victories over defending-NCAA-champion City College of New York and nationally ranked Long Island and West Virginia that season.

In Arizona's first appearance in the NCAA Tournament, in 1951, in the regional semifinal, the Wildcats rallied from a 50–29 deficit against Kansas State but came up short, 61–59. The rally in front of what amounted to a Kansas State home crowd in Kansas City drew the praise of the media covering the event.

Johnson and Bob Honea had combined for a team-best 15 points each to fuel the rally. "[Arizona] just didn't know they were beaten," Stu Dunbar of the *Topeka Journal* wrote. "They couldn't get relaxed at first then later on, they didn't need to. That 21 [Johnson] is quite a fancy article—a great player."

Johnson was one of 11 original inductees into the UA Sports Hall of Fame and he met his early billing; he is indeed one of the best all-around athletes in UA and Tucson history.

Johnson became an Air Force pilot after his Arizona career, sacrificing opportunities to play for the Boston Red Sox and for the NBA's Milwaukee Hawks. He flew more than 100 missions during the Vietnam War and retired as a colonel in the Air Force in 1978.

He passed away at 79 in 2010.

39 Brian Williams: The Enigma

Lute Olson says it without hesitation: "He's far and away the best athlete I ever had here." That's a clear-cut statement about Brian Williams, but so little else about the ultratalented but enigmatic Williams was so easily defined. He was just...different.

Williams, the son of singer Eugene Williams, a member of the Platters, was passionate about music and travel and philosophy and art and any number of other pursuits in which he could consume life in the biggest gulps. But basketball? That was just something he did some of the time.

The 6'11" post player often moved in mysterious ways among the basketball world. In 1999, having changed his name to Bison Dele to honor his Cherokee and African heritage, he walked away from $36 million and the three years left on his contract with the Detroit Pistons. Just three years later, he was presumed dead, killed in July 2002 along with two others on a boat somewhere in the South Pacific at the hands of his older brother, who had changed his name to Miles Dabord. Dabord died in a California hospital in September 2002 following a suicide attempt.

Williams' best friend on the Wildcats was guard Matt Othick. They had known each other during their high school days in Las Vegas, and Williams spent time living with the Othick family. Williams played at the University of Maryland as a freshman before transferring to Arizona, presumably at the urging of Othick.

"He was a bizarre character, to say the least, but what a talent," Othick said. "He was an unbelievable player. He just didn't like basketball. He never liked it.... My mother is an artist. In high school, my dad and I and all my buddies would be watching games in his office, and Brian would be in talking to my stepmother about art. I swear. He was different."

Williams became eligible at Arizona in the 1989–90 season, and he averaged 10.6 points and 5.7 rebounds per game, eventually settling in at power forward next to freshman seven-footer Ed Stokes. Williams averaged 13.7 points and 7.6 points as a junior before declaring for the NBA Draft.

"He practiced hard all the time, but he wasn't going to be the guy who was going to be at McKale at 9:30 at night, working on his shot," Olson said. "But he had great hands. Great touch. Quick feet. What an athlete. Unbelievable quickness. The only guy who could beat him in sprints was Kenny Lofton." Othick recalls Williams' demeanor in the hotel before Arizona's 77–55 loss to Alabama in the second round of the 1990 NCAA Tournament in Long Beach, California. Othick's brother and friends from Las Vegas were in town for the game. "And I was looking at him like, man, there's something wrong with Brian today. I don't know what's going through his mind," Othick recalled. "My brother walks in with all his buddies and goes, 'Brian, you ready to play tonight? We're going to crush Alabama.' And he goes, 'No, I'm not ready.' That's how his mind was. He had days when he just didn't want to play basketball."

Williams was suffering from sore knees at the time, but his mind-set probably didn't help. He failed to score, grabbing only two rebounds in just 14 minutes against the Crimson Tide.

"But then he put up some of the greatest single-handed performances I've ever seen," Othick added. Such was the mystery of Brian Williams.

His NBA career was similarly uneven, but he did help the Chicago Bulls (alongside Steve Kerr and former UA teammate Jud Buechler) win the NBA title in 1997 after signing with the team late in the season. Williams appeared in 19 postseason games, averaging 6.1 points, 3.7 rebounds, and 17.7 minutes per game.

Oftentimes, Williams called teammate Michael Jordan the "Black Jesus." If so, what was Williams? "I'm surely not Judas," Williams joked in telling the *Tucson Citizen*. How about Matthew? Williams said, "If he was cool, then I'm him."

His best individual season in the pros came with Detroit a year later, when he averaged 16.2 points and 8.9 rebounds. One season after that, he walked away from basketball and all those millions at just 30 years old.

Othick and his brother, Trent, a film and theater producer, considered making a movie about Williams' life, but Matt said they weren't satisfied with the quality of the script they had written. *Sports Illustrated* and *ESPN the Magazine* are among the national outlets that have tried to illuminate the Williams mystery. Venerable TV drama *Law & Order* based a ripped-from-the-headlines episode in 2003 on his disappearance.

"Nobody really knows what happened," Othick said. "It's so sad."

40 Bruce Larson

Bruce Larson has the distinction of being the only former Arizona player to become the Wildcats' head coach.

He played as a reserve for Arizona coach Fred Enke Sr. in the 1948–49 and 1949–50 seasons, and he replaced Enke as the head coach in the 1961–62 season. Taking over for Enke, who at the time was the winningest coach at Arizona, with a 509–324 record in 35 years, proved to be a difficult task. Enke retired due to illness.

Larson was forced to coach in antiquated Bear Down Gym and managed Arizona's transition from the Border Conference to the more competitive Western Athletic Conference, starting in the 1962–63 season. He also led the program through a time of national unrest during the civil rights movement.

"Players wanted to demonstrate," Larson said in *Arizona Wildcats Handbook*, authored by John Moredich. "Bear Down was even set on fire before one game. The damage was not enough, so we still played."

Before returning to the Arizona program to serve as an assistant under Enke in 1959, Larson had coached Eastern Arizona College and Weber State College to prominence. He coached what is today Weber State University to a runner-up finish in the 1958 national junior college tournament, then a national championship in 1959.

"We came in on an era when Arizona only recruited Arizona kids," Larson recalled in 2014. "It was rare to get somebody from out of state. Schools stayed within their bounds."

He, however, didn't. It was Larson who spotted Joe Skaisgir on the recruiting trail and convinced him to come to Arizona. He played for Larson one year, after Enke Sr. had gotten ill and was later forced to retire.

"[Larson] and I had good chemistry," Skaisgir said. "He understood the way I played. I enjoyed his philosophy about basketball. He was a great man."

Ernie McCray thought the same. "I would have loved to have played for Bruce," said McCray, a star senior on the 1959–60 team. "He was the most forward-thinking coach I had anything to do with in my young life.

"His X's and O's...he would say things that made you think, *Oh, I hadn't thought of that.* Bruce started talking about *why* we were doing things and what we're trying to do, like a schematic. That was new. He had a philosophic approach. We just had plays [under Enke]."

One of Larson's assistant coaches at Arizona later became a significant figure within the program in his own right: former athletic director Cedric Dempsey, who eventually was elevated to the NCAA's executive director.

Dempsey, who served under Larson from 1964–66, recalls limitations that affected Larson's ability to experience the kind of success Fred Snowden and especially Lute Olson enjoyed at Arizona. "Bruce is one of the better technicians I've ever been around," Dempsey said. "Had he had the tools that certainly came after that, I think he would have done the same thing.

"I was the first full-time staff person as an assistant coach. Until that time he always had graduate assistants. I was teaching graduate courses. They wouldn't let me recruit. Bruce did that. I could scout and do that [but] I wasn't truly a full-time assistant."

Larson's best season was Dempsey's first year with the program, a 17–9 mark in 1964–65. It was Larson's highest finish in the WAC, second. He had only two winning records in the next seven seasons, for an overall record of 136–148 in 11 seasons. He was ultimately forced to resign in 1972, and took a position within the Arizona athletic department and continued to serve as a professor of exercise and sports sciences at the school. He eventually retired from UA in 2001 at the age of 73.

In a 2009 interview with former *Tucson Citizen* columnist Corky Simpson, Larson commented that a lack of a recruiting budget was too difficult to overcome. He said he enjoyed his time coaching, eventually being replaced after the 1972 season, Arizona's last in worn-down Bear Down Gym. "We transitioned from the Border Conference to the WAC, and back then it was a pretty good basketball league," he said. "It was very competitive."

"I enjoyed working with him," Dempsey said. "I learned more about basketball from him than anyone I've been around."

41 Jud Buechler: Jack of All Trades

Where else could you find information on Jud Buechler than on Surfshot.com? The website, unsurprisingly, is about all things surf, sand, and water.

And there's just a little part that's basketball, too, since basketball is how the former Arizona star made his name after a stellar college career and a professional career that was beyond belief. After all, how else do you describe a player who played 12 years in the NBA and made more than $11 million?

He earned three NBA titles as a reserve on the famed Chicago Bulls playing behind the likes of Jordan, Pippen, and Rodman. And he also played alongside former Arizona teammates Steve Kerr and Brian Williams to get that done. "The reason I ended up playing for the Chicago Bulls was because of Steve," Buechler said. "Steve and I are good friends and it worked out. I turned out to be a player who fit in that system.... It was nice to have three Arizona guys on a world championship team. And it was a blast."

As it's been described before, Buechler, Arizona's dogged 6'6" small forward, has had the existence of a guy in a beer commercial, living the life of Riley. To top it off, he's a talented all-around athlete with surfer boy good looks.

Who would have ever thought his life would turn out as it has? Consider the volleyball-playing guy out of Poway High in Southern California, who also happened to be a pretty good basketball player. "I think I was a guy who worked real hard," said Buechler, who is currently a club volleyball coach in the San Diego area.

Buechler was so talented in basketball—in a jack-of-all-trades, master-of-none way—that he played every position except center at Arizona. "When I got there I played point guard, and my second

Jud Buechler drives toward the basket against UCLA's Trevor Wilson in the 1990 Pac-10 Tournament.

year I battled at the two spot," he said. "As a junior I started at power forward, and then my senior year I was a small forward. I'm really proud of the player I became, putting in the work." By the end of his career he was an All–Pac-10 Conference selection, and the team MVP.

"He was fundamentally as sound as any player we ever had," Arizona coach Lute Olson said.

Yet there were some doubts his career would end up like it did. "I think there was a turnover [committed] by him late in freshman season that cost us the game," Olson said.

When asked about that, Buechler said he didn't need to be reminded. UA lost to UCLA 84–83 in McKale Center in 1987. "You don't forget those," he said. "It was devastating [for the team] and it was devastating to me, and it was something I had to deal with emotionally. I had to get past that and regain confidence."

Buechler acknowledged that bad games happen. You play in so many games that it's bound to happen at some point. But that one "was the first big blow to my career to that point and I had to grow from that," he said. "I look at it as something I had to deal with, but it could have been a reason why I went so far in the NBA and making it through. I had to grow as a player."

After the play and the game, Olson said fans were so distraught that he got the "feeling that they thought Jud wasn't going to be a good player...but I didn't feel that way. He went on to have a great career and played a lot of years in the pros."

Whether it was at Arizona or in the pros, Olson said, "Jud was always ready to play." In fact, he was the ultimate team player. And that's what made him so special. He knew his role and filled it to his maximum ability.

"I think Jud was just a great-hearted guy to begin with, and he cares about people, whether it's on the court or off the court," said former UA assistant Kevin O'Neill, who as an assistant in the mid- to late 1980s. "It showed through the way he approached people on the team. And I know for a fact he was the same way in the NBA. People wanted to have Jud on their team. There were so many intangibles that came with him other than his ability, which was always undervalued in college and in the NBA, that made him the perfect guy to have on your team. And Jud was one tough guy. He had the big smile all the time.... Well, that shouldn't fool anybody. He was tough. He was hard-nosed. He'd do anything to win. He didn't care about scoring. He didn't care about stats. He didn't care about publicity. He only cared about winning and would do anything to win."

And he did plenty of that. In his collegiate career, he was part of three Pac-10 championship teams, finishing his career 107–26 at UA. "You don't get to certain levels without being highly competitive," Buechler said. "I took a lot of pride in outworking people. I was a good athlete, but not as good as some of the others, so it wasn't like I could afford to not go 100 percent all the time. I embraced that underdog role, the hardworking, grind-it-out role."

The spotlight clearly shined on him in his senior year, when he was a team captain and later named the team MVP by averaging 14.9 points and 8.3 rebounds a game. "I took real pride in that," he said.

Of course he did. That was Buechler's way. Strong, stout, and steady. He ranks seventh in all-time games played at 131, biding his team as a bench player and taking advantage of his playing time whenever he had a chance. He also started in more than 70 games.

It was his performance in the annual Fiesta Bowl Classic that may have first showed fans that he could really play. "That kind of put me on the map," he said. "I really didn't have any monster games, but I just kind of led by example and work ethic."

And it rubbed off on the others. In fact, he was part of the famed "Gumbys." "He never sat on the bench and complained," Olson said. "He was the first guy up during timeouts. He encouraged guys...but that's just who Jud is. He doesn't have a selfish bone in his body. But would I have thought after he finished his career at UA he'd have played 12 years in the NBA? Well, no is the answer."

42 George Kalil: UA's Super Fan

There he sits in Section 4, Row 1, and Seat 2 or 3. He's as consistent as the Tucson sun. George Kalil has seen more Arizona basketball games in person over the last 40 years than any other fan, coach, player, or, well, anyone. According to Kalil, he's missed only about a dozen, maybe slightly more.

"It didn't make any difference how we played or who we played. Everything was always great with George," former Arizona coach Lute Olson said of UA's Super Fan. "George basically had basketball and he had his business."

He proved his fidelity to the program in March 2014 when he donated $1 million to help UA with its restoration project at his second home, McKale Center. After years of being asked for large donations, he was ready to give "and they were ready to take it," he said. "I handed over a check for $1 million. They were shocked. I was shocked...I'm just glad I did it."

His love for UA started in the early 1970s as a kid growing up in the heart of the city just four blocks from Bear Down Gym. He later became a constant figure in the stands. And he's been part of the life of seven UA coaches through the years.

"I hadn't had a vacation in five years and I went on a road trip," Kalil said of how it all began. "I've enjoyed it—the players, the managers, the families, coaches. It's truly a special family to me."

If you've been to a game at McKale Center no doubt you've seen Kalil sitting, hands clasped, behind the bench. If the team is on the road it's more than likely you've seen him on TV, right behind the bench. He's unassuming, but seemingly always there.

His first game was March 2, 1973, when UA traveled to Fort Collins, Colorado, then Laramie, Wyoming, after there was an advertisement in the paper rallying for fans on the Wildcats' road swing. He was urged to go because he hadn't been on a vacation in years. Arizona lost to Colorado State 79–72, and, yes, he still remembers.

It was that loss that prompted him to go purchase a drum so he could help rally the team to win. Kalil and his drum became legendary in the Western Athletic Conference. Arizona won the next game, against Wyoming. And it came with him to games for the next seven years. It was only retired when the chancellor at BYU created an ordinance stating that no fan could bring their own musical instrument. "That's how they got rid of that," Kalil said. "He later admitted the ordinance was for [my drum].

"I had a whale of a good time. I don't cause any trouble. That's what I've prided myself on: I don't cause any problems." Yet during the Olson era that wasn't so clear. When Olson was named coach in 1983, Kalil asked Olson if he could travel with the team. After all, it had been something he had done through the years. Kalil remembers the conversation being in a public restaurant.

"His answer was, 'We'll see,'" Kalil said, laughing. "He was very polite, but it was like a situation when you have a child come up to you and you have guests and the dad says, 'We'll see.' That's what I got."

For three months, Kalil stewed. "I wasn't sure if I'd get on that boat," Kalil said. Olson joked that he had heard Kalil "was worried sick about it." "I said I needed the summer to think about it," Olson said. "Knowing George, I bet he woke up every day wondering what the deal was."

In the meantime, Olson's assistant Scott Thompson picked the brain of Kalil, president of Kalil Bottling Co. and a Tucson staple, about everything involving the program. Who could the program trust? Where could it get dry cleaning? A lot of the little things, Kalil remembered.

A couple months after Olson was hired, the Olsons had a party, and to this day, Kalil said, he isn't sure how he got invited. But it was there that he became an official member of the team.

Bobbi was knitting in the backyard and talking to a few of the players outside. Bobbi turned to George and asked if he was going to be traveling with the team. He wasn't sure how to answer. He told her the situation as he knew it and that he hadn't heard back from her husband.

"She put the knitting material in her lap and took my hand and said, 'You're officially part of the traveling party,'" Kalil recalled. "I didn't know what to do. Do I turn and look to Lute? I didn't turn, but he was eight feet away. They talked over everything but I'm not sure if they talked about me."

Through the years he became her constant companion. They had lunch or shopped or whatever. He typically found his way on the bus—except for one time. Olson had been notorious for punctuality. One day, Kalil wasn't on the bus; he was on the fourth floor of the hotel, making his way down. The bus left without him, and he had to take a taxi to the arena.

Years later, after an upset loss in the mid-1980s, Kalil was on the bus and doing the best to cheer the team up, knowing it was a tough loss. "George is there, saying 'Nice game' to all the players. And he said something to me and I just gave him a dirty look," Olson said. "Later on he asked Scott Thompson, 'When can we start smiling again?' Scott said, 'As soon as we win.'"

Thankfully for Kalil, there have been wins galore.

43 Joe Skaisgir: Two-Year Wonder

One of Arizona's best junior college transfers is not a name that rolls off the tongue—but it should.

Tom Tolbert and Bennett Davison are two of the more popular junior college transfers because each was part of an Arizona Final Four team, in 1988 and 1997, respectively, under Lute Olson. Yet in terms of overall productivity, no one tops Joe Skaisgir, a junior college jewel who transferred from Henry Ford Community College in Dearborn, Michigan, in 1960.

Skaisgir's performance with Arizona is all the more astounding since he did not play basketball in high school. He stuck with his promising baseball career as a first baseman before attending junior college. He then transferred to Arizona because the climate was more conducive to baseball than in Michigan.

Yet he flourished on the hardwood. Skaisgir, a 6'5", 200-pound forward and team captain for Bruce Larson in 1961–62, was the first Wildcat to score more than 1,000 points combined in two seasons. "And we only had a 24-game schedule," he added. "I feel very good about scoring all those points in two seasons."

He earned all of his points as the focal point of opposing defenses. He was bullish around the basket despite having the size of a small forward, and he played with substance over style. Larson remembered Skaisgir as a player "with great hands," but not quick. He was also a very good baseball player—a good all-around athlete and someone who could possibly play in today's game.

Larson said he had a great feel for the game and had a great temperament. "Joe can go out and get his 20 points and 15 rebounds and nobody really realizes it," Larson was quoted as saying in a 1962 *Tucson Citizen* article. "He's just not the flashy, showboat type of ballplayer. But don't think for a moment he's not a great one."

Skaisgir scored 529 points in 1961–62 and added 505 the next season for a career total of 1,034. When he left the program, Skaisgir held multiple school records:

- Field goals made in a season (208)
- Field goals made in a game (17 vs. Hardin-Simmons, January 4, 1962)
- Career scoring average (19.9 points per game)
- Rebounds in a game (26 vs. Cal State-Los Angeles, January 31, 1962)

He tied Bill Reeves for that last record, a mark that still stands today as the highest single-game total in school history.

"That night it just seemed every rebound came in my direction," he said. "I worked hard in that game, getting good position. I didn't realize I had that many until we got off the floor. I had no idea. It was quite amazing." What's more, he could have had more but he sat the bench late in the game.

Skaisgir also threatened Ernie McCray's single-game record of 46 points, set against Cal State-Los Angeles in 1960. Skaisgir came just two short, scoring 44 in that 1962 game against Hardin-Simmons. "I would have loved to have played with [McCray]," Skaisgir said. "He played inside, and that would have helped."

And here's something that likely will never be accomplished again: Skaisgir, during the 1960–61 school year, led the basketball team in scoring (19.4) and then put on his cleats, grabbed a bat, and led the Wildcats baseball team in hitting with a .425 average.

All these years later, he not only ranks second in career scoring average at Arizona (behind Coniel Norman's 23.9 points-per-game average from 1972 to 1974), he is first in rebounding at 11.2.

"[Attending Arizona] was the best time of my life, really," said Skaisgir in the summer of 2014. "I thought I made the right choice of going to UA in playing under Coach Enke and Coach Larson."

Larson told the *Tucson Citizen* in 1962 that Skaisgir ranked among the Wildcats' greats at that time. The list included Linc Richmond, Leon Blevins, Fred Enke Jr., Leo Johnson, Roger Johnson, and McCray. "As a shooter and rebounder, Joe is right up there with any of them," Larson said. "His shooting is probably his greatest weapon. He's as good a shooter as anyone I've coached or been associated with. He has exceptionally good hands and unusual mobility for a big man, too."

NBA scouts watched Skaisgir closely in 1962, but the Arizona standout opted to chase his baseball dreams instead. He played only three years in the minor leagues before injuries cut short his career.

"I had the choice of going pro in basketball or baseball and I chose baseball," he said. "I look back on that and think that may not have been the best choice. But baseball was my first love. I played it all my life. When the opportunity came to choose a school…I chose baseball. Coach Larson allowed me to play both sports if I made the baseball team."

Skaisgir was inducted into the Arizona Sports Hall of Fame in 1977.

44 Arizona vs. UNLV

It is one of the most agonizing, heartbreaking moments in Arizona history. Foul or flop?

Arizona was ranked No. 1 going into the 1989 NCAA Tournament and had rolled past Robert Morris and Clemson in the first two rounds. Then came old adversary UNLV, a team the Wildcats had beaten 86–75 earlier in the season at McKale Center. And it all came down to *that* moment: UNLV freshman guard Anderson Hunt with the ball, angle right, the final seconds ticking away. Hunt, on the dribble, dipped his left shoulder, gave Arizona guard Kenny Lofton a push, and Lofton went sprawling backward on the court. No foul. Hunt all alone for a three-pointer. And he made it, clinching a dream-killing 68–67 loss for the Wildcats.

Coach Lute Olson is on record saying it was a flop, that it would have taken more than that shove to knock down Lofton. But with different referees, perhaps it's a foul. If Lofton had stayed standing, perhaps Hunt would have missed. We'll never know. But the sting endures.

"That was the worst thing ever," said Matt Othick, a freshman guard on Arizona's 1988–89 team. "It makes me sick to my stomach," he added, talking about the end of the game. "When I was young, it didn't, but now that I don't have a title, it makes me really sick. We played so bad in that game."

It was worse still because Othick was from Las Vegas and had switched his commitment from UNLV to Arizona, after getting out of his letter of intent to New Mexico on a technicality after the Lobos had fired coach Gary Colson. "I had to hear about it and hear about it and hear about it, people telling me, 'You should have gone to Vegas,'" Othick said. "And I was like, 'You guys have no idea how much better we were than you.'

"When you're a freshman, you think, 'Oh, we're still going to win one or two titles.' But after my junior year, I was like, 'Man, why didn't we win *that* title?'"

The Arizona-UNLV rivalry burned white hot for several years, as the teams clashed over recruits, battled for supremacy in the West, and chased national titles. UNLV coach Jerry Tarkanian famously and derisively referred to Olson as "Midnight Lute" after

Arizona coaches swooped in to steal junior college center Tom Tolbert from the Rebs at the last minute.

The history between the schools goes back longer than that—Arizona's 114–109 overtime victory over UNLV in the 1976 Sweet 16 was one of the Wildcats' most significant NCAA Tournament victories—but those games in the late 1980s are what fans on both sides most remember.

The 1988 game in McKale was huge. Keith Jackson and Dick Vitale were on the call for ABC. *Sports Illustrated*'s Alexander Wolff was in attendance, writing later:

"Short of ivory-handled pistols at measured paces, Nevada–Las Vegas coach Jerry Tarkanian and Arizona coach Lute Olson couldn't have found a better way to resolve their Wild West feud than they did on Saturday—with a basketball, a national TV audience and two splendid deputies, Stacey Augmon and Sean Elliott. 'He's never beaten me,' Tarkanian said of Olson before engaging his fellow desert fox in Tucson. 'I think it bugs him. I know it bugs him. But I've never said anything to him about it.'"

That game would provide Olson with his only win in five tries over Tarkanian's Rebels. Olson shut down the series after the Wildcats lost in Las Vegas in February 1990. Olson commented afterward that Hunt cursed at him and his staff after diving for a loose ball near the Arizona bench. Hunt denied the accusation, claiming it was Olson who swore at him as he walked back to the court.

Olson swear? Not likely. Either way, the series was over.

"The thing that I indicated in setting up the schedule was I [wanted] to play against teams that have the same rule book that we had, and who followed it," Olson said. "After we played them a couple of times, then we ended that series."

But it wasn't the end of it. In 1991, a year after UNLV won the national championship and was favored to do so again with a team

Lute vs. Tark

Jerry Tarkanian's deteriorating health prevented him from speaking in front of the crowd in September 2013 at the Naismith Memorial Basketball Hall of Fame ceremony at Springfield, Massachusetts, but he taped a message that could be heard from Las Vegas to Tucson.

One of Tarkanian's most significant rivals was Lute Olson, Arizona's Hall of Fame coach. Their history dates back to when Olson succeeded Tarkanian at Long Beach State in 1973, only to inherit a program placed on NCAA probation.

During a taped speech at the Hall of Fame ceremony, Tarkanian talked about his coaching "comrades" and his "fiery and competitive, even argumentative" past with members of the coaching profession.

"I have loved the game of basketball since my earliest memories," said Tarkanian, with his wife, Lois Tarkanian, standing near him for support. "Basketball has been good to me. I've been able to be comrades with some fine individuals in the coaching profession.

"Sure, we can be fiery and competitive, even argumentative, but we all loved the game, that special game of basketball. Deep down, we'll understand the other. Thank you for your friendship."

Tarkanian did not name names, but Olson's name immediately came to the minds of many.

His bitter past with Olson and Arizona gnawed at Tarkanian decades after their on-court rivalry ended. "People said a lot at our expense," Tarkanian told *Sports Illustrated* in a 2010 interview. "The Arizona assistants, they were always telling the parents of our recruits that the mob is going to get your sons or the hookers are going to get your sons if they go to UNLV. We heard it all."

That followed disparaging comments he made about Olson, Arizona, and the Wildcats fans in a "Shark Bytes" blog once published online by the *Las Vegas Sun*. In March 2010, he wrote about silencing Arizona's fans at McKale Center with a win over Georgetown in the 1991 NCAA Tournament there.

"Our fans who traveled to the game said they were treated so badly," Tarkanian wrote. "They would go into restaurants and have a hard time being served. To this day, John Thompson will tell you that was the only time Georgetown got cheered on the road.

"[The Hoyas] were always considered the villains because they were a pretty rough and physical team. But when they took the court against us in Arizona, they received a standing ovation. You could say we got the last laugh. We beat Georgetown and advanced to the Final Four."

In December 2008, Tarkanian wrote that beating Arizona and Sean Elliott in the 1989 Sweet 16 was one of his greatest victories. An excerpt:

"I was so happy. It was one of my favorite victories, because it was Arizona. We wanted to beat Arizona bad because of earlier in the year, the way they celebrated on that floor [after beating UNLV 86–75 in Tucson]. Our players went nuts in the locker room. We went back to the hotel and celebrated all night. A bunch of our boosters went to the airport the next day to see Arizona go home. People were drinking and yelling, 'Arizona go home! Arizona go home!'"

Olson says the coaching rivals did soften to each other over the years, and there's photographic evidence. At the 2014 Final Four, Tarkanian's son, Danny, took a photo of the great coaches together—Tarkanian sitting in a wheelchair, Olson with his hands on Tark's shoulders, both smiling at the camera.

Danny tweeted the photo, writing: "People in Tucson and Vegas wouldn't believe this photo op #FinalFour."

that was undefeated entering the NCAA Tournament, the Rebels played in McKale Center for the first and second rounds.

Officials set up the Rebels in Arizona's locker room. At the time, there was a decorative oversized half basketball that adorned the entrance to the Wildcats' locker room. "It meant something to them," Tarkanian wrote in a 2008 blog for the *Las Vegas Sun*. "I don't know why." UNLV's players, in a show of blatant disrespect, autographed Arizona's basketball. "I didn't know the players did it," Tarkanian continued.

Said Olson, "That's just typical of the guys that [Tarkanian] dealt with. They just had no appreciation for what was the right thing."

Arizona resumed the series with UNLV in the 2006–07 season—Olson's last on the sideline—and the programs figure to be regular partners again under Sean Miller's watch in Tucson. "It's a natural series," Olson said. "And I'm glad to see Sean has picked that up."

45 Derrick Williams

There was Sean Elliott and then there was Derrick Williams. They are two of Arizona's best-ever players.

The former was the player former Arizona coach Lute Olson benefitted from when he signed with Arizona in the mid-1980s. Williams was the player Sean Miller reaped under similar circumstances, in the late 2000s.

Each was pivotal to his coach. But who would have ever guessed that Derrick Williams would have created such a stir for Miller at Arizona? "He made it a reality," Miller told TucsonCitizen.com shortly before Williams became the second overall NBA pick. "He really earned his way into the place he is now. I look back to 24 months ago. We were working hard just to convince Derrick to come [to Arizona]. One thing is sure: 24 months go real fast. It is amazing."

So was Williams' career. When Miller arrived at Arizona on an April afternoon in 2009, he had to convince players Tucson was their place. USC coach Tim Floyd had resigned at Southern California to begin the domino effect of Trojans recruits defecting, and Miller was the beneficiary. In came Solomon Hill, Lamont "MoMo" Jones, and Williams, who at the time was the lowest-rated recruit of the three. (He was ranked 95th by Scout.com, and not ranked in the top 150 by Rivals.com.)

"I don't think I should have been rated that low," Williams told *Basketball Times* a season and a half after arriving at UA. "But people have their opinions. All it does is fuel my fire to be one of those top players."

He was—and in huge fashion, eventually becoming UA's second player to go No. 2 in the NBA Draft, joining Mike Bibby

(1998). He went to the Minnesota Timberwolves, where he played 2½ years before being traded to Sacramento in 2013.

So far, his draft status and the expectations that came with it have not been met on the court—although there have been glimpses of success.

"He came into the league as an offensive weapon, No. 2 pick, athlete, versatile," said Sacramento coach Mike Malone to the *Sacramento Bee*. "Now he has to make his mark as a guy who can also guard his position, whether it's the three [small forward] or the four, and that takes a certain mind-set. He's shown he can do it, but it goes back to: Does he have the mind-set to do it consistently?"

"I would probably say I'm a little bit behind just because I really haven't gotten the opportunity to get out there and play," Williams told reporters. "I've seen some guys on other teams that got drafted top five that play 40 minutes a game whether they're playing good or bad.

"I think sometimes that's a good thing and it can be a bad thing. When you're being thrown into the fire and being able to learn from mistakes and things like that, I think that does work. I haven't really had that opportunity, besides when I [first] got here."

It was certainly a meteoric rise to get there in the first place. In his freshman season at Arizona, he averaged 15.7 points per game and was named a freshman All-American. He was also named the Pac-10 Conference Freshman of the Year.

A season later, he was all but an unstoppable force, becoming the Pac-10's player of the year, averaging 19.5 points and hitting 60 percent of his shots. He also averaged 8.3 rebounds a game. But it was his three-point prowess that made him tough to stop; he hit 56.8 percent of his three-point shots—a mismatch nightmare.

"I'm just a lot more skilled than people think I am," Williams said.

When he eventually made it to Chicago for the NBA pre-draft camp he was dead-set on convincing anyone and everyone who would listen that he was more of a small forward than a power forward, despite being used in the latter way at Arizona. "I'm not a power forward. I want to clear that up," he said at the NBA camp. "I'm a small forward that can play the four....

"I'm not going to get away from being in the post if I have a mismatch. That's what I did this season. I had a lot of mismatches. If I have a slower guy on me, I'm going to take him outside and drive past him. If I have a smaller guy on me, I'm going to be able to post him up."

He did plenty of both things in his sophomore season, and in highlight reel form.

When TucsonCitizen.com did a poll of Williams' best plays, it seemed as if there wasn't enough room for all of them. So it chose four. Here were the results after a reader poll.

- The game-saving block vs. Washington: 29%
- The game-saving block vs. Memphis: 6%
- The game-winning three-point play vs. Texas: 23%
- The one-handed put-back dunk vs. Duke: 39%

In fact, his game-saver against Washington was voted the best all-time play in the 40-year history of McKale Center. Welcome to the Internet age, when all that's remembered is what happened recently.

Still, there's no arguing that Williams had an impact. And in his final season, he did it with an injured hand, one he suffered on January 27 against UCLA. The school and coaches declared it was a "sprained right pinky," but it was more than that. After the season, Williams admitted it was broken, only making his season even more impressive.

Williams admitted after the season that the injury came very close to ending his sophomore season. "If I cracked it a half inch lower, I would have had to have [had] surgery," he said. "If I had to sit out, I would sit out, but I wasn't going to sit out if there was no reason. I just wanted to continue to play with my teammates for as long as I could."

46 Craig McMillan: The First McDonald's All-American

Before there was Jerryd Bayless or Aaron Gordon or Stanley Johnson, there was Craig McMillan, a 6'6" shooting guard from Cloverdale, California.

Indeed, long before the former three even knew what a McDonald's was, McMillan had become the first McDonald's All-American to ever sign with Arizona. He was also a *Parade* All-American back in the day when *Parade* All-Americans were a *big deal.*

"He was crucial," former Arizona coach Lute Olson said of his first major recruit. McMillan was part of a recruiting class that included Joe Turner, Rolf Jacobs, Bruce Fraser, and John Edgar. It was Olson's first full-fledged recruiting class after having come in at the last minute a year before.

"I think once [McMillan] came," Olson said, "I think others thought, *That's a program we need to start looking at.*"

Yet when McMillan announced he was going to go to Arizona his friends wondered, *Why Arizona?*

So, how did Arizona, a team just two seasons removed from going 4–24, land him? Well, McMillan, who finished as the fifth-best scorer in California high school history, liked what he saw in Arizona winning 11 games in Olson's first season. He liked the campus. He liked the atmosphere and coaching staff. He had seen progress and witnessed Arizona go on a small winning streak to end Olson's debut season.

"I just figured I had a chance to get in and have a bigger role," McMillan said. "I might have gone somewhere else because they weren't great initially. But you could see the team develop."

In fact, he said Arizona was "always high on my list. I don't think that they thought that. They came in for the last recruiting spiel and I just told them I was going; they didn't need to go into the spiel."

Olson laughed when looking back at that. "Coach [Ken] Burmeister and I went to Cloverdale on the recruiting trip and I told Coach that we'd have to approach it in a different way because Craig had a scholarship offer from Stanford," Olson said. "We needed to be clear about how important he would be to the program. Once we finished with our presentation I asked him, 'What do you think?' And Craig said, 'I want to come!'"

Olson was taken aback. No one was more thrilled, but he was as shocked as anyone to hear the news. "What else could I say but 'great'?" Olson asked. In fact, the coach almost had to kick Burmeister to be quiet because McMillan had already said he was coming; there was no more selling to do.

Two seasons later McMillan was part of one of Arizona's biggest last-second wins when it beat Oregon State on a miracle shot at McKale Center. UA won 63–62 in overtime when McMillan picked up a deflected ball on a length-of-the-court pass from Steve Kerr. It was appropriately named "McShot."

"Craig's Mr. Clutch," Kerr said. "When the game's on the line, go to Craig."

In looking back at the play, McMillan joked that he didn't have to do that much in part because the ball landed in his lap and all he had to do was lay it in. "Twenty five, 30 years later people are still talking about that," he joked.

"As a team, we practiced the play often," said McMillan, now a successful coach at Santa Rosa Junior College. "It is always a long shot at best when you have the ball at the opposite baseline with two seconds, but we were fortunate that it was a good pass and that the ball got tipped right to me for the layup."

Two years later, he was more known for his defense, using his 6'6" frame against smaller guards and being the roving player when UA went to a box-and-one defense. Behind Sean Elliott, Kerr, Anthony Cook, Tom Tolbert, and the rest, he helped UA reach its first Final Four in 1988, his senior year. He finished his career averaging nine points and starting 109 games.

"To tell you the truth, I don't think I have much of a legacy there," he said. "It was a group of guys who turned the program around. We got in at the ground floor in what has eventually turned into a basketball dynasty."

47 NCAA Tournament Appearances

When Lute Olson came to UA in 1983, Arizona's basketball program had played only five NCAA Tournament games in the first 44 years of the national championship tournament. What's more, three of those five games were in one year, when Fred Snowden's team beat Georgetown and UNLV before losing to UCLA in the West Regional final in 1976. Yes, there had been NIT appearances, and an NCAA Tournament bow in 1951 when the Wildcats went 24–6.

But what a turnaround. In the 30 years since Olson's first season at Arizona, the Wildcats have played in *76* NCAA Tournament games. From 1985 to 2009, Arizona reached the

NCAA Tournament in 25 consecutive years, two years shy of North Carolina's record 27.

Olson took the program to the next level, an elite championship plateau. His 1996–97 national title team holds the distinction of being the only program to beat three No. 1 seeds in the NCAA Tournament. Miles Simon (the Final Four MVP that year), Mike Bibby, Michael Dickerson, A.J. Bramlett, Bennett Davison, and company defeated top-seeds Kansas, North Carolina, and Kentucky.

The victory over Kansas in the Sweet 16 is widely considered the most significant in the program's history because of how dominant the Jayhawks had been that season. Kansas had four future NBA players in its starting lineup: Paul Pierce, Jacque Vaughn, Raef LaFrentz, and Scot Pollard.

The top-ranked Jayhawks were 34–1 entering the game. They became the first No. 1 seed to lose in that year's tournament. Arizona was 21–9 and the fifth-place finisher in the Pac-10. Yet the Wildcats took an early 10–2 lead and maintained an edge against the Jayhawks.

"The message it probably sent was we weren't intimidated at all," Simon told reporters of his team's game-opening burst. "We had something to prove tonight, and we came out and did it."

After a thrilling overtime win over Providence in the Elite Eight and victory over North Carolina in the Final Four in Dean Smith's final game as a coach, the Wildcats faced Rick Pitino and Kentucky in the NCAA title game. Behind Simon's game-high 30 points, Arizona defeated Kentucky 84–79 in overtime in what was the pinnacle of the program.

The Wildcats advanced to their fourth Final Four four years later and came close to winning another title before losing to Duke in the national championship game. Since then, the Wildcats have not advanced to a Final Four, a 13-year drought that has included Arizona's transition from Olson to Sean Miller at head coach. The

Wildcats program, forced to regenerate without Olson, missed the NCAA Tournament for the first time since 1984 in Miller's first season, 2009–10.

After an Elite Eight appearance in Miller's second season, the Wildcats again missed the tournament in 2012. In the last two seasons, Arizona's program has picked up steam in the NCAA Tournament, advancing to the Sweet 16 and Elite Eight.

The 13 years without a Final Four trip is the longest drought since before Olson arrived in 1983. It took only five years for him to coach Arizona to its first Final Four in 1988 with the two most popular players in the program's history, Sean Elliott and Steve Kerr.

The Wildcats' magical season, which culminated with a school-record 35 victories, included four consecutive victories in the NCAA Tournament to reach the national semifinal against Oklahoma. The Sooners prevailed, but Arizona's run served noticed that as long as Olson was coach the Wildcats would be a perennial NCAA Tournament threat.

Six years later, in 1994, the potent backcourt of Damon Stoudamire and Khalid Reeves led the Wildcats to their second Final Four, where they lost to eventual champion Arkansas. The Wildcats' Final Four appearance that year came after humiliating first-round losses in the previous two years against No. 14–seeded East Tennessee State and No. 15 Santa Clara. The loss to Santa Clara was only the second time in the history of the NCAA Tournament that a No. 2 seed lost to a No. 15 seed.

"I don't feel jinxed," Olson told the media about the consecutive forgettable losses. "At this point, I'm just frustrated that we couldn't play more the way we're capable of playing."

After those two first-round setbacks, Olson's program had only two first-round losses in the next 11 seasons. In that span, Arizona advanced to three Final Fours, which included the national title in 1997 and title-game appearance in 2001. And Olson did not become known as a first-round failure but instead as a Hall of Famer with NCAA Tournament success. His March Madness record at Arizona was 39–23, a respectable winning percentage of 62.9 percent. He is one of only eight coaches to coach in five or more Final Fours and one of 11 who has taken two different teams to the Final Four (his Iowa team advanced to the Final Four in 1980).

48 Ooh Aah Man

Some schools have famous mascots. Instantly recognizable fight songs. Classic colors, classic uniforms. Famous traditions. But no one, other than Arizona, has ever had the Ooh Aah Man.

"He's unique," said former UA coach Lute Olson.

In one of the happiest accidents that ever happened at Arizona, the Ooh Aah Man—known in real life as Joe Cavaleri—entertained fans for more than three decades, standing at midcourt during timeouts, stripping off clothes, and contorting his arms to form letters and lead cheers of "A-R-I-Z-O-N-A" and "U of A...U of A."

He was a fixture at McKale Center until failing health, including a diagnosis of Parkinson's disease, forced him to hang up the blue-and-red striped socks in 2013.

"I think it's really funny that after all these years of doing this during the games, the reaction was still the same," Cavaleri said after retirement. "Most of the players of the opposing teams watched me instead of listening to their coach. I would glance over at their huddle and they would be looking at me doing my thing and laughing.

"I remember one game in 1990, we were playing Oregon State and Brent Barry was sitting on the end of the bench. He was

The Ooh Aah Man, Joe Cavaleri: one of Arizona's most colorful characters.

Three Questions with the Ooh Aah Man

Q: How did Lute Olson react to you?
I really didn't think that Lute liked me at first. I think he thought I was crazy. After I became a fixture at the games, however, I think he started to like me. It was Bobbi Olson that loved my wife and me. I think she was the one responsible for my being invited to the tournament games. Bobbi made it a point to say hello to my wife and [me] at every game we attended.

When we missed two games because my wife miscarried our first child, the next game we were at, she came over to our seats very concerned about what happened to us and asked how we were. We told her what had happened and she hugged us both with genuine tears in her eyes. She was one great lady and I loved her very much. Then I knew that Lute liked me, too, because she told me so.

Q: How did stripping off items of clothing become part of the routine?
During the 1979–80 season, my friend Ron Riviezzo, better known as Aldo, had a uniform made for me. It was a leotard bodysuit with a cape like Superman had. Like Superman, I would have to take off my clothes to do my thing. When I first did it, I really struggled getting my pants off over my sneakers. Fred Snowden saw this and called me into his office to ask me about it and my act. When I explained what I wanted to do, he gave me a pair of Leon Wood's tear-away pants. I really loved Coach Snowden. My striptease act was born. It wasn't until the mid-1990s that I started to add more clothing to the act."

Q: What is your favorite memory as the Ooh Aah Man?
I think my favorite memory would have to be winning the national championship in 1997. The University of Arizona called me and asked if my wife and I wanted to go to Indianapolis for the Final Four. I told them that my wife couldn't come because we had two small children and one on the way, and that I would like to go but I didn't want to bump a pom-pom off the trip this time. They said I could come, but I wouldn't be allowed on the floor. I said fine, I would find a way to cheer in the stands.

When we went to the first game, I dressed in full uniform just in case. It was good that I did because little did I know it would become a big part of the game. Halfway through the first half, I turned to the people in my section and did an Arizona spell-out.... When I got up the second time to cheer, I tore off my pants and took off one shirt, and that got the whole crowd fired up. I did two loud spell-outs. Then I pointed to the band

and then the student section for a U of A cheer, then the boosters and parents for a 'U of A' then behind me for a 'U of A.' We did it a few more times then I raised my arms and got everybody to cheer 'U of A.' It was fantastic. It was so loud.

When we played for the national championship against Kentucky, I was ready. I got to my seat and everybody was ready to cheer. I did my thing during timeouts and we won in overtime. That was it. We were national champions. Riding back to the hotel on the bus with the parents was incredible. It was one of the most rewarding things I have ever been a part of.

redshirting his freshman year. I was kneeling down on the floor right next to the bench. He asked me what I was supposed to be, and I told him what I did. He looked at me like I was nuts.

"My timeout came and I went out and did my thing. When I came back to sit down on the floor next to their bench, he gave me a high five and smiled and told me that I was great. When the game was over and we had won, he told me that the reason we won the game was because of me and the way I got the crowd all fired up."

Surprisingly, the tradition all started at a UA baseball game. Cavaleri was coming from a wedding reception, wearing a tuxedo, when he stopped at an Arizona baseball game. The Wildcats were trailing, and Cavaleri started leading cheers from the stands: "*Ooh aah, sock it to 'em, Wildcats!*" he yelled. Sure enough, Arizona came back to win, and a super fan legend was born.

Cavaleri began to be recognized around Tucson, and not just because he was a bartender who worked at several popular spots around town. He soon began firing up crowds at basketball games, first when Fred Snowden was the coach, through all the Lute Olson years and into the Sean Miller era before retiring the Ooh Aah character at the age of 61.

"It meant everything to me to be the Ooh Aah Man," Cavaleri said. "I loved it so much. To go out on the floor and get everybody in the stands to cheer was an incredible feeling. I still to this day do not know why they cheered with me. But I do know that if it wasn't for the fans I would never have been the Ooh Aah Man.

"It was such a great feeling to go to schools where my son would play basketball and get recognized and sign autographs and talk to people who I had never met before."

Indeed, Ooh Aah was so ingrained in the program that he became part of the official traveling party during the NCAA Tournament. He recalled in an *Arizona Daily Star* story being in the team hotel in Kansas City the night when the Wildcats lost to Oklahoma in the 1988 Final Four.

He was on the balcony when someone called down to him. "Are you going to jump?" Steve Kerr asked.

"I don't know. Are you?" Cavaleri replied.

"Well, I was thinking about it." Kerr had just suffered through one of the worst shooting nights of his career, the one game he always says he can never forget. That night, Ooh Aah Man tried to ease the pain.

"I could give you a Steeeeeeve Kerrrr one more time," he offered. Kerr laughed. Ooh Aah laughed.

In little ways, Ooh Aah just made things better. Even after his retirement, he attended some home games in seats near the floor. Sometimes, during a timeout in the second half, there he was, standing at his seat, leading the familiar cheers.

"Even though I am now officially retired I don't consider myself done as the Ooh Aah Man," Cavaleri said, "I will always be the Ooh Aah Man until the day I die."

49 Bear Down Gym

Historic Bear Down Gym is a gymnasium no longer. The creaky wooden court has been replaced by blue carpeting, the basketball stands taken out in favor of cubicles. The place where Ernie McCray scored a school-record 46 points in 1960, and where the Wildcats won 81 straight games from 1945 to 1951, is now a place where students strive to earn high marks on research papers.

In June 2012, the Arizona Board of Regents approved a $13.5 million renovation of Bear Down Gym that should take almost four years to complete. The building, which is on the National Register of Historic Places, has become a temporary place for admissions offices as well as tutoring services.

Once the project is complete, Bear Down will boast classrooms. But the look of an old-time gym will remain, with the open roof structure and bleachers protruding from the walls. Championship banners will still hang from the rafters.

Bear Down Gym, where the legendary Fred A. Enke coached during his entire career, from 1925 to 1961, was also a nonbasketball venue beforehand—when the Navy occupied it during World War II. The U.S. War Department used Bear Down Gym as a barracks for 500 students as they went through a quick-study Naval Indoctrination School, just prior to being shipped off to war. Many of the young sailors and officers who lived and trained at Bear Down Gym gave their lives during the war. Legend has it that their ghosts frequent the old gym, looking to continue their college education.

The initial cost of the construction of Bear Down Gym in 1926 was $130,000. It was built to house close to 3,600 with bleacher seats. Originally named Men's Gymnasium, it was renamed after the motto "Bear Down" was spoken by football player John "Button" Salmon to his teammates on his deathbed in 1926.

Arizona was 5–8 against ranked teams at the hallowed gym. The most notable victory was against second-ranked Long Island 62–61 on January 29, 1951. That season was one of the best in Arizona's history, as Enke's team finished 24–6 and captured its sixth consecutive Border Conference title.

That season also included the point-shaving scandal that rocked the Long Island program. The quickness of Leo Johnson limited Long Island All-American forward Sherman White to 14 points. White fouled out with 8:15 remaining. The Blackbirds led by as many as 18 points but faltered after White drew his fifth foul. It was the Arizona Wildcats' 73rd straight win at Bear Down Gym.

Long Island coach Clair Bee blamed the refs for the outcome. "You will never get good teams to come to Tucson because of this condition," Bee told the Associated Press. "If I had the best team in the nation, I couldn't beat Arizona on this floor in Tucson." Bee made this complaint despite Arizona being whistled for 24 fouls compared to Long Island's 19. Less than a month after losing to Arizona, White, who averaged 27.7 points a game and was the Sporting News National Player of the Year that season, was arrested for the point-shaving scandal. He was banned from playing in the NBA.

The next impressive win over a huge opponent at Bear Down Gym was over No. 8 San Francisco 71–56 on January 28, 1965. An over-capacity crowd of 3,823 watched Arizona senior forward Albert Johnson post 16 points and 15 rebounds in the upset over the Dons, who were 12–1 entering the game. San Francisco lost to UCLA in an NCAA Tournament Elite Eight game at the end of that season.

"We caught the building at the end of its time," said UA standout Warren Rustand. "We had been in there, so we knew every possible dead spot on the floor, and as a defense we'd guide their offense to that dead spot. It was a great place to play, fun and filled every night."

50 Matt Muehlebach: Mr. Triple-Double

Matt Muehlebach was miserable. It was halftime during a 1990 Pac-10 tournament quarterfinal game in Tempe. The guard had missed all of his three-point attempts against USC and had a measly two points.

"I was pissed," he said. "I was like, *I am having the worst game of my life*. I go to the locker room and I kind of have my head down. I'm self-loathing."

And then coach Lute Olson, as was his custom, went through the halftime rebounding totals—usually as a way to motivate the big guys.

"He would say it mockingly," Muehlebach said before lowering his voice and talking slowly to mimic Olson. "It was, 'Williams, two. Rooks, one.'" Then the coach got to Muehlebach. "Eight," Olson said. And just like that, a mood was changed, an idea was born. *Hey, I could get a triple-double.*

"I'm sure a lot of people would say, 'Oh, I never had an idea,'" said Muehlebach, who otherwise never had more than six rebounds during his junior season. "But I had an idea at halftime because of the rebounds. I remember thinking, *Hey, that is pretty close to 10, and I know I have a lot of assists*. I got a couple of rebounds right away in the second half, and I was like, *I have a shot*."

He had six assists at halftime and recalls getting to 10 fairly easily in the second half. The problem was, he still didn't have the points. Arizona was routing USC—the Cats would ultimately win 80–57—and Muehlebach kept looking at the bench to see if the coaches were getting ready to take him out. Finally, he got his 10th point at the free-throw line, and with it, the triple double: 10 points, 11 rebounds, and 10 assists.

"I think someone told the bench, because when I came off they were all fired up," Muehlebach said.

Despite a 2-of-8 shooting effort—that included missing all five attempts from behind the arc—it was the first triple-double in school history, and only the third ever in the Pac-10. Muehlebach joined the excellent company of Cal's Kevin Johnson and Oregon State's Gary Payton.

"Matt had a super game," teammate Jud Buechler told reporters after the game. "I'm a bit jealous."

Filling the box score wasn't the whole story, though. Muehlebach—whom Olson called the best defensive guard in the Pac-10 that season—hounded dynamic USC freshman Harold Miner all game long; Miner shot 5-of-20 from the field.

Hmmmm. Miner missed fifteen shots with Muehlebach guarding him. Can we credit Muehlebach with some sort of *quadruple* double? "It's funny, because all I was worried about was locking in defensively and not getting my ass kicked by Miner—again," Muehlebach said. "It's funny how when you focus on defense, *aha*, all those other things come easy."

Others would go on to post triple-doubles at Arizona—including center Loren Woods with points, rebounds, and *blocked shots*—but Muehlebach was the first to reach the milestone. And he remains the only four-year Wildcat to go undefeated at McKale Center (64–0) and is the only UA player to have four regular-season championship rings.

"I'm like a guy who has five good jokes at a party or a couple of magic tricks," Muehlebach said, laughing. "I have a few of these unique things that no one has done."

His career was rock solid. He was mostly a towel-waving Gumby from the bench as a freshman in 1987–88, but he finished his career with 89 starts, 1,006 points, and a 41.9 shooting percentage from three-point range (163-of-389).

"Wow, you talk about a competitor," Olson said. "He was just a tremendous competitor and a good team guy."

He went on to practice law in Tucson and embark on a media career, first as an analyst on UA radio broadcasts and then also branching out into TV work.

Muehlebach, without question, has way more to his name than being "Mr. Triple-Double."

51 Salim Stoudamire: The Moody Sharpshooter

For Salim Stoudamire, it was all about the body language and the smirks. Of course, it was also about that picture-perfect shot that had Arizona coach Lute Olson declaring his then-senior the best shooting guard in the country back in 2005.

It was hard to argue, with Stoudamire hitting so many big three-pointers to aid UA in getting to the Elite Eight in his final season. His big shot against Oklahoma State in the Sweet 16 was monumental, putting Arizona in the Elite Eight in Rosemont, Illinois, for a legitimate attempt at its fifth Final Four.

There was his big buzzer-beater against UCLA, over Arron Afflalo in McKale Center, and the Pac-10 clincher against Arizona State in Wells Fargo Arena.

Call him "Mr. Big Shot." Indeed, "He's about perfect when it's down to that last shot," Olson once said about Stoudamire.

"He was the best shooter in college basketball," said current UA assistant Joe Pasternack. "I can easily say that."

He could attest to it because, back when Salim was hitting three-point daggers, Pasternack was an assistant coach for California and saw his talent firsthand. It was the same team that Richard Midgley doggedly played for in the mid-2000s. In those days, Midgley hounded Stoudamire in what turned out to be epic defensive battles. In 2004, California found one way to stop Stoudamire... get him flustered.

Midgley gave Stoudamire a forearm shot 21 seconds after the opening tipoff, and never relented. Stoudamire appeared out of sorts and out of sync the rest of the way. "He jacked me," said Stoudamire of the forearm later that week. "But he's kind of a dirty player. I'll bet that their coach told him to come out and do that to set the tone for the game to let us know that they weren't going to play around."

Pasternack said the shot was not intentional but something that just happened. Either way, Arizona struggled throughout the game, losing 87–83. Stoudamire scored seven points, hitting just three of nine attempts from the field. "They denied me the ball, but I did what I haven't been doing the past couple of games, and that's get frustrated," Stoudamire said.

A season later, Stoudamire was prepared when they again faced the Bears. Arizona won 87–67, even though Stoudamire wasn't that much of a factor with six points. "We're pretty good if I only take one shot and score six points and we still win by 20 on the road," Stoudamire said afterward. "I really don't care. People are going to try and get me frustrated, but it won't happen. It's dumb to try that."

Teams tried everything to get into Stoudamire's head. They also counted on Stoudamire getting into his own head—something that happened often. Stoudamire was suspended or disciplined a few times, and often had a talking-to when he would get that hound-dog look on his face.

Arizona coach Lute Olson recalled a game with Arizona State. Arizona was winning handily, but Stoudamire sauntered into the huddle and wasn't all there. Olson asked him what was wrong. "I feel like a robot out there," Olson recalled Stoudamire saying. "I said, 'You do? Let me tell you what a robot does. He gets his jacket and goes down to sit at the end of the bench and watches the game.' In the second half they made a run at us and Salim is looking down the bench to see if I'm going to crack and put him back in before we lose. Well, I wouldn't put him in."

Arizona eventually won 70–68. But it was part of the continuing problem Stoudamire would present. "I went into the locker room after the game and said 'Salim, is there a problem?'" Olson said. "Did we win or lose?" Stoudamire told him they won. Olson prompted him to go see him in his office after the weekend was over. "I made sure he'd have the weekend to think about it," Olson said. "I did that on purpose."

Another time when Olson felt there were attitude problems, he suspended him against Marquette in a game that had NCAA Tournament ramifications even though it was early in the season. "He asked if he'd be able to make the trip and I said I wasn't sure," Olson recalled. "I wanted to see how he handled things. But he came down to the manager's table and was really in tune with what was going on." Olson called him in the day before the game and said he could make the trip but he wouldn't play. And that how he conducted himself would determine whether he played a week later. "He turned into the team's biggest cheerleader," Olson said. "He was right there with Josh Pastner on the bench cheering."

Olson's point was made, although Stoudamire did slip into his moods every now and again. "The thing I tried to get across to him was that 99 percent of the people never get a chance to meet him," Olson said. "All they know is what they see on the court. 'You make me depressed watching you, just by the way you react. Your teammates don't know if you are upset with them or upset with yourself.' I just told him I wasn't going to put him out there and have him display that attitude to our fans. It was then he got a lot better."

Stoudamire turned out to have a very good career, finishing 111 points ahead of his cousin Damon's all-time scoring total with 1,960 points, good enough for fourth on the school's all-time scoring list. He's tied for ninth all-time in field goals made (615, with Chris Mills) and is the all-time leader in three-pointers (342). He's second to Steve Kerr in three-point percentage all-time (45.8) and second all-time in free throw percentage (87.0).

Unfortunately, it didn't translate into a stellar NBA career. After getting drafted by the Atlanta Hawks in the second round of the 2005 NBA Draft, Stoudamire lasted just three years. Most recently, he has made attempts at playing in the D-League and overseas.

52 Ben Lindsey

In an Arizona Board of Regents meeting in 2011, almost 30 years since Ben Lindsey had any relevancy with the Arizona program, the embattled former coach voiced his displeasure about a university-generated basketball history book labeling his brief time with the program as "infamous."

In Brian Jeffries' foreword to *University of Arizona Basketball,* the Wildcats' radio play-by-play voice writes just that: Lindsey's time was "infamous."

"What in the world makes you think you are entitled to define my coaching legacy in this manner?" Lindsey asked the board of regents. "So why don't you take this book of yours and throw it in the trash with all the other garbage?" Strong words from a coach who led the Wildcats to one of the worst seasons in the program's history. Arizona was 4–24 overall and 1–17 in the Pac-10. It was the lowest win total for the Wildcats since they had finished 4–22 in 1958–59.

Lindsey had compiled a 317–137 record with two NAIA titles at Grand Canyon College. He had just been hired at Fort Hays State in Kansas when Arizona athletic director Dave Strack came calling. Lindsey was hired after Jack Hartman turned Arizona down after the 1982 season in UA's attempt to find Fred Snowden's replacement. Hartman at first agreed to coach Arizona but then changed his mind, deciding to stay at Kansas State.

After his firing, Lindsey sued Arizona and was awarded $1.17 million in lost salary. An appeal by the university reduced that amount by $480,000.

Arizona offered three reasons for Lindsey's termination during the court proceedings:

1. The communication relationships between Lindsey and certain players on the basketball team.
2. Lindsey's prospects for a successful recruiting effort.
3. The technical tasks of rebuilding the basketball program.

The university claimed that some players requested the opportunity to meet with new athletic director Cedric Dempsey during the season and complained about Lindsey's performance. Dempsey tried to avert a meeting behind Lindsey's back, but the players insisted on a private meeting, according to the appeal by the university.

Eventually, seven players met with Dempsey to voice their displeasure about the coach. The appeal claimed that players complained about last-minute changes in the game plan before the team had the opportunity to practice the suggested changes. Lindsey testified that some of the players recruited by Snowden had difficulty adjusting to his methods.

Brock Brunkhorst, a guard from Phoenix, was one of them. He signed with Snowden despite Lindsey's attempt to recruit him for Grand Canyon. Brunkhorst was a sophomore when Lindsey coached the Wildcats. "The sophomore year was a disaster," Brunkhorst told the *Tucson Citizen*. "It was a waste of a year. I knocked heads with Lindsey right off the bat. He was recruiting me in high school, and I think he held that against me from the start, that I didn't go to Grand Canyon. I quit the team for a few games my sophomore year. I didn't agree with his philosophies and how he did things. I'm just thankful Cedric had the foresight to cut the suffering real quick."

Call it infamous or don't, but the terrible season under Lindsey was a blessing in disguise. It provided Dempsey with the opportunity to land Lute Olson, who filled the coaching vacancy and attacked the challenge of turning the program around. Five years later, Arizona was in the Final Four.

53 The Gumbys

Arizona guard Bruce Fraser once said that being a Gumby was "a cursed, charmed existence." It was, as fellow Gumby Sean Rooks once further explained, like being on both ends of a totem pole—the 1987–88 Wildcats were No. 1 in the country, which was great, but there was also a bunch of guys at the end of the bench who hardly ever played—not so great.

Still, they made the very best of it. Which is why the Gumbys—mostly a collection of young players who had to wait their turn—became the most lovable group of reserve players in school history. Sure, there was Sean Elliott and Steve Kerr and all the other starters, but it was those towel-waving, foot-stomping, hand-slapping, cheer-creating bench players who best exemplified the joy, the loyalty, the selflessness of the earliest glory years under Lute Olson.

"They were great," Olson said. "Their enthusiasm from the bench was really, really important. They were great practice guys. There wasn't anybody who felt that they should have been playing more—at least that I found out about."

Arizona's Gumbys came to be several years after Eddie Murphy, donning a green foam suit on *Saturday Night Live,* repopularized the animated TV character from the 1950s. The story goes that Kerr once bought a rubber toy Gumby, which Fraser—who would later call himself "the Grand Poobah of the Gumbies," Kerr told the *Seattle Times*—saw as a symbol of his own plight.

"I said to him one time, 'What's this about the Gumbys?'" Olson said. "He said, 'Gumby is just not appreciated.'"

Fraser once told the *Tucson Citizen*: "A Gumby gets used. He expects to get used. Even when you're not, you think you are."

Fraser, who was a senior on the 1986–87 team, accepted his role as a scout team foil and took to putting the toy Gumby in his sock during games for good luck. One night during a rout at Washington State, Olson put Fraser into the game... and Gumby came popping out of his sock onto the hardwood.

The legend really grew during the next season, when Fraser was a student assistant, joining a scout team that included the likes of Rooks, Matt Muehlebach, Harvey Mason, Jud Buechler, Brian David, Mark Georgeson, and Craig Bergman. They developed choreographed moves, such as the "three-point can-can shuffle," "the windmill," and the "Dick Enberg," the last of which is when the bench players would respond to a great play by yelling the broadcaster's signature "Oh, my!" and putting their hands over their heads.

The Gumbys became so rambunctious that the Pac-10 thought it had to legislate their behavior. The league sent a letter to officials encouraging them to penalize a bench that stood up on the sideline, unless it was in response to a big play.

"Some of the opponents thought they were making fun of them," Olson said. "But that wasn't the thing at all. They were just supporting their teammates."

But while they were having fun, the Gumbys yearned to play. These were some future stars, after all. "What really sucks is not just not playing, but you get abused in practice. *Abused*," said Muehlebach, who was a freshman guard on that team. "You're playing guys who are bigger, older, stronger, smarter. You're constantly getting your ass kicked every day."

Then came a moment that we'll call "Gumby's Revenge." Arizona played at Iowa on December 12, 1987, a huge game that marked Olson's return to Iowa City.

"We would always sit around, saying, 'We're pretty frickin' good,'" Muehlebach said of the Gumbys. "Well, the night before the Iowa game, the Gumbys demolished the starters [in practice]. We got so hot and we demolished them. We were like 24-of-30 from three-point range. We were kicking their ass."

Olson was paying attention. The scout team was the first to 15 points. Olson said, "Play to 20." The Gumbys still won. Olson kept moving the mark higher and higher, giving the starters a chance to catch up, but the Gumbys kept on with a huge lead.

"He finally said, 'That's it. Let's shut it down,'" Muehlebach remembered.

The next day, when Olson would normally run a light shootaround before the game, he had the starters scrimmage again against the Gumbys in an effort to restore the first-teamers' confidence. "And they were pressing us," Muehlebach said. "They were motivated. They kicked us, and we were like, *OK, call the dogs off.*"

It worked. The Cats went out and beat third-ranked Iowa 66–59.

Gumby Sean Rooks gets some playing time against UCLA.

As the season went on, the Gumbys' story became bigger and bigger. Fans wore Gumby gear to McKale Center. Some even dressed in big foam costumes. It became a national story.

As it turned out, it wasn't at all like Fraser had initially envisioned. A Gumby was—and still is—very much appreciated by the Arizona faithful.

54 Al Fleming

One of the original members of Fred Snowden's Kiddie Korps, rebounder extraordinaire Al Fleming of Michigan City, Indiana, was literally with Arizona before he was recruited in 1972.

How's that? Well, the first name of Fleming's mother was Arizona.

"Needless to say, if you gave Fred Snowden a card like that to play, there was no way Al Fleming was not going to play basketball at the University of Arizona," former teammates Bob Elliott and Eric Money write in the book *Tucson: A Basketball Town*.

Fleming, who lost his life to kidney cancer at age 49 in 2003, still holds the Arizona school record for most rebounds in his career.

Fleming, a 6'7" power forward, finished with 1,765 points and 1,190 rebounds when his career ended in 1976. At the time, both were school records. His scoring total still ranks 10th on Arizona's career list. He's in good company: Fleming, Bob Elliott, and Sean Elliott are the only Wildcats to rank in the top 10 on both career scoring and rebounding lists.

As a senior, Fleming was a key member of the Wildcats' Western Athletic Conference championship team. Arizona earned its first NCAA Tournament berth since 1951 and made it to the

West Regional final, where the Wildcats lost to UCLA in Pauley Pavilion.

"His leadership took us there, no doubt," Bob Elliott, Fleming's college roommate, told the Associated Press after Fleming's passing.

Gayle Hopkins, an All-American track athlete at Arizona who later coordinated alumni functions for the athletic department, told the *Tucson Citizen* that Fleming was "a super fine person, and there has been no better ambassador for the school."

Fleming was drafted in the second round, the 30th choice overall, by the Phoenix Suns of the NBA, but he was waived before the season started. He was a member of the Seattle SuperSonics in 1977–78, when they reached the NBA Finals. After that, he played professionally in Sweden, Italy, Israel, Portugal, and Uruguay, then retired from the sport at age 28 and moved back to Michigan City.

He was working as a recreational supervisor for a prison in his hometown when he passed away after a five-year battle against cancer.

"Five years—that is a long time to deal with something that you know is literally eating you alive," Fleming told the *Arizona Daily Star* about his battle with cancer. "In your mind, you'd better be strong. You better get that part of you built up."

Fleming also holds the scoring record at McKale Center for an Arizona player—41 points against Detroit, coached by Dick Vitale, in 1976. He scored 33 by halftime, also an Arizona record. Fleming, who led Arizona in field-goal percentage in each of his four years at Arizona, holds the school record with a 66.7 percent mark in 1973–74.

55 Warren Rustand: The Perfect Leader

If there was anyone in the program who was Steve Kerr before Steve Kerr was Steve Kerr, it was Warren Rustand.

Rustand was well-accomplished and perhaps underrated as a basketball player, yet very good at what he did. One of the most impeccable leaders in Arizona basketball history, he was a steady guard who did not experience a losing season under Bruce Larson from 1962 to 1965.

Only a handful of Wildcats were deemed team captains for more than one season, and Rustand is among them. He was bestowed that honor by Larson in 1963–64 and 1964–65. Fittingly, the next two-time captain was Kerr, two decades later (1985–86 and 1987–88).

"[Being captain] was all about leadership, and I think Kerr is about leadership," said Rustand in 2014. "It's not about shooting baskets or playing defense, but it's about leadership. As you look at sports there are people who come along programs once in a while who change the nature of those teams. There were a lot of guys who had more ability than I did, but there was more."

Larson agreed. Rustand played for UA in the mid-1960s and was part of UA's first winning season in more than a decade, in 1963–64. "His leadership has meant a lot to us," Larson was quoted as saying during the 1963–64 season by the *Tucson Citizen*. "He sets an example by his actions. Russ doesn't do a lot of talking, but when he does have something to say, the other players listen to him."

Rustand, a career 81.4 percent free-throw shooter, was the first Arizona player to be selected as an Academic All-American and to play in a national all-star game (the 1965 East-West game).

He was named All-WAC in three consecutive years, leading the Wildcats in field goal percentage and free-throw percentage those three years.

He also served as UA student body president and received the 1965 Freeman Award as Arizona's outstanding graduating senior.

"I had a great time at the University of Arizona and I had a great time with my teammates and I loved playing basketball," Rustand said. "I played during a great era." He remembers the Western Athletic Conference being a superb conference, with powerhouses Texas Western, Arizona State, and New Mexico among the best teams in the country at the time. "It was an unbelievable league during that time," he said. "People who look at the Pac-12 now tend to forget the first few years of the WAC were tough because there were some of the best teams. It was such a great time to play basketball because the competition was ferocious. We had a good team and good coach. Campus life was real nice. It was a great time."

Rustand, an Arizona Sports Hall of Fame inductee, and former U.S. Congressman Mo Udall are two of the most distinguished former Arizona basketball players who served the country in Washington, DC. Rustand served as the appointments secretary to president Gerald Ford during his time as a White House Scholar. He was also the CEO or chairman of 17 companies and on the board of directors for 50 public, private, and not-for-profit organizations.

After his Arizona career, Rustand was drafted by the San Francisco Warriors of the NBA but instead chose to serve as assistant coach at Arizona in the 1967–68 season. He also coached and administered youth basketball for 20 years and worked as a sports reporter for KVOA-TV from 1969 to 1972.

"Pro basketball was never on my agenda to do; it was never a big dream," he said. "I had other dreams to accomplish in my life. I wanted to go to graduate school. I wanted to run companies and wanted to help my community in a different way. My leadership interests didn't involve pounding a basketball. Although I think the NBA is interesting, I think it's kind of boring."

Rustand, 71, is still going strong as an entrepreneur, educator, and public servant. He continues to conduct motivational speeches for businesses and prospective business owners. He is now the CEO at Providence Service Corp.

"Character is defined by how you treat those who cannot help you and cannot hurt you," Rustand said during one of his recent motivational speeches. "It's how we treat those people who don't have the power to influence us in any way. It's the wait staff who help us at our tables. It's the people who make our beds in our hotel rooms. It's the homeless person on the street that we have the power to choose to help or not help." Perhaps Rustand's indefatigable style comes from his father, Stanford Rustand, who reportedly drove 1,080 miles round trip from Whittier, California, to watch every Arizona game at Bear Down Gym. He did not miss any games during Rustand's four years at Arizona, including his son's freshman year when freshmen were ineligible.

56 Jerryd Bayless

Perhaps the best way to describe Jerryd Bayless' one season at Arizona was that he was the right guy at the wrong time.

His performance in the 2007–08 season was a bright spot amid an otherwise dark and uncertain time, when coach Lute Olson was on a leave of absence. Bayless had been recruited by Olson out of St. Mary's High School in Phoenix, but he ended up with Kevin O'Neill as the interim head coach.

Bayless, a combo guard, tried to shut out the turmoil as best he could, averaging a team-high 19.7 points while also producing 4.0 assists per game and shooting 40.7 percent from three-point range (59-of-145) in his only season as a Wildcat. The team struggled, especially late in the season, and finished 19–15 overall, with an 8–10 record in the Pac-10.

"I loved coaching Jerryd," O'Neill said. "Nobody ever worked harder. At any level I've ever been at it, no player worked harder on his game than Jerryd Bayless did that year. No player."

It was also clear to the media, which O'Neill allowed into the postgame locker room, that no Arizona player took losing harder than Bayless. "He did," O'Neill said. "This guy's whole life, heart and soul, was in basketball. It still defines him today. He's the same guy."

Bayless, who was chosen a second-team All-American by *Sports Illustrated*, declared early for the 2008 NBA Draft, becoming the first one-and-done player at Arizona.

"I've thought carefully about my options since the end of the season, discussed it with my parents and others who could give me appropriate guidance, and made this decision with a clear mind," Bayless said upon announcing his decision. "It's the right time for me to move on."

Olson responded that he was disappointed he did not have an opportunity to coach Bayless, who averaged 33.2 points in his senior season at St. Mary's and led his team to second place in the Arizona state tournament. A McDonald's All-American, he averaged 37.9 points as a junior.

No freshman in Arizona history has ever scored as many points in a season as Bayless, with 592. He also became the first player in Arizona history to score 30 or more points in three consecutive games when he accomplished the feat against ASU, Cal, and Stanford—all at McKale Center.

His 39 points against the Sun Devils on February 10, 2008, are the most by a freshman in the program's history. He followed that up with 33 points against Cal on February 14 and 31 points against Stanford on February 16.

Bayless was great off the dribble, almost always able to draw contact. His 187 successful free throws are the fifth-most in a single season in school history, and his 223 attempts rank eighth.

"He's an unbelievable kid with great character, and he's a great competitor," Olson said.

When Bayless played in the NBA Summer League in Las Vegas before his second season in the NBA, he was visibly upset that he had not been coached by Olson, who had recruited him to Arizona in the first place. In recent years, however, Bayless' disappointment has subsided. He has attended Arizona games and even taken part in video productions shown at McKale Center before games.

The 11th overall pick in the 2008 draft, his NBA career has been uneven. To date, he has played for six teams in his first seven years. Although he has more time left as a pro, Bayless has also begun to look at his life after basketball. He started an AAU team in Phoenix in 2014, with the hopes of potentially coaching in the future. He signed with Milwaukee in the summer of 2014.

"My first message to them, and really any young basketball player who is trying to better [himself], get a college scholarship and possibly make a career in the game, is just to stay focused," Bayless wrote on his blog at JerrydBayless.com. "If that's your dream, then continue to pursue it no matter what. I think that's a message that everyone in the younger generation should receive. If there's anything that you really want to do, that you dream of accomplishing—whether it's being a basketball player, or a lawyer or whatever you choose to do—stay focused, no matter what it takes, stay focused and if you want it, you can achieve it."

57 Jim Rosborough

Jim Rosborough cleared the other assistant coaches off the bus. Managers, trainers, support staff, too, until it was just him and the players remaining.

The Arizona Wildcats were in Storrs, Connecticut, to play the UConn Huskies, but head coach Lute Olson wasn't there. He had remained in Tucson while his wife, Bobbi, was in the final stages of battling ovarian cancer in December 2000.

It was an emotional time, but when Ros was done talking, everybody felt fine. "I have been told after the fact, by the guys, that the minute I finished my talk they were all ready to go play," Rosborough said.

He had that gift to make everyone calm, make everyone feel good. For 18 years on the Arizona sideline, Rosborough was the loyal lieutenant, the savvy scout and strategist, the popular assistant who had the personal warmth to counterbalance Olson's sometimes aloofness.

And in that 2000–01 season, he stepped up as the interim head coach, not only at UConn but in holding the team together after Bobbi's death on January 1, 2001. Olson had told the team at a shootaround on December 28 that he would be taking a leave of absence. "It was a horrendous, horrendous time for everybody," Rosborough said. "He's in the locker room, crying with the guys and telling them what's going on."

Arizona lost 75–74 to Mississippi State that night in the title game of the Fiesta Bowl Classic at McKale Center, the Wildcats' first loss in the 16-year history of the tournament.

"Losing that game, could everything have headed south?" Rosborough said. "It could have." He talked to the team in the locker room about the 1994–95 Duke team that collapsed under interim coach Pete Gaudet when Mike Krzyzewski had to take a health-related leave of absence. "I said, 'That is not happening here. We're going to be fine,'" Rosborough said. "Then we have a team meeting later that week and got some things aired out that apparently were bothering a lot of kids."

Arizona went 3–1 in its next four games under Rosborough, including two routs on the Washington road trip. "I think the kids would tell you we came out of those four games feeling really good about ourselves," Rosborough said. "And then Lute called me after we got back from Washington. He said, 'Well, do you mind my coming back now?'" Well, of course not.

With Ros in charge, the 2000–01 Arizona team—"maybe talentwise, the best team that has ever been at Arizona," he said—stayed the course and put everything together to make a run to the national title game. For as much as Rosborough still steams over the goaltending call on Loren Woods with 1.8 seconds left in a 71–69 loss at UConn, he absolutely boils at the officiating in UA's 82–72 loss to Duke in the championship game.

"We heard this the next summer from anybody we saw when we went out recruiting—they honestly and truly felt it was the worst-refereed title game they had seen to that point," he said. "Now, you can always say that, but we heard it all over the place.

"I think Krzyzewski is clearly one of the top two or three coaches who has ever been, but I'll tell you, he works those refs. And he was down there all over those refs that game, and maybe that had something to do with that. That's my viewpoint. It's not necessarily sour grapes, but it's the truth."

Rosborough was at Olson's side for his entire run at Iowa (1974–83). He first came on as a graduate assistant, hired because of his recruiting ties in the Chicago area. He didn't join Olson in Tucson until 1989, after spending three seasons as the head coach at Northern Illinois.

Through the years, Ros pretty much did it all. He ran the summer camps. Was a friendly face to the media. Handled countless administrative duties. Known for his game-planning, he prepared the scouting report on Kentucky when Arizona won the national title game in 1997. Olson elevated him from assistant to associate head coach after that season.

It was a wonderful relationship—beneficial for both men, and Arizona—but it came to an unfortunate end. After the 2006–07 season, in which the Wildcats lost to Purdue in the first round of the NCAA Tournament and had seen a recent slip in discipline and overall quality, Rosborough suggested to Olson that Miles Simon "didn't quite get the whole picture" as an inexperienced assistant coach. Simon had just completed his second season on the UA staff.

"Maybe that was a learning period for him," Rosborough said. "To be honest with you, he was a little bit of a liability.... And I heard from other people around Lute that he was aware of that."

Still, Olson went in a different direction in a staff shake-up. He opted to bring in Kevin O'Neill as the lead assistant, offering Rosborough something of a basketball operations position. Ros declined. "For 27 years, I was loyal to him and helped him and looked out for him," Rosborough said.

Rosborough stayed in the athletic department, working with athletic director Jim Livengood, as Olson took a health-related leave of absence in the 2007–08 season. The head coach announced his return after the season, when he made it clear O'Neill would not be back. Rosborough and Olson met to discuss an on-court reunion.

"He said, 'Jim, I will take care of it' and we shook hands," Rosborough said. "I walked out the door, waiting to hear." Olson never called back.

From that time in the spring of 2008 to the summer of 2014, Rosborough said he has had no relationship with Olson and that they haven't said more than "four sentences" to each other in passing.

"The ending was awful," Rosborough said. "But I will say this to the day I die: There's not a better coach around. I mean, a great, great practice coach. I owe this guy everything. He was kind of like a father figure to me. Any success I ever had, I owe to him.

"The only time it was not good was the last 10 minutes, when he wanted me to do this other stuff. Otherwise, he let you do your job and he was a great person to work for. He was loyal to us; I was loyal to him. But the last 10 minutes were not good. Until he reaches out to say something, I'm pretty well done with the guy. I did everything I could to help him. I'm not embarrassed to tell you that."

Across all sports, Rosborough has his place among the great Arizona assistants, which include pitching coach Jim Wing under Jerry Kindall, and defensive line coach Sharkey Price under four football coaches.

"My wife has said to me numerous times: 'After you guys won the title in '97, why didn't you look to go somewhere?'" Rosborough said. "The answer to that is, it wouldn't have been better. We had players who were great kids. You're winning. You're on top of the heap. I really liked my time there. There was stability for 18 years to get my kids raised, to get ingrained in the city of Tucson. There isn't a bad thing I can say about it. I could not have asked for more out of that time."

58 Luke Walton: Living the Good Life

His commitment came one late September day in 1997, when the UCLA Bruins powder blue really turned blue—and red.

UCLA may or may not have been a factor in his recruitment, but it was on that day Luke Walton, the son of former UCLA great

Bill Walton, chose Arizona as his college. He went 6–3 against the Bruins in his career.

"My dad didn't put any pressure on me to go to UCLA or anywhere else," Walton said at the time. "He respects coach Lute Olson very much, so he was very happy when I told him I was going to Arizona."

His commitment came just months after Arizona had won the national title, and it spawned a college career that lasted five years at Arizona, including a redshirt season in 1998–99.

"If I could stay more than five years," Walton said during his senior year, "I would." Why not? He had huge success and was part of it all as Arizona went to the NCAA Tournament every year, was in the national title game in 2001, and was the No. 1 team in the nation in 2003.

"It was such a great time in my life. I had so many good memories," Walton said. "I made so many friends. It's unbelievable. Just [recently] we won a rec league title with [former teammate] Rick Anderson. You make these friendships and Tucson just gets behind you. You can't describe the fans' commitment to you. It's a feeling I'll never forget."

In fact, Arizona is also where he met his wife, Bre Ladd, a former UA volleyball standout. Teammate Richard Jefferson was his best man. Andre Iguodala was at the wedding, as was Jason Gardner, Channing Frye, and, of course, Lute Olson. Arizona proved to be a life-changing place for Walton, one of three basketball-playing sons of the Hall of Fame great.

Luke Walton, now retired from the NBA, is part of the first father-son combination to win multiple NBA titles. Bill won two (1977, 1986) and Luke won two with the Los Angeles Lakers in 2009 and 2010.

"That's what Luke has always been about: winning and doing whatever it takes to win," Lute Olson said of Walton when he was going for NBA titles. "And it's his total game that makes him special and the fact that he makes everybody better."

Arizona seemed as if it were always good with Walton around. In his five years, Arizona went 107–29. Olson said Walton "understands the game and does things you just can't teach."

It all started January 13, 2000, when it was announced he was going to make his first start. The nod came because his best friend, Jefferson, had suffered a broken right foot against Stanford the week before. "Now, it's his turn to deliver," Bill said at the time.

"Mentally and physically, I think I am ready," Walton said at the time.

"[My dad] just said to continue to play my game and not try to do too much," Luke said. "I have to be more productive than I have been but not get caught up in all the [hoopla]."

How could there have been any? He entered the game averaging just 2.7 points, 3.1 assists, and 2.1 rebounds, after all. He was hitting just 25 percent of his shots.

"That'll come," he promised. And it did. And nothing was better than when he had Arizona's sixth triple-double in school history—27 points, 11 rebounds, and 10 assists.

"It may be as good a performance as we've ever had at McKale Center," Olson said. "You think back to Sean Elliott's performances, but Luke did it with his defense, too. He was an excellent passer and scorer. I don't think we've had a guy do it in so many ways."

If there was one thing Walton had it was a feel for the game—unteachable instincts from growing up around his father and seeing plenty of basketball. He said he could envision himself passing the ball even before he was about to pass the ball.

Is it in the genes? "It's hard to tell what it is," Walton told the *Tucson Citizen*. "It could have something to do with my dad. I heard he was a good passer," he laughed. "I haven't seen many of his games."

Luke Walton's "good life" includes two NBA championships.

Either way, Luke Walton's time at Arizona resulted in what turned out to be a great career. He finished 22nd on the school's all-time scoring list with 1,179 points, fifth in assists with 582, and ninth all-time for a single season with 194. He's the only player in the program's history to have more than 1,000 points, 500 rebounds, and 500 assists. He was also a two-time All–Pac-10 pick and the most outstanding player of the league tournament in 2002.

In 2014, he was named to the Pac-12 Hall of Honor. "It's a great honor. I love the Pac-12," Walton said. "The years at Arizona were some of the best of my life. To be able to play with the players I did and have the coaching staff I had...it's just an amazing feeling."

59 Lute vs. the *Daily Star*

Any coach who stays in one place for a quarter of a century is going to go through times when he faces criticism from the local media. That's part of the job.

Yet the relationship between Lute Olson and the *Arizona Daily Star*, Tucson's morning newspaper, often went beyond a merely uneasy coexistence. It wasn't just about a he said–he said situation, or a negative critique of a coaching situation. There were times, even as the Wildcats were pursuing a national championship in the NCAA Tournament, when this adversarial relationship was the dominant storyline of the day.

It was a relationship that got off on the wrong foot almost from the start. In March 1985, the *Star* published a story on the front page of the paper alleging that Olson had engaged in improper behavior by having the team's basketball uniforms bought from Sand-Knit, owned by MacGregor Sporting Goods, which had

Olson on contract serving as a consultant and running clinics. Was it a clear conflict of interest, with Olson essentially giving the company kickbacks?

As it turned out, the *Star*—which had exposed major improprieties in UA's football program several years earlier—had rushed the story and gotten its facts wrong. The university had purchased the uniforms from Sand-Knit in 1983, before MacGregor bought the company in 1984. So, there was no quid pro quo with the uniform contract.

In a front-page correction, Star managing editor Jonathan I. Kamman called the error "grievous and deplorable." Some picketed at the newspaper offices. The paper even received bomb threats.

Facing demotions, sports reporter Rich Dymond and sports editor Sam Pollak resigned. Olson steamed, telling the Associated Press the story was "the worst piece of journalism, the most vicious attack with the most distorted facts in my memory."

The erroneous report nearly had dire consequences for the Wildcats, too. Olson, who had recently declined to throw his hat in the ring for the vacant head coaching job at Kentucky, agreed to meet with UK officials in Lexington. "Given the circumstances of the day, I think there's a definite need for me to be available for talks with Kentucky," Olson told the *Tucson Citizen*, the city's afternoon newspaper. "When people can come out with a flat-out character assassination, with fabrications through and through, then I owe it to my family to look at what other people have to say."

Olson looked, but ultimately decided to stay in Tucson. One of Kentucky's missteps: Not realizing how important Bobbi Olson was to the process and failing to include her in meetings. "That was a big mistake," Olson said.

As Olson built further success at Arizona, his media foil became *Daily Star* columnist Greg Hansen, mainly stemming from a column on May 6, 1991, under the headline OLSON UNAVAILABLE IN TIME OF CRISIS.

Brian Williams had recently declared early for the NBA Draft, Sean Rooks had made some troubling comments about, in Hansen's words, "an abyss between the coaching staff and the players," and Khalid Reeves was facing a charge of alleged sexual assault on campus. (He was later exonerated by the university.)

Wrote Hansen:

> **Where was Olson?**
>
> He had flown to San Diego to represent the university in a gala fund-raising effort. That's nice.
>
> But isn't his first obligation to his players? Wouldn't it be nice if the coach found it necessary to be at Reeves' side in time of crisis? Wouldn't Reeves' mother, who entrusts her son to attend school 3,000 miles from home under Olson's guidance, appreciate and expect Olson's personal counsel? Has Olson become bigger than his team?
>
> As the coach fiddles in some faraway ports, his team burns. His fans wonder what in the hell has gone wrong.

In his autobiography, Olson writes, "There have not been that many people in my life with whom I didn't get along, but one of them was *Arizona Daily Star* columnist Greg Hanson [sic]." Perhaps the misspelling was intentional.

Olson, furious over the accusation that he was unavailable to his team, disputed Hansen's claims of absenteeism. In a sit-down meeting, he showed the *Star*'s editor and sports editor a calendar that highlighted 283 consecutive days of work. In *Lute! The Seasons of My Life*, Olson writes that he told the *Star*'s editors, "I want you to know I will never talk to Greg Hansen again in my life." During the Wildcats' NCAA Tournament run in 1994, Olson used the big stage to fire back at some in the media who had previously been critical of his team. The headline on the ensuing Hansen column: Olson holds grudge like no one else.

That spurred such a backlash that, three days later, the *Star*'s managing editor, Bobbie Jo Buel, took the unusual step to write a story on the front page of the paper's sports section to address the issue. She began, "Why does Greg Hansen say all those mean things about Lute Olson? That's the general theme of phone calls and letters to the Star these days."

She went on to excerpt Hansen's basketball columns through the season to give readers a "recap of the toughest, roughest things Hansen said over the season" and to help them discern the truth of the matter.

For many years, Olson and Hansen did not speak directly. Instead, Hansen's colleagues would ask the questions in press conferences that Hansen wanted asked.

Is there a happy ending? In 2000, as Bobbi was suffering from ovarian cancer, she told Lute that she hoped he could patch things up with Hansen.

Writes Olson in his autobiography, "When she died, Greg wrote an unbelievable article about Bobbi. It was just beautiful. I called him and asked him to come to my office. 'Okay,' I said, 'we're starting from day one right now. I can't tell you how much I appreciated your column.' Ever since that day we've had a good relationship. Thanks to Bobbi."

60 Michael Dickerson

Usually when an NBA player averages 15.4 points in his first five seasons, he's considered a can't-miss prospect. Unfortunately for Michael Dickerson, he missed out on a long and successful NBA career because of a series of hamstring and groin injuries. He was forced to retire from the NBA at age 28 in 2003 while with the Memphis Grizzlies.

"This is a sad day for me," Dickerson said in a statement. "I am grateful to the entire Grizzlies organization for their unwavering support and encouragement throughout my career, and especially the lengthy process to attempt to rehab my injuries." Dickerson had played only 10 games in his last two seasons because of the serious groin strain.

His scoring ability and defense on the wing helped Arizona win the 1997 national title. He ranks No. 8 on Arizona's career scoring list with 1,791 points. He was a two-time All–Pac-10 selection.

Since his retirement he's been an every-so-often visitor to Tucson, visiting with Kelly and Lute Olson and their family. He's also been a frequent houseguest to the Olsons. "He's a terrific young man and the kids think the world of him," Lute Olson said.

Houston drafted him in the first round in 1998, the 14th pick overall. He was traded to the Grizzlies organization (then in Vancouver) after his rookie season. His best season was in 1999–2000, when he averaged 18.2 points, 3.4 rebounds, and 1.4 steals for the Grizzlies.

After a five-year hiatus, Dickerson, then 33, attempted an NBA comeback in 2008. He was ultimately released during the preseason by Cleveland and Memphis. He played briefly in Spain in 2009 before opting to tour the world, seeking the opportunity to train young players abroad. He visited India and Tibet with the financial support of his NBA contract, which paid him $43 million in 2002, a year before he was forced to initially retire.

At Arizona, Dickerson was always substance over style. He was the quietest player on the Wildcats' 1996–97 national title team, always keeping to himself. His calm demeanor could be mistaken for being passive, but Olson rarely had as hard of a worker and as tough of a defender on the wing.

When asked about his hefty NBA pay after retirement, Dickerson told HoopsHype.com in 2010: "[The money] didn't make it easier at all at the time. It really doesn't mean anything to me."

Dickerson continues to train prospective college players in Canada, working at camps in Toronto and Vancouver. His work ethic and skill should be beneficial for the young prospects. Former Arizona assistant coach Jim Rosborough told the *Arizona Daily Star* during the Wildcats' 1996–97 championship season that "no one spends more time on his shooting than this kid. I've never seen a kid put in as much time as Michael does."

One drill Dickerson must be teaching his players in Toronto and Vancouver is shooting without taking a dribble. Catch and shoot. Catch and shoot. Over and over. He was a master of that while at Arizona.

"He just comes off the screen, and, pop, there it is," Rosborough told the *Arizona Daily Star*. "Michael has worked so hard on that move in practice and in the gym alone, that when he gets in a game situation, it becomes second nature."

61 Arizona vs. Arizona State

The Arizona–Arizona State rivalry wasn't much of one after Lute Olson arrived in Tucson. Olson's Wildcats won 16 of their first 17 games against the Sun Devils, and 24 of their final 25. (For the record, he was 43–6 against the school up north.)

Here's another sign of dominance: Olson had as many 30-point victories over Arizona State (6) as he had overall losses.

None of this means that the in-state rivalry has been docile, or uneventful. And it's been filled with one truly ugly incident, a classic gesture from Olson and the best (literal) punch-line in Arizona history.

Arizona had won at Arizona State 83–82, on Valentine's Day in 1998, although there certainly wasn't any love lost between the teams that day. ASU's Eddie House and some of the Wildcats verbally sparred outside the locker rooms, a tone-setting event for what happened a week later, when the travel partners embarked on a road trip to Oregon.

Each team ended up at the Electric Station restaurant in Eugene on the same night. "We had come out from dinner and Miles [Simon] was outside already, and Eddie House was out there running his mouth—again—just popping off," said center A.J. Bramlett. "When I came out there, I just got involved verbally and didn't think anything was really going to happen."

And then, at least in Bramlett's version of the story, House took a swing at him. "We got into a fight in front of a very nice restaurant with [plate-]glass windows," Bramlett said. "It wasn't something I had planned on happening, but in the heat of the moment, you have to do what you have to do."

And Bramlett did. The altercation ended with House on the ground. Legend has it—and Bramlett doesn't deny it—that he then delivered this classic walk-off line: "You want more of this national championship ring?" He might have felt good right about then, but he began to worry on the bus back to the hotel. What would Olson think? The coach called Bramlett to his room. Was he in trouble?

Far from it. Here is what Bramlett recalled Olson saying about the incident with House: "A.J., if he's going to be a jerk, then he got what he deserved."

"And that was the end of it," Bramlett said. "Coach surprised me with that one. But he's a smart man."

Olson had his own limits. Which brings us to January 3, 2004. By this point, Olson had endured two decades of barbs and insults from Arizona State fans, who once even pelted his team with candy on the way to and from the locker room.

With his team up by 20-something points late in the game in Tempe, Olson responded to the student section by turning to the fans and simply pointing to the scoreboard. Arizona won 93–74.

"I was like, 'You know, I have learned every new word from them you can learn,' and I finally just had enough," Olson said. His move only fanned the flames, of course. Students began chanting, "Lute's an [expletive]! Lute's an [expletive]!" ASU coach Rob Evans later called Olson's gesture "classless." The following month, however, Arizona State president Michael Crow apologized in person to Olson for the poor behavior of his student body.

As far as classless behavior, though, it doesn't get worse than what happened in 1988 in Tempe. A group of fans taunted Steve Kerr during warm-ups with chants of "PLO! PLO!" and "Where's your dad?" in reference to the 1984 assassination of Malcolm Kerr, who was the president of American University of Beirut when Palestinian terrorists shot him in the head.

"They yelled despicable things at him, obviously trying to destroy his concentration," Olson wrote in his autobiography. "It was more than disgusting. Several of our players had to be restrained from going into the stands after the hecklers."

The gambit failed. Kerr responded by shooting 7-for-7 from the field, hitting all six of his three-point attempts, and scoring 22 points. Arizona won 101–73. "It's hard to believe that people would do that, but it had happened to me one other time before, a couple of years ago, also at Arizona State," Kerr told the *Los Angeles Times* a few days after the game. "But that time it was just one or two people, so it wasn't noticed much. Saturday, it was about 10 or 15 people, in unison.

"When I heard it, I just dropped the ball and started shaking. I sat down for a minute. I'll admit they got to me. I had tears in my eyes. For one thing, it brought back memories of my dad. But, for another thing, it was just sad that people would do something like that."

Though the Olson era is done at Arizona, the flames of rivalry still burn hot between the Wildcats and the Sun Devils.

62 Solomon Hill: Patience Pays Off

Every rebuilding project needs a strong foundation, and that is what Solomon Hill was to coach Sean Miller.

Hill took a crooked path to Arizona, committing to the Wildcats when Lute Olson was still coach, switching to USC after Olson's retirement, and then circling back to UA after scandal hit the Trojans program. Turns out he was exactly what Arizona and Miller needed all along.

While Derrick Williams became the supernova star in that recruiting class, he left for the NBA after leading the Cats to an NCAA Tournament regional final in his sophomore season. Hill, meanwhile, was the enduring bedrock from which Miller was able to launch future success.

Hill will always be the example of how to do things the right way. The versatile forward was the team's best practice player. He added a new element to his game every year, improved his body every season. He was unselfish on the court.

And then he got rewarded. In modern college basketball, there often is a stigma on a player who stays for his senior year, but Hill's patience and dedication paid off. After tying a school record by playing in 139 career games, Hill landed as the 23rd overall pick in the 2013 NBA Draft, going to the Indiana Pacers.

Miller recalls a conversation he had with Hill late in his sophomore season. "He was really emotional and upset, and we kind of had one of those meetings you remember forever," Miller said. "Part of what he was saying was, a lot of players he was ranked with or ahead of in high school were on track to the NBA, leaving after their first and second years. Well, why isn't it happening for him?

"What I explained, and we explained back to Solomon: you can't ever rush the process. Sometimes it happens early, sometimes it happens later. But if you stick with it, your talent will eventually win out."

The coach was right, and Hill's talent indeed won out. He was a first-team all-conference selection in his final two seasons, helping Arizona get to the 2013 Sweet 16.

He stuck with the process for all four years, improving his scoring average from 6.7 points per game as a freshman to 13.4 as a senior. "I was proud to be part of the rebuilding phase," Hill said.

Hill's improvement was especially seen in his shooting ability. He went from four made three-pointers as a freshman to 17 as a sophomore, 37 as a junior, and then 57 in his final season.

He had value far beyond scoring, though. As a junior, he was second on the team in scoring (12.9 per game) and the leader in rebounding (7.7) and assists (2.6).

He had another long talk with Miller after that season, asking if it would be worth it to come back for his senior year. "His point was, you're damaged goods if you come back as a senior," Miller said.

The coach's response: Don't worry about any stereotypes. It's just about getting good enough. "'Right now, if you're not a first-round pick, don't play with that,'" Miller remembers telling Hill. "'You're too good of a kid, you're too talented.'

"He listened. He got his degree.... As a coach, that's probably the most fulfilling part of the job when that happens. He's a special kid."

He became the 18th first-round pick in Arizona history, and the second under Miller.

Minutes after Hill was drafted, Miller took to Twitter to write: "Don't know if I have ever been happier as a coach than when I saw Solomon become a first round pick in the NBA! #HonoredTheProcess @nba"

That nicely sums up Hill's legacy at Arizona: Honor the process.

63 Arizona vs. New Mexico

You've heard of home-court advantage. How about home-clock advantage?

Arizona coach Lute Olson could live with the questionable officiating—he'll tell you he had to swallow plenty of home cooking from the refs at the Pit in Albuquerque—dating to his Iowa days when he played in a tournament there—but some alleged help from the scoreboard timer pushed him over the edge. And that's why a gem of a basketball series between Arizona and the University of New Mexico has been on extended hiatus.

There were 4.6 seconds left in a game at the Pit on January 16, 1999. Arizona led 78–77 in front of a raucous crowd of 18,018. New Mexico had to inbound the ball from underneath its own basket.

Point guard John Robinson II took the initial pass and had to weave through traffic before he got near the top of the key. Then he passed down low to Damion Walker, who put up a layup attempt that Arizona's Michael Wright got fingertips on before the ball went through the basket.

Uh...all in 4.6 seconds?

"I wanted to beat the Lobos in the Pit like crazy," said Albuquerque native A.J. Bramlett, a senior center on that Arizona team. "Being on the court, it just seemed easy to know there was no way they could have done what they did in that amount of time. Coach was just animated. His jacket had come off already and he was lining up the officials."

Lobos coach Dave Bliss said later his team had never been able to complete that play in 4.6 seconds in practice. "We had our TV people break it down by the 10th of the second," Olson said. "It took [New Mexico] 7.2 or 7.5 seconds or something."

Well, probably not that long, but the timer's slow start of the clock, allowing the coast-to-coast score, burned Olson then—"either the guy is inept or very dishonest," he said days later—and it still gnawed at him 15 years later. "That's when I said, 'That's it,'" he said. "You know it's going to be tough because the fans are so active and all that, but when we have to worry about the timer also, then we weren't going to continue the series."

The teams played their last contracted game in Tucson the following season. New Mexico won 70–68 on December 21, 1999, snapping second-ranked Arizona's 37-game home winning streak at McKale Center. And that's been it for UA-UNM.

With the memory of the series still fresh, though, Arizona did have to play in the 2002 NCAA Tournament in Albuquerque. Olson recalls allowing his team to watch the end of a tournament game in the arena while he finished up pregame work in the locker room. "All of a sudden I heard this, '*BOOOOOOO!*' Olson said with a smile. "It was our team coming out of the ramp. Oh, boy, they hated us."

There have been rumblings in recent years of renewing the series—which spans 125 games and dates to 1917—but nothing was on the schedule as of the summer of 2014. (Arizona leads the series 83–42.)

"You wouldn't even understand how big a deal that is here," said Bramlett, who still lives in Albuquerque. "I still hear daily from people wanting the rivalry to be renewed. It's funny because it's such a big deal here, but I doubt people in Tucson are thinking about New Mexico, you know what I mean? It's an interesting kind of dynamic."

Bramlett, who was in attendance rooting for the Lobos as a kid when they beat No. 1 Arizona at the Pit on January 2, 1988, learned all about that dynamic in a hurry when he committed to Arizona over his hometown team. "From one day to the next, I pretty much turned from the favorite son to a traitor," Bramlett said. "I was hated by the whole city, pretty much."

Given how Sean Miller has scheduled against Mountain West powers San Diego State and UNLV, it might not be long before the old flame vs. the Lobos is relit. "I would like to see the rivalry come back," Bramlett said. "They were great games. They were exciting and there was a lot of passion on both sides. If they did renew it, I'll be there—with all my Arizona gear on."

64 Kiddie Korps

Before there was a Fab Five at Michigan in 1991, there was the Kiddie Korps at Arizona in 1972.

Oddly enough, both all-freshman starting lineups had a "Motown" feel to them. Two of the Fab Five's starters were from Detroit (Chris Webber and Jalen Rose). Likewise, two of Arizona's Kiddie Korps members were also Detroit natives (Eric Money and Coniel Norman), and Fred Snowden, Arizona's head coach, was an assistant at Michigan before moving to Tucson.

The Wildcats' storied recruiting class, Snowden's first as head coach, also included Jim Rappis from Waukesha, Wisconsin; John Irving from Wilmington, Delaware; and Al Fleming from Michigan City, Indiana.

The combination of Money, Norman, and Rappis on the perimeter mixed with the dominant inside game of Irving and Fleming earned Arizona its first No. 1 recruiting class according to *Street & Smith's* magazine.

"The night we played the Red-Blue scrimmage was uncharted territory," former Arizona player Steve Kanner is quoted as saying in the book *Tucson: A Basketball Town*, which is coauthored by Money. "There was tremendous excitement surrounding Coach Snowden and his Kiddie Korps.

"The talent level in the program took an immediate step up. That night was the first showcase. Motown had come to Tucson."

Bruce Larson, the coach Snowden succeeded, had not recruited nationally because of Arizona's budget. Arizona hired Snowden with the promise to allow him to attract players from all parts of the country, and Snowden delivered.

Snowden hired as his lead assistant Jerry Holmes, who had East Coast recruiting ties because of his Pennsylvania background. The combination of Snowden from the Midwest and Holmes from the East allowed the Wildcats to draw from a countrywide well for the first time, becoming a national power. Moreover, the NCAA allowed freshmen to become eligible in Snowden's first season in Tucson (1972–73) and McKale Center opened its doors that season.

Everything fell into place for Snowden to turn Arizona basketball around with the Kiddie Korps, who were forced to mature immediately together. "These kids are proving something to themselves that not many kids their age get to do," Snowden was quoted as saying in an Associated Press report after the Wildcats upset UTEP and New Mexico in consecutive games. "They're learning they have to be adults now."

Three members of the Kiddie Korps—Money, Norman, and Fleming—later played in the NBA. Norman remains at the top the Arizona charts by scoring 23.9 points a game (Money ranks sixth at 18.6). Fleming is still Arizona's top career rebounder, with 1,190.

Irving, who became homesick, transferred closer to home to Hofstra after his freshman year. After sitting out a year, he led the nation with 15.4 rebounds a game. He is one of only two Hofstra players who tabulated more than 1,000 points and 1,000 rebounds in his career.

Rappis emerged as one of Arizona's catalysts in the Wildcats' Elite Eight season of 1975–76. He was selected an All-West Regional player in the NCAA Tournament that season. He was also a two-time Western Athletic All-Academic selection.

Attendance for Arizona games went from roughly 3,000 at Bear Down Gym to 14,000 at the new McKale Center in 1973. Tucson indeed became a basketball town because of the influence of Snowden and the Kiddie Korps.

The Wildcats went from 6–20 in Larson's last season to 16–10 in Snowden's first. The Wildcats improved to 19–7 the following season with Bob Elliott, an Ann Arbor, Michigan, recruit who replaced Irving as the starting center.

Money and Norman left for the NBA after their sophomore seasons. Despite their loss, Arizona continued to improve, going 22–7 in 1974–75 and 24–9 with a WAC title and Elite Eight appearance in 1975–76.

There's no argument: the Kiddie Korps established a foundation for that success to happen.

65 Jordan Hill: A Raw Talent

Jordan Hill was the least-heralded part of the 2006 recruiting class. Chase Budinger was the jewel of the trio that included Nic Wise, the pocket-sized point guard who committed to UA during his freshman year in high school.

"I know I wasn't a recruiting star, but I know I'm a very good player," Hill told the *Tucson Citizen*. "If fans give me a chance, I promise I won't let them down."

One day on the recruiting trail, coach Lute Olson saw the lanky and raw power forward play well in an AAU game, which started the process of him becoming an Arizona Wildcat. Olson then called assistant Josh Pastner to make sure he rushed over to see Hill as well.

"Jordan's a great feel-good story for anyone willing to dream and anyone that believes in the power of love and prayer," Gary Graham told the *Atlanta Journal-Constitution*. Graham was the coach of Hill's AAU team Smyrna Stars. Hill signed with UA out of Patterson School in North Carolina, the place he ended up after needing more schooling to become eligible for college.

"There was no ranking on him [at the time]," Pastner told the *AJC*. "It just shows the importance of evaluating. It's so much more important than you think. And Jordan gets a lot of credit. He worked so hard. You could always tell the ability was there.

"But who knows what would have happened if he hadn't hooked up with Gary Graham? Who knows how things might have turned out if he didn't get that chance or the chance to work with Chris Chaney at the Patterson School?"

A season after signing with UA, Hill, a 6'10", 235 pounder, started to make an impression. As UA was getting ready for its weeklong trip to Canada to play in exhibition games, Hill was flourishing.

"It's like the light is going on," Olson said. Everything went on. He had defensive timing, a knack for jumping and blocking shots, and he was an extremely hard and determined worker.

"That was one guy I didn't really know about before he came here," Marcus Williams said. "I had never really seen him play. He is definitely somebody we really need. I wouldn't be surprised if he actually plays more than people think because he really gets after it defensively, finishes well around the basket and eats up rebounds."

Said Olson, "We're not surprised by his ability because we always thought it was there. But we thought with him having limited experience on the high school level, we thought it would take him a little bit longer.

"He's a very coachable young man. He's very focused. You don't have to tell him something twice."

As it turned out, Hill turned out to be one of Arizona's best big men in the Olson era. In his freshman season he averaged 4.7 points and 4.1 rebounds per game. In his second year he became an honorable mention All–Pac-10 pick and was part of the conference's all-defensive team. He ended his second season leading the conference in field goal percentage, at 62 percent. By his junior year, he was good enough for the NBA, leading UA with an average 18.3 points and 11 rebounds per game.

He holds the school record for rebounds for a season, with 375, while his career rebound average (7.9) is the sixth best in school history.

No player in the previous 10 years had come so far so fast compared to Hill, who declared for the draft after UA made a run at the Sweet 16 under Russ Pennell and Mike Dunlap. "I just want to thank the fans of Tucson, my coaches, and my teammates for all of their support," Hill said in declaring for the NBA Draft. "Playing at Arizona has been a great experience and puts me in the position to move to the next level. It's always been a dream of mine to play in the NBA."

In the summer of 2009 the New York Knicks drafted him as the eighth player overall, making him the 10th lottery pick for an ex-UA player since 1989. He's now a key contributor with the Los Angeles Lakers.

66 Chase Budinger: From Volleyball to Basketball

He has been considered Lute Olson's best-ever recruit. And that's a tall order for any recruit who has ever played for the Hall of Fame coach. But that's just what Chase Budinger was when he came out of La Costa Canyon High in the San Diego area.

Budinger, of course, was one of the best high school volleyball players in the world when he decided to play for Olson, becoming the school's 14th McDonald's High School All-American. He was considered the top player in a class of recruits (including Jordan Hill and Nic Wise) that would help Arizona get back to the Final Four after what had been a tough year by Arizona standards: 20–13 in 2005–06.

"I'm probably the one that stands out between us three," Budinger told the *Tucson Citizen* at the time. "I've come in with a lot of hype, but they don't say anything about that. They don't care. All I care about is the team and people who are inside the circle. Whatever is said on the outside goes in one ear and out the other."

There was no question to Olson that he was special from the first time the coach saw him play, as a freshman. "He was a great athlete," Olson said. "I watched him play some volleyball as well as basketball. I thought he was a perfect fit for the program. He's a great guy and he was a team-type guy."

And an Arizona guy—long before he signed and long after. Olson recalled getting a call from Budinger in the spring after he had committed to ask if "Josh [Pastner] could stop calling me. Tell Josh I'm coming to Arizona. I don't want to hear from him until I get to school [in the fall]."

Budinger proceeded to show up and did not disappoint, although he struggled a time or two. He even landed in the top 10 in career scoring average with 17.0 per game. And he finished at No. 11 on the school's all-time scoring list in just three years. Only Sean Elliott (1,820) and Bob Elliott (1,701) scored more points in their first three seasons. He also ranks second in minutes per game (35.4).

Despite all the superlatives, what he'll be most known for is a single game. Arizona was at home against Houston, and UA came roaring back after trailing by double digits late in the game. The spark was ignited when Houston guard Aubrey Coleman appeared to intentionally step on Budinger's chest and face after being called for charging with 9:51 left in the game and Houston up 63–51. The incident became an instant must-see YouTube clip.

"I never meant to step on him," Coleman said through the school shortly after the incident. "I have never been in an incident like this before, and I have nothing but respect for him as a great player. I love the game too much to do something like that intentionally. I want to say I'm sorry from the bottom of my heart. I know that God knows what is in my heart, but I am hopeful that Chase will understand and forgive."

Upon returning to the team hotel, Coleman later wrote Budinger a personal apology and later tried to reach him via phone soon after. "He wanted to contact me, but I pretty much told his people I didn't want to talk to him," Budinger said. "I just didn't want to talk to him at all. I didn't care. He tried to say it was an accident and everything. I thought it was a bunch of BS."

The Wildcats went on to win seven consecutive games, giving the team hope for an NCAA berth. It did lose the next four before eventually getting into the tournament and making a run to the Sweet 16.

That was a season that almost didn't happen for Budinger, who almost declared for the NBA Draft but decided to return—in part because Olson had declared he was returning from his medical leave of absence. Budinger did test the NBA waters, but a week before the draft decided to return.

"The opportunity to play for Coach Olson, in my mind, best prepares me to have a successful NBA career," Budinger said. "I want to enter the NBA with great certainty of my future potential and believe the chance to develop further under Coach Olson enhances that opportunity."

"I'm thrilled that Chase decided to come back," Olson said at the time. "Selfishly, I feel the decision is in Chase's best interest. I feel in a year he will be a top-10 pick."

As it turned out, Olson returned to the court but then, just before the first practices, retired.

After the season, Budinger declared for the NBA Draft but was shockingly left on the board until the second round and 44th pick. He was eventually dealt to the Houston Rockets and is now with the Minnesota Timberwolves, who signed him to a three-year deal worth a reported $16 million in 2013.

67 Channing Frye: Mr. Improvement

It was easy to see what Arizona coach Lute Olson saw in Channing Frye when he recruited him out of Phoenix St. Mary's High School: he was a guy with "great character" and lots and lots of potential. In fact, Olson said Frye's legacy may end up being this: he's one of the most improved players to ever play for him and one of the smartest, most thoughtful, and thought-provoking.

In fact, if there was ever a go-to guy for a quote it was Frye, who seemingly always came up with an anecdote or an analogy when it came to offer perspective. Figure that in a surprising loss to Washington State in his senior year, he compared the loss to a person putting sour Skittles in their mouth. Yes, *that* crazy face.

"He's very intelligent," Olson said. "What I liked about him when I saw him in high school was that he just ran the floor and just worked his tail off all the time." He was a lanky and gawky sort who looked like he needed a meal more than he needed a basketball. No question he was a project. To this day, Olson still reminds him of the kid he used to be: a guy who needed to get bigger and stronger.

"We got a commitment out of him when he was a junior," Olson recalled. "Of course, ASU after that said, 'We wouldn't have offered him anyway.' But in terms of improvement, when he finished high school he was ranked the 178th best senior in his class. A short four years later, he was the first of that class taken in the pro draft (in 2005).

"Channing was an unbelievably hard worker. He worked hard on the weights. He worked hard on his conditioning. He was great to coach," said Olson.

What really hooked Frye, considered a project when he was being recruited out of high school, was that Olson always "handwrote his letters" to Frye and many other recruits. "I took a lot of pride in that and my parents said it meant something," Frye said about the recruiting letters.

On Frye's unofficial visit he was sold after sparking friendships with Luke Walton, Jason Gardner, and Gilbert Arenas. "It was about winning, and I got addicted to that," Frye told Fox Sports Arizona.

Arizona also became a brotherhood for Frye, a 6'11" center who rated in the recruiting class behind Salim Stoudamire, Will Bynum, Dennis Latimore, and Isaiah Fox.

"It's rare in basketball to find true friends and guys I consider brothers," he said. "I'll talk to them the rest of my life."

And there is plenty to talk about. One night is clearly there if they choose to speak about it at all. It was the game in which Illinois roared back from 15 points down in the waning minutes of regulation to beat Arizona in overtime to get to the 2005 Final Four. It was also the final game of Frye's career.

He had 24 points, 12 rebounds, and six blocked shots in the contest. Unfortunately, his three-pointer proved to be Arizona's last goal in regulation. It came with 6:03 left.

It's a game he's often thought about, but he chooses to remain positive about it. To be fair, few Arizona fans choose to even talk about the game, one that would have put Arizona in the Final Four for the fifth time.

"It's the night I became a lottery pick," Frye told Fox Sports. "That's how I see it. I would have much rather have lost on a last-second shot," Frye said. "To be honest, it is what it is. It was a game we were not supposed to win."

He's long been a put-things-in-perspective type. He'll be in his 10th season in the NBA, and has become one of the best

Channing Frye and the Letter

Arizona coach Lute Olson did something he had never done before in late February 2005. He wrote a letter to the Pac-10 Conference office to denounce its selection of the Pac-10 player of the week, defending his own player Channing Frye, whom he felt should have been given the award. Even Frye was surprised with the tone of the letter.

> I am appalled at what has transpired recently within our conference...Channing Frye just concluded one of the most impressive road trips, in terms of individual performance, in the history of this conference.... It is completely beyond my comprehension how you and your staff cannot have the instincts or common sense to do what is right.... Just in case you missed the games and/or did not see the box scores, Channing was 24-of-28 from the field and 8-of-8 from the free throw line last weekend.
>
> ...It must take the box score hitting you square between the eyes before you finally see it. Therefore, in addition to the aforementioned shooting exploits, Channing also had 13 rebounds, five blocks, and three steals, while playing 81 minutes! I ask you, what does it take? Would you like Channing to take tickets at the door and also sell concessions? I may advise him to do so at the upcoming Pac-10 tournament. If I seem incensed and furious, your senses are correct. To put it loud and clear...I felt it was totally disgusting not to have Channing Frye recognized. [He] stands for everything that is right with college athletics....
>
> He deserves better. He deserves to be recognized for his hard work and dedication, and whether it is through this letter or the national media, I will see that it gets done.

Frye would later say he would have rather "got that win at Washington than get that award."

"I don't ask for anyone's appreciation," Frye said in a *Los Angeles Times* interview. "I just try to go out there and be a winner. I don't care about any individual awards. It's good, and it's just probably a reflection of our system and our team, but I don't ever ask anyone to appreciate me or think that I'm the best at anything. I just want people to say Channing was a winner when he was here and he was a successful person."

three-point big-man shooters in the league. If you ask him, he's always been able to shoot. Olson, however, thought otherwise.

"I told Channing, we could have you shoot threes and have Jason Gardner rebound, or Jason Gardner shoot threes and you rebound," Olson said. "But he always had great touch. It's great to see him doing well now, when you think of him being out of basketball last year."

In 2012, he was diagnosed with a virus that causes an enlarged heart. He sat out the 2012–13 season but returned in 2013–14 with the Phoenix Suns. He agreed to a four-year, $32 million deal with the Orlando Magic in July 2014.

"I've been blessed with the opportunity to come out here to do what I love," Frye said while visiting a hospital for children in Phoenix. "Whenever you have health scares, you really appreciate the little things. For me, seeing these kids fight for their lives…this was the best way I could give back."

68 Brian Jeffries

Brian Jeffries has come a long way since his days as a sideline reporter for Arizona football games and the pregame host of Arizona men's basketball games. There's a reason why he's the Voice of the Arizona Wildcats. Anyone who has heard him on the radio or in person knows the voice. Deep, distinguished. If there were a color to it, indeed, it would be red and blue.

No one has seen more Arizona basketball games in person over the last 25 to 30 years than Jeffries. In 2012, he was inducted into the Arizona Broadcasters Hall of Fame.

Ex-Cats in Announcing

Former Arizona Wildcats seem to be everywhere in the media. Most of them are very good. But none is probably as good as a fictional talk show host Corey Williams created in the mid-1990s.

Williams, who today is a game analyst for ESPN and FOX, used to sit in the back of the team bus and pretend to be a guy he called Chucky White, who would "interview" the players.

"We talked about everything," Williams said. "Because it was a fake show, it was an indirect way for guys to show their grievances and talk about the program."

He recalls one time when forward Ray Owes asked to participate. "Ray Owes was super quiet and was never on the show," Williams said. "But one day, and I don't know what happened, he asked to be put on the show. And he just went off. 'You guys don't pass me the ball. I hit 55 percent from the floor and have a better shooting percentage than all of you.' It was funny. It was a team bonding thing.

"Everyone is off the hook because it's all fake. Coaches rolled their eyes, but honestly it was a way for a guy to blow off steam and to take shots at the staff without getting in trouble because it was all in good fun."

Yeah, until one day, when Bobbi Olson inadvertently ruined that fun. She walked onto the bus and, instead of sitting next to Lute, told her husband that she was going to sit with the guys at the back. "Right then and there the 'Chucky White Show' was canceled," Williams said. "There was no way we were going to continue. Oh, hell no. Mrs. O is coming back here, so we can't say anything. Everyone was on the best behavior. She came back and asked, 'What are we talking about tonight?'

"We had nothing," Williams said, laughing. "Show is suspended until further notice."

Williams borrowed on that experience to launch himself among an impressive group of ex-Cats in announcing.

Steve Kerr was an analyst for NBA games and the NCAA Tournament, including the Final Four. Miles Simon is active for ESPN in-studio and at college games. Sean Elliott is an analyst for the San Antonio Spurs and Fox. Matt Muehlebach branched out onto the Pac-12 Networks to complement his duties sitting next to Arizona radio play-by-play man Brian Jeffries.

Tom Tolbert is a talk show host of some renown for sports radio giant KNBR in San Francisco. Luke Walton and Jud Buechler have dabbled in front of the camera.

Still more: Former UA assistant and interim head coach Kevin O'Neill started working for the Pac-12 Networks late in the 2013–14 season. Kenny Lofton has been on TV as a commentator on the Los Angeles Dodgers. One more connection: Alex Flanagan, the wife of former Arizona fan favorite Kevin Flanagan, has been a longtime reporter for Fox, ESPN, and NBC.

"Some schools have a coaching tree," Kerr told Jeffries in 2014. "We have a broadcasting tree, I guess."

Let's just give Arizona basketball a new nickname: Broadcast U.

"I love my job because it really doesn't feel like a job," said Jeffries, 60. "There's a lot of work that goes into it but it's stuff you love to do. You love the preparation."

Of course, it helps to be able to comment on a winning team, and for more than 30 years the Wildcats have been winners. Not that it's made it easy for Jeffries, who became Arizona's play-by-play guy in 1985.

"It's gratifying to be part of it all," he said. "I've often told people that when you've lived through an era you never know when it'll end or know how long it will go. You wonder if it'll ever be repeated."

Lo and behold it has—and Jeffries has often had a front-row seat directly or near the head coach, whether it be Lute Olson or Sean Miller. "Right now, it looks like we will see [a championship] again [with Miller as the coach]," Jeffries said. "Being around it is pretty special."

It's exactly what he wanted growing up in the Seattle area. He listened many a night to radio announcers and noted how they were identified with the program they covered. "When I got the job my plan was to keep it," he said, smiling. "I don't have control of that."

There were times when he may have looked elsewhere. When he first was hired in the mid-1980s, contracts were for three years because radio rights were up for bid. "My job was three years at a time, at one point five years," he said. "I looked because I wondered, *What if the station lost the rights and the new guys didn't want to hire me?*"

In 2007, he celebrated his 20th year as the Voice of the Wildcats, and a year later signed with current rights holder IMG to become the director of broadcasting. "Now, as long as I do my job and I try to keep better at it, the chances of losing my job are a lot less than what they were," he said.

The contract with IMG runs through 2024, "so there's some security, so I stopped looking."

He's missed just six, maybe seven games, in his tenure, calling every other bounce pass and assist—likely more than 1,500 games. "The first couple of times I missed it was bizarre because I'm watching [on TV] and felt like I was a million miles away," he said.

But he's been there for the big moments: Arizona's national title in 1997, UA's Final Four in 1994, Arizona's title game in 2001, and UA's trip to the Final Four in 1988.

"I'll never forget that…first Final Four. Of course there's the championship game. That'll always be there. And the team's run behind interim coach Russ Pennell [in 2009] because that was so unexpected."

With Lute Olson, deep runs were always expected. Jeffries and Olson shared a bond because of all the pregame, postgame, and weekly interviews. "He was great, always gracious," he said. "Always made time for me. We had a great rapport. He was always very thorough and never tried to cut it short. The weekly show we did was fun. Even though it's not the favorite thing for coaches to do, I think he enjoyed talking to the fans one-on-one like that."

His five years with Miller have been "very much the same" in that he and Olson are both "good communicators and thoughtful in what they say."

"Sean is never in a hurry," Jeffries said. "He's always there to talk and willing to answer."

And yes, he's a fan—but he still tries to keep a distance. It's the broadcast journalist in him. "You got to separate yourself [from it]," he said. "If you don't, then you lose your objectivity. I've always wanted to represent the team. You have to give them space. Even though I'm one of them, it's healthy not to become too close."

He'll be that way until he no longer does it. "Until they tell me I'm not good at it. That's when I'll be done," he said.

69 Wildcats in the NBA

Former Arizona assistant coach Josh Pastner once relayed something he had heard about the large number of Wildcats in the pros. "You can't swing a bat in the NBA without hitting a Cat," he said. And that's a statement you can take to the bank.

Really, you *can* take that to the bank, because that's what nearly three dozen of Lute Olson's recruits have done—and some continue to do—to the tune of more than $1 billion in NBA salaries. Yep, a cool—*very cool*—$1 billion. With a *B*...

Olson's recruits—those who signed at Arizona under Olson, played for him, and finished their college careers in Tucson—reached that NBA salary milestone during the 2013–14 season, hitting $1,005,824,715—give or take a few thousand, depending on the database you're researching.

That grand total doesn't include endorsements, appearance fees, playoff bonuses...anything like that. And it doesn't include the more than $60 million made in MLB by basketball-player-turned-All-Star-outfielder Kenny Lofton. It also doesn't consider the substantial multitudes of millions made by Lute's recruits while playing basketball overseas.

Andre Iguodala

It happened after one of Andre Iguodala's multitude of fantastic games at McKale Center. UA senior Luke Walton turned to the media and said, "He is going to be one of the best players to ever come out of Arizona by the time he is done here...if he stays."

Iguodala *was* that good, and he continues to be that good with his array of talents. He had the vision of a point guard, the shot of a shooting guard (though it could have been better), and the rebounding ability of a power forward. Iguodala was the first player in school history to lead the team in rebounds, assists, and steals in the same season.

Iguodala can thank Walton, then a senior on the 2002–03 team when UA was ranked No. 1. "We went at each other so hard [in a scrimmage]," Walton told Deadspin.com. "He finished with 30, I finished with 20-something, and I said, 'This kid is going to be really, really good.'"

At one point, Iguodala told Arizona coach Lute Olson he wanted to be like Walton, a see-the-court type with a great basketball IQ.

"Luke was great for me," Iguodala told Deadspin.com. "I had great numbers in high school; I scored a lot of points. But Luke showed me how to play basketball stress-free, like how to pass, how to position yourself, how to sacrifice yourself for a teammate."

Iguodala's talent was rarely questioned, although he was considered more of a track star than a basketball player in high school.

How about this? "I'll tell you this: he's better than I thought he was," said Jerry West, a Golden State executive and silhouette for the NBA's logo. He then turned to Iguodala and said, "You would have loved playing with me. And I would have loved playing with you."

What better compliment from an NBA icon is there than that?

Iguodala, a 6'8" forward, was flattered. And he's one of the many NBA players who have found prolonged success in the NBA after life at Arizona—albeit a short life for him.

Iguodala left after two years. It was all but a foregone conclusion after his sophomore year, during which he was caught on the big screen on his cell phone as UA prepared to run out on the court at the Pac-10 Tournament. Two weeks later he was ducking into the women's locker room to avoid a reporter's question about possibly going to the NBA.

He was that different. And so proud to be the first player to make Lute Olson curse.

"Bitch, bitch, bitch," Iguodala remembers Lute saying. "All you do is bitch." They laugh about it now. But when Iguodala announced he was going he thanked the man who brought him to Arizona. "I want to thank Coach Olson, the coaching staff, my teammates, and the fans of Tucson for their support," he said. "I feel the time is right for me to fulfill a lifelong dream of playing in the NBA."

He just finished his 10th season in the pros and is still going strong at the age of 30. Life is good for Iggy, the player Los Angeles Lakers star Kobe Bryant said is "Pippenesque" when it comes to length and covering ground. Iguodala has long been known for his defense.

"I've been a fan of his since he came out of Arizona," Bryant told the *Los Angeles Times*. "I've always tried to look out for him as much as I could, talk to him about the game and things like that. I'm just happy for him to be in a situation where he feels comfortable."

It was like his decision to come to Arizona. It came after he chose Arkansas and the chance to play for then-Razorbacks coach Nolan Richardson. But after Richardson was bought out of his contract, Iguodala decided to leave. Georgia Tech, Kansas, and Maryland were the other (so-called) choices.

"Arizona was in my top three before, but I knew that's where I wanted to go after Nolan left," Iguodala said. "I just said I was considering other schools because I didn't want to close everyone out."

The friendship he started with Hassan Adams may have been the difference. The connection formed when they played together at the annual Jordan Classic. Adams committed first; Iguodala, well, later. "I was surprised because we had already talked about both coming here," Adams told the *Tucson Citizen* about their respective decisions. "He just didn't know what he was going to do. I just gave him my number and we kept in touch. I told him this should have been his first choice."

Iguodala was inducted to Arizona's Ring of Honor in 2012—he was the 20th member included—after he was a member of the gold-medal-winning Team USA at the 2012 London Olympic Games. Other Arizona Ring of Honor members include: Sean Elliott, Jason Gardner, Luke Walton, and his current coach Steve Kerr, who was named the Golden State Warriors coach in May.

"That's some good company," Iguodala told Nuggets.com. (Iguodala was with Denver at the time of the announcement.) "I'm truly honored and blessed to be acknowledged as part of the Ring of Honor."

Six of Olson's players have, or will, reach nine figures in NBA salaries, including Gilbert Arenas, whose total salary includes the $62 million he was paid by the Orlando Magic to basically go away for the final three years of his contract. The team used the league's amnesty clause to waive Arenas, thereby removing his contract from its salary cap, although it was still on the hook for all that dough.

Eight of Lute's recruits were still drawing NBA paychecks in 2013–14, including a cup of coffee for Mustafa Shakur. The seven others—Chase Budinger, Channing Frye, Andre Iguodala, Jason Terry, Jerryd Bayless, Jordan Hill, and Richard Jefferson—still have ample earning power.

Beyond the piles of gold, there has been a golden reputation for the vast majority of players coming out of Arizona, a trend that likely will continue as Sean Miller quickly loads more players onto the NBA conveyer belt.

In 2006, *Sports Illustrated* surveyed NBA coaches and scouts about college programs, and this is what Olson said at the time: "They said Arizona was the most NBA-friendly," Olson said. "I thought that was a great compliment to the guys who have come out of here—that they know how to play, they are fundamentally sound, and they are good team members, whether they are on the court or on the bench."

That was true even for those who didn't even stay all four years. Take Iguodala, who left UA after two seasons and was the ninth overall pick of the 2004 draft, selected by Philadelphia. "After Andre practiced a while with Philadelphia, he called and said, 'I can't thank you enough for what I learned at Arizona. There has been nothing here that I didn't know coming in,'" Olson said.

Based on figures from basketball-reference.com, the *USA Today* salary database, and various news stories (there are sometimes small

Gilbert Arenas is one of the best known—and highest paid—Arizona products in the NBA.

differences in the figures), here is what Lute's recruits earned in the NBA through the 2013–14 season:

Player	NBA salary	Player	NBA salary
Gilbert Arenas	$181,904,131	Chase Budinger	$7,977,968
Mike Bibby	$107,576,621	Loren Woods	$3,468,931
Richard Jefferson	$106,607,034	Tom Tolbert	$2,919,500
Damon Stoudamire	$100,535,041	Anthony Cook	$2,295,000
Jason Terry	$96,372,744	Salim Stoudamire	$2,187,000
Andre Iguodala	$86,192,891	Ben Davis	$715,847
Michael Dickerson	$50,425,662	Hassan Adams	$709,881
Sean Elliott	$40,626,666	Miles Simon	$672,500
Chris Mills	$37,370,000	Reggie Geary	$492,250
Channing Frye	$35,338,889	Ed Stokes	$272,500
Luke Walton	$33,903,340	Ray Owes	$220,000
Bison Dele	$22,159,500	Mustafa Shakur	$145,120
Sean Rooks	$17,173,000	A.J. Bramlett	$118,974
Steve Kerr	$16,119,000	Pete Williams	$70,000
Jerryd Bayless	$15,606,520	Marcus Williams	$52,209
Jordan Hill	$15,204,687	Matt Othick	$13,000
Jud Buechler	$11,365,000		
Khalid Reeves	$9,013,309	**Total**	**$1,005,824,715**

70 Gene Edgerson

He had the hair, the knee pads, the long socks, and the scowl. And he had the grit and the growl when he was in uniform. Gene Edgerson knew how to work it...on and off the court.

"I got smart and took something and ran with it," said Edgerson. "It was who I was generally. But why not take something, use it, and market it to your advantage? But at the end of the day, I played my ass off. The high socks, knee pads, and all that was entertainment. The core of me was about giving it all I had."

And he did (more on that later).

But what you probably didn't know was that Edgerson is part of Arizona trivia: What player in Wildcats history played in two Final Fours?

Yes, it's Edgerson, the 6'6", 230-pound power forward from New Orleans St. Augustine High. He was 132–35 in his five years at UA. "I never would have thought that, but I was fortunate to win a championship," Edgerson said. "But for me to be in a position was great. I had many dreams as a kid and I recall watching 'One Shining Moment' all the times I watched the championship games. I envisioned being part of winning a championship, but being able to participate in two is a dream that I never dreamt."

Yet he did just that. As a freshman he played 15 minutes and was pivotal in the overtime win against Kentucky. He hit two free throws (going into the game hitting 39 percent from the line) and pulled down five rebounds.

His personal highlight in Arizona's run to the title—and probably the reason why he was so good down the stretch—came when he dunked on Raef LaFrentz in the Sweet 16 game, when UA upset No. 1 Kansas, 85–82. "That right there just boosted me for the rest of the tournament," Edgerson said in Arizona's national championship book. "That was the kind of thing I was doing when I first started working out with the guys in the beginning of the year in the gym. That just showed me that I was capable of being a dominant force on the offensive end."

Dominant he was, throughout his career. And not so much statistically, but with his personality and candor. He told it like he saw it. And did what he needed to do to get his education, something he promised Lute Olson and his mom, Susan, he'd do when he signed with UA.

"I took advantage of [the scholarship] and took care of business when I had to," he said. "I know a lot of guys who I played with who didn't at the moment. At some point they realized they needed

The Big Hit

Gene Edgerson "never intended to hurt" Brigham Young player Bret Jepsen on that November 28 night in 1998. It just turned out that way... unfortunately.

"It was my intent to send a message, but never my intent to hit the kid in the head," Edgerson said 16 years later. "The hit I meant to give him was in the chest. Yes, I was going to hit him back because he went after me, and as a player you have to protect yourself. If the referees aren't going to do it, you have to."

Edgerson said he had communicated with the referees, as did Olson, about the rough play going on near the basket. "But they were so arrogant they didn't want to listen," said Edgerson, who admitted to being frustrated because the referees had turned a deaf ear to him.

Arizona went on to win the game 78–74 in overtime, but it was overshadowed by the hit by Edgerson and the injury to Jepsen, who suffered a Grade 2 concussion and was knocked out about 30 seconds in the second half.

Replays showed that the problems had begun earlier. Two plays before Edgerson struck Jepsen, they were tied up over a possible rebound. The next time down the floor, in an attempt to block out Edgerson, Jepsen put his elbow and forearm near Edgerson's neck. A play later, Edgerson threw the elbow that floored Jepson.

"No one sent me out to do such a thoughtless thing," Edgerson said at the time. "I take full responsibility for my actions, and I am not making any excuses. Those who know me know that I am a nice person, good student, and a hard worker. I humiliated myself with such poor judgment, and I assure everyone that it will not happen again."

Upon review of the game, Edgerson was suspended the next game, against Wyoming. Soon after the incident, Edgerson sent an apology letter to Jepsen.

"Was I wrong? Well, yes, you're supposed to turn the other cheek. But at that point I think I had already turned the cheek a couple of times," he said. "I couldn't anymore."

A year later, Jepsen, then a senior, decided to call it a career after suffering from a viral infection and from relapses related to the concussion.

the education and went back. But it's so much easier to take care of business at the time than coming back and having to work a little bit harder later."

While in school, Edgerson was known as the "Kindergarten Cop" because he student-taught in local schools toward his degree. He also sat out as a redshirt in 1999–2000 to get the degree.

"Basketball wasn't the most important thing," said Edgerson, now an education consultant. "I wanted to play professional basketball after school and did in the D-League and with the Globetrotters, but, hey, if you can't be honest with yourself, who can you be honest with?"

He knew his skills were limited, at least when it came to the NBA, so he moved on. "I had to go another route," he said. "I gave it a shot and it didn't work out. I was OK. But I was glad I had my education. It's opened up other doors besides basketball."

He shares that message with kids today when he speaks to them. His motto: education comes first. As he has said, "basketball is all fine and dandy, but it won't be around for the rest of my life."

Or to put it another way, "It's like priests having a calling from God. Something told me it was to be my job to be a kindergarten teacher," he told the *Tucson Citizen*.

Fourteen years later after concluding his UA career, he's still one of the fan favorites when he visits for games. And, he appreciates everything UA has done for him. "It was the best thing to ever happen to me, coming from where I came from and living in poverty," Edgerson said. "Having the opportunity to do it and the experience was priceless. Being able to play basketball and taking advantage of a free education. I have friends who have to pay student loans. I didn't have to do that because I took care of business not only in the classroom but on the basketball court, too.

"I wanted to win. I hated losing. I didn't come from a losing program. It was embedded in my DNA to win. It was about taking advantage with a dive or rebound so our team could get a second opportunity to win. That's the way you play.

"I knew what I could do and what I couldn't do. A good basketball player always knows what he can do to take advantage. So I just made up for it by playing hard. Winner and a team player… that's all I wanted to be known as."

71 Gotta Watch Olson-Frieder

Arizona State coach Bill Frieder is sitting in the office of a plastic surgeon, asking if there is anything the doctor can do to help with that hound-dog face.

"I can try," the doctor replies with some skepticism.

That was the set-up for one of the classic commercials featuring Frieder and Arizona coach Lute Olson that ran in the state of Arizona in the 1990s. If you're of a certain age, you recall the ads with a smile. If you're a younger fan, or a hoops-head-come-lately to the UA basketball party, do yourself a favor and search "Lute Olson vs. Bill Frieder" on YouTube, where several of the TV spots are preserved.

In this particular commercial, after Frieder gets his loan approved for plastic surgery, he happily responds, "Doc, make me the best-looking coach in Arizona!"

Cut to after surgery when Frieder picks up a mirror, looks... and then lets out a scream as, indeed, he now looks exactly like the best-looking coach in Arizona: Lute Olson. Perhaps unsurprisingly, Olson said that commercial is his favorite. Frieder's favorite is the one in which he is revealed to be the maniacal pilot of a small airplane as Arizona is trying to get to the big game on time.

The stately Olson and the frumpy Frieder made perfect comic opposites. The commercials were played for laughs against the backdrop of a larger purpose, especially after an ugly incident in the rivalry in 1988, when ASU fans taunted Steve Kerr about the assassination of his father.

"The original idea was to bring the schools together, to show that you could compete and then you could be human beings and not have what had gone on the years before that, like the Steve Kerr situation at ASU [which was] absolutely intolerable and inexcusable," said Frieder, who was the Sun Devils' head coach from 1989 to 1997.

"And then after we did the commercials for a year or two, they became legendary, to the point where we made a lot of money doing them. Everybody in the state loved [Olson]. After three, four years of commercials, I think more people in the state knew me from the commercials than they did from [me] being the basketball coach at ASU."

Frieder was always willing to be Olson's foil on television, to be the self-deprecating one. "ASU fans were upset about the fact he would do it," Olson remembered.

There's the one in which a saleswoman fawns over Lute. After he leaves, Frieder comes up to her with a pile of Christmas presents. "This must be your lucky day," he says.

Still swooning, she looks at his bank card and replies, "It's not every day you get to meet a famous basketball coach, Mr.... uh, Fridder?"

"It takes you all day to shoot a 30-second commercial, which wasn't fun," Olson said. "But it was fun to see when the finished product came out."

It was totally worth it.

Visit the NCAA Vault

Brent Musburger's voice greets you as Arizona and Oklahoma tip off from the Final Four in 1988. On the first possession of the game, Sean Elliott scores two points.

This is, at least for now, as far back as you can go to see the Wildcats in college basketball's way-back machine, "the NCAA vault," which is available on YouTube. It's a treasure trove of selected, complete games from the NCAA Tournament.

That loss to the Sooners was a huge disappointment for the Cats, and it's the game Steve Kerr will never forget. The best shooter in the history of Arizona went 2-of-12 from three-point range that night, finishing with six points. "I still think about that game," Kerr said at the 2014 West Region. "There isn't a day I don't think about it. In fact, I'm thinking about it right now."

Sigh. Not all of these games have happy endings.

The NCAA has 16 of Arizona's tournament games archived online. Presented without commercials, the games run about 80 minutes in real time, so that's more than 21 hours of UA history just waiting for you to experience again—or discover for the first time. It can't get much better than that.

The good and bad—it's all there. It might be tough to stomach the first-round losses to East Tennessee State (1992) and Santa Clara (1993). In that latter game, that darn Steve Nash drives left past Damon Stoudamire for a difficult running layup off the glass for the second basket of the game. It was that kind of game.

But if reliving the losses isn't for you, click on Arizona's 1997 Final Four win over North Carolina and then the title game victory over Kentucky. In September 2013, former UA center Joseph Blair helped organize a charity event in downtown Tucson, where fans could come to watch a public showing of that 84–79 overtime win. The game was shown on a big screen at the Fox Theatre.

Lute Olson and several members of the title-winning team were in attendance for the event. As they were brought up to the stage to answer a few questions, in front of about 1,000 fans, every single ex-Cat mentioned they had never gone back to watch the title-winning game before that day. After all, they said, they were right there when it happened and can replay it in their heads.

"It's great watching this," Miles Simon told the crowd that night as the game was paused in overtime. "I'm still kind of anxious and nervous. I don't know if we win or not," he joked. "Seeing my teammates and seeing how hard they are fighting and how each member of the coaching staff was pulling for each other, that's the memory that will [last]."

The NCAA vault also holds three games from Arizona's 2001 run, including the championship game loss to Duke. And more pain: the 2003 Sweet 16 loss to Kansas and the 2005 meltdown against Illinois.

One of the better memories preserved is the 2003 double-overtime classic against Gonzaga (and it's worth it just to hear Dick Enberg say, "Oh my!"). The Wildcats held on to win 96–95 as the Bulldogs' Blake Stepp missed a leaning eight-foot bank shot at the buzzer.

"What made that game so special was that both teams played really well," said Gonzaga coach Mark Few. "It was an epic game."

It was indeed. And you can watch it whenever you want.

Here is a list of Arizona games available at the NCAA vault:

Year	Opponent	Year	Opponent
1988	Oklahoma	2001	Duke
1992	East Tennessee State	2002	Oklahoma
1993	Santa Clara	2003	Notre Dame
1994	Arkansas	2003	Gonzaga
1997	North Carolina	2003	Kansas
1997	Kentucky	2005	Oklahoma State
2001	Mississippi	2005	Illinois
2001	Illinois	2011	Duke

"I thought we really did improve the relations of the school[s]," Frieder said. "Didn't have any big situations those eight years that I coached. Took [his successor] Rob Evans all of 30 seconds to screw that all up, but me and Lute brought the parties together."

And Frieder knows people are still being entertained, thanks to YouTube. "They text me things like, 'I just watched your commercials' or 'They just showed your commercials at a get-together,'" Frieder said. "It's amazing."

72 Kevin O'Neill

Kevin O'Neill had an inkling that things would end badly when he was announced as Arizona's head coach in waiting on December 18, 2007. It turns out he was right about that.

"I think it's hard for those things to work out," he said.

At the time of the announcement, O'Neill had been the Wildcats' interim head coach for about six weeks after Lute Olson began an indefinite leave of absence. Would he be back? If so, when? There really was no crisis handbook for athletic director Jim Livengood to follow. In selecting O'Neill as coach-in-waiting, the hope was to patch together continuity in recruiting, but that plan—and the entire 2007–08 season—eventually unraveled.

"It's one of those things where it's hard for everybody in that situation," O'Neill said. "It's hard for the players. It's hard for the assistant coaches. It was a difficult situation for everybody. It was a difficult situation for Livengood. Really hard."

O'Neill, the onetime Arizona basketball recruiting savant from 1986 to 1989 (the assistant who famously once dressed in a gorilla suit to get a recruit), ended up being the villain of the story. Fair? People will have their own opinions on that. It was, to say the least, the ultimate square-peg, round-hole scenario.

"Those guys were all good guys, and they weren't hard to coach," O'Neill said. "What happened was, I'm a different guy than Lute—different style of play, different personality, different everything. Those guys signed to come and play for Lute. I had to do it the way that I knew best, and I think that was hard for some guys to deal with, but believe me, none of it was any of the players' fault."

The Wildcats had won four games in a row in late January when Nic Wise—the team's only true point guard—suffered a knee injury. He ended up missing seven full games. Earlier in the season, the team struggled when Jerryd Bayless missed four games with an injury. "When Nic got hurt, that really killed us because we didn't have much depth and Jerryd had to move over to the point," O'Neill said.

As the season with an uncertain future became more of a burden, the players grew increasingly disenchanted with O'Neill's style (more abrasive personally and more deliberate on the court). Arizona lost nine of its final 13 games, including a first-round NCAA Tournament loss to West Virginia.

"I think instead of winning 19 games, we could have won 24 or 25 if those guys hadn't had injuries. We were too thin to withstand injuries to our guard corps, and that made it difficult," O'Neill said.

Arizona went 19–15 overall and fell to seventh in the Pac-10 with an 8–10 mark. In addition to everything else going on, O'Neill had the misfortune of being an interim head coach during what might have been the best-ever season in the Pac-10. "The Pac-10 was a *monster*," he said.

Consider the talent. The league produced six players who were among the top 15 selections in the NBA Draft after the season: USC's O.J. Mayo (3), UCLA's Russell Westbrook (4), UCLA's Kevin Love (5), Stanford's Brook Lopez (10), Bayless (11), and Stanford's Robin Lopez (15).

Olson's original plan to bring back O'Neill as an assistant—which was heartily endorsed by guys like Steve Kerr and Tom Tolbert who were familiar with O'Neill from his first stint—was fueled by the desire to introduce more toughness and discipline on the coaching staff. He was to be "the hammer." But when Olson took his leave, the players were left with far too much hammer, and they didn't like being the nails. (When Bayless was asked years later about O'Neill by national college basketball writer Jeff Goodman, Bayless merely responded, "No comment.")

Josh Pastner

When Josh Pastner got his turn at holding up Arizona's NCAA championship trophy that April night in 1997, he felt an overwhelming feeling of accomplishment, and a sense that every day at Arizona—come April—it would be like that.

Joy and jubilation as a champion. Of course, the reality of it was, it wasn't likely. He came to know that reality as a player a year later, when Arizona fell short in the Elite Eight in Anaheim, in 2001 as an assistant coach, and now as head coach at Memphis.

Life isn't always about hoisting NCAA titles. But on March 31, 1997, it was for Arizona, and Pastner was a walk-on and an integral part of the Cats' title run. "I loved every second of it," said Pastner, looking back. "I was blessed to be around some great coaches—Coach Olson, Coach Jim Rosborough—and some great players. They are now some of my best friends. And, of course, I was around one of the great fan bases in the entire country."

If there was one player who got the most bang for his buck it was Pastner, a lightly recruited player (if he was at all) and child prodigy who wanted to be a coach from the age of 10. By 13 he was publishing "Josh Pastner Scouting Report," referring to Houston's high school talent. At 16 he was leading an AAU team that later won the national title and had the likes of future NBA-ers Emeka Okafor, T.J. Ford, and Daniel Gibson. Three years later he was applying to be the Los Angeles Clippers head coach.

Pastner was a media darling, and if you didn't see him on camera during a game it meant you either weren't watching closely or that he didn't know where the camera was positioned. He was front and center in nearly every shot—to his credit. He was also listening to everything.

"I tried to soak in every word of Coach Olson's and Coach Rosborough's to learn the game," he said. "I knew I wanted to coach, and when you're around someone like Coach Olson you learn. I wanted to take advantage of all that, especially the master craftsman of Coach Olson."

When he joined Arizona in 1996 he was dubbed "the next Steve Kerr" for his basketball acumen. "I worked hard. I didn't even go to my prom because I was thinking basketball," he said. "I wanted to outwork people. I wanted to play. But once I got to UA and realized and [understood] that mom and dad didn't give me great athleticism, I was out. I had a sense of hope I'd be like a guy like Steve Kerr, but once I got there the reality set in."

Years removed from his retirement—and their time together—Olson often refers to Pastner as his "son." Not many players or former coaches have been given that distinction.

One time during Jim Rome's radio show, Josh called in when former UCLA player Toby Baily was a guest. Pastner spoke for a bit and then, Rome said, "Hey, I know you! You're Lute's little helper."

Pastner went 42–0 as a player, getting in only when Arizona had big leads. He made nine total baskets in his career. But he was another one of Arizona's favorite sons.

"I love Coach Olson because without him I am not where I am today," he said. "He gave me an unbelievable opportunity, and a lot of my principles and the things I do have come from him. There are no words I can say that would put the true meaning of how I feel for Coach Olson."

But in the spring of 2009, Pastner, then 31, said good-bye to Arizona and the Wildcats, taking an assistant coaching job with John Calipari at Memphis.

He may be a Tiger now, but he'll forever be a Wildcat. "I love Tucson," Pastner said. "It's one of the greatest places in the world to live. I didn't want to leave, but I also knew it was the right time to leave. I needed it for my personal development and to get out of my comfort zone. It wasn't easy."

He had other opportunities to leave to become an assistant coach elsewhere, but "I couldn't pull the trigger because I wasn't ready. And the timing wasn't right. And I loved where I was at."

You could tell. On his senior night—a game in which he played near the end in a win against California—he cried when it was all over.

"I didn't want it to be over," he said. "I wanted it to last forever. It was hard for me and that's why it got emotional. When I was at Arizona I was there morning, noon, and night working with the guys. It was hard."

His former teammates swear by him. Mike Bibby said Pastner was always there rebounding for him; Michael Dickerson credited Pastner for helping the team win the 1997 title because he was so insistent on getting the team up and ready to go get extra shots in.

This is how crazed Pastner was. On the team's first meeting in 1996—remember, he was a walk-on—he brought the team together and told them "We're going to be in the gym every night and we will win the national championship."

"If I had a freshman do that now that I'm a head coach I'd say, 'What are you doing?' How dumb was I to do that?" he mused. "But thank goodness that the team accepted me. And it worked."

It worked so well, in fact, many former players called on his behalf for Pastner, then an assistant at Memphis, to become UA's head coach when Russ Pennell and Mike Dunlap were done in 2009. Eventually, Sean Miller was hired.

"I loved every one of them," he said. "It was a natural [thing for them to back him]. But the only way they were going to hire me was like how they hired me at Memphis—that I was the last man standing," he laughed. "I recognized that no one was going to take the job. They had to give it to somebody. I do love my teammates for having my back. I loved my time there. And I love them when we're not playing them."

Although O'Neill had a year left on his contract at $375,000, Olson basically fired O'Neill in his televised comeback press conference on April 1, 2008.

O'Neill certainly is one of the most polarizing figures in Arizona basketball history. Fans might be surprised to learn he had a strong contingent of supporters within the athletic department during his second stint. But at the same time, his tell-it-like-he-thinks-it-is style didn't play well with others, and it's hard to point to anything he did to ease the unusual and difficult situation.

"When I left, I said nothing negative, and I wouldn't say anything negative now," O'Neill said. "But in any situation that was as difficult as that, somebody is going to be made out to be the villain."

73 Jim Livengood

When then–Arizona athletic director Jim Livengood was looking to hire a basketball coach after Lute Olson's retirement, he first tested the waters with Michigan State's Tom Izzo.

"I knew that would be a hard move in terms of getting him out of East Lansing," Livengood said. So it was.

Livengood moved on: Memphis coach John Calipari became, arguably, the top target. Livengood flew during the 2008–09 season to Palm Springs, California, where Calipari was giving a talk to a business group.

"It was maybe January, early February," Livengood said. "I met with him for quite a long time." There was some promising discussion... and then Kentucky fired Billy Gillispie in late March. "The minute that Kentucky job opened up, John made that decision," Livengood said.

It's the nature of a coaching search—especially one that lasted all season, given the timing of Olson's retirement—that all manner of famous names would be mentioned as possibilities for a job as plum as Arizona's, but yet nothing could get super serious until after the coaches in question had completed their seasons.

The job could have gone to USC's Tim Floyd. He declined.

Xavier's Sean Miller became an on-the-radar candidate about two weeks before the 2009 Final Four, Livengood said. They gauged each other's interest on the phone before each flew to Albuquerque during Final Four weekend, driving north to Santa Fe to meet with university president Richard Shelton, who was there for the weekend.

Livengood chuckles at the Southwestern culture shock for Miller, a Pittsburgh native who had spent all of his 40 years on the East Coast and in the Midwest. "To say that there was a little bit of awe would be a total understatement," Livengood said. "He didn't know places like this existed."

On Sunday, April 5, after returning home to Cincinnati on UA booster Paul Weitman's plane, Miller called to tell Livengood he would stay at Xavier but wanted to sleep on the decision. Miller changed his mind in the morning, dialing up Livengood in the wee hours of the morning in Tucson.

"Elation would not even come close to describing my feelings when he said, 'Jim, I'm coming,'" Livengood said. "And it wasn't so much that it was just a relief, it was that this is the right guy. Everybody I talked to was just emphatic that this was a star. He certainly was a great coach. The basketball part was really secondary; he was really a good person. He was going to do it the right way, treat kids right."

Calipari, who had recruited Miller to Pitt as a player and coached with him as an assistant with the Panthers, was "huge" in helping Miller make an informed decision about Arizona, Livengood said. Another key figure was Jason Levien, a former

NBA agent who was serving in the front office of the Sacramento Kings at the time. Levien was close to Jack Murphy, Livengood's son-in-law, who had spent eight years in various roles with the Arizona basketball program.

"Jason was a huge help to Sean in terms of working through a contract and what would happen," Livengood said. "At that point in time, we had a really good board of regents, but several of our regents wanted to be really careful and not spend a lot of money."

Through some fits and starts and unexpected twists, Livengood had landed his man at an original deal of $2 million per year, certainly one of the athletic director's enduring legacies from his 16 years on the job at Arizona. About eight months after hiring Miller, Livengood announced his decision to depart UA and take over as athletic director at UNLV.

Although Livengood wasn't there in person to see it, was Miller's successful first five seasons—two league titles, two Elite Eights, and a Sweet 16—what he expected?

"The easy answer is yes," Livengood said. "But you never know. Nothing has surprised me because I think he is so well grounded, and he's such a phenomenal recruiter.... It's not a question of if Sean is going to go to a Final Four and win a Final Four. That's a question of when."

It all worked out well for Livengood, Miller, and Arizona. But where would Livengood have turned next if Miller had stayed at Xavier? That answer will have to wait. Livengood said his would-have-been next target is still coaching "at a very high level" for the 2014–15 season and doesn't want to reveal the name until he's no longer at that program.

"We've talked a number of times since Sean's hire," Livengood said of the mystery man. "He wasn't a fallback at all. He probably would have been hard to get, but I think we would have been able to do that."

74 Kevin Parrom, Never Quit

One of the greatest moments of Sean Miller's first five seasons at Arizona didn't involve a dunk, a game-saving block, a half-court heave, a league championship, or an NCAA Tournament victory.

It was simply a hug. *The Hug.*

Kevin Parrom, a versatile 6'6" wing, never earned All-Conference accolades. He didn't average double-digit points in any season. He wasn't drafted. He didn't go on to NBA glory.

Yet he became one of the lovable characters in Miller's relaunch of the Arizona basketball program—and not just for his toughness and hustle and the way he could grab a defensive rebound and glide down court as a one-man fast break. It was that Parrom overcame injury, loss, and senseless violence with so much grace. Which is the lead-up to the Hug.

It was November 13, 2011, and Arizona was playing an otherwise forgettable home game against Ball State. Parrom hadn't played in the Red-Blue Game, either of the team's two exhibitions, or any of the first two games of the regular season. The word was he might have to redshirt while recovering from gunshot wounds to his right leg and left hand, which he had suffered when he was home in late September to visit his ill mother in the Bronx.

And then, with 15:24 to go in the first half of the BSU game, there he was, after the first media timeout, on the court. The crowd, slowly realizing he had checked in to the game, rose to a standing ovation.

Parrom, with his right foot braced and taped—and with a .22-caliber bullet embedded near his right hamstring—played 18 minutes, with six points, four rebounds, and two assists. When Miller took out Parrom from the game with 32.7 seconds left, the atmosphere at McKale got a bit misty. They embraced tightly on the court, Miller's right hand cradling the top of Parrom's head, a moment of heartfelt recognition for the player's difficult journey.

"He's just such a warrior, such a great kid, a kid who's been through more than any person ever deserves to be through," Miller said after the game. "We're so much a better team with Kevin, but that's not even the story....

"You go through what Kevin went through, nobody has any idea how much time we spent together, talking, meeting, me trying to be hard on him knowing it's almost unfair for me to be hard on him, but that is what is required for him to continue to forge ahead.

"I'm just grateful that he is on our team. It's just really awesome to see him out there."

Parrom's mother, Lisa Williams, died of breast cancer in October 2011. And Parrom's grandmother had lost her battle with breast cancer a few months earlier in July.

In between those two losses, he was shot. While staying in his father's apartment in the Bronx, he invited over a female friend. Before 1:00 AM on September 24, Jason Gonzalez, the girl's ex-boyfriend, forced his way into the apartment and struggled with Parrom before reaching for his gun.

"I'm looking at the guy and he has no soul," Parrom told the *New York Daily News*, "no reason for living."

Gonzalez fired four times and fled. He was eventually arrested, pleading guilty in February 2013 to a charge of attempted murder.

Parrom survived, but there was a question of whether he would ever play basketball again. With a little luck, a lot of medical know-how, and a strong will... he came back far ahead of any schedule. And then, just as he was really beginning to look like his old self on the court, he suffered a broken bone in his right foot on January 28 and missed the rest of the season. (He had previously missed part of his freshman season with a stress fracture in his foot.)

In April 2012, he was selected as one of the winners of the 2012 Wilma Rudolph Award from the National Association of Academic Advisors for Athletics. The award honors student athletes who have overcome great personal, academic, and/or emotional odds to achieve academic success.

As a senior, a year later, he averaged career-highs with 8.3 points and 4.9 rebounds per game. More important, he graduated in May 2013, as he promised his mother he would do.

Parrom, who originally committed to Xavier before Miller and his staff (including New York City recruiter Book Richardson) left for Arizona, provided the toughness that fueled the collective mindset the coaches eventually installed in Tucson. The Wildcats would be "soft" no more, as Parrom illustrated in a game at Arizona State as a freshman.

Parrom prevented Ty Abbott from a fast-break layup with a hard foul from behind, immediately getting right in Abbott's face. Parrom, always active on social media, went on Twitter after the game and delivered the line that became a mantra for all Miller teams: "No Easy Buckets."

He went on to play professionally, mostly in the NBA's D-League, after finishing his UA career in 2013. The fan favorite became known as T-Loc (Tucson local) for the way he embraced his new home.

"It was one of the reasons I came here, because of the family setting in Tucson. I love it," Parrom said after his comeback game in 2011. "It was good to feel the crowd stand up for me. I really needed that."

And then he talked about that one special moment: "That hug was just great."

75 Joseph Blair

If Joseph Blair's contributions in Tucson had ended in January 1996 with his academic ineligibility midway through his senior year, he would be remembered as a very good big man for the Wildcats. As it is, he's praised simply for being a good man.

Blair, after a successful 13-year career playing basketball overseas, returned to Tucson and founded the Blair Charity Group, whose mission, according to its website, is to "develop the youth and young adults of Southern Arizona through accessible programs, sports camps, clinics and leagues that build leadership, life skills and community engagement."

With his natural charisma and ability to be oh-so-comfortable with a microphone in his hand, Blair became a visible man-about-town, hosting events and lending his time and name to a variety of community functions—basically, just giving back. Ask anyone: Blair matured into a guy who "gets it."

"I really liked Joseph when he was here," said former UA assistant Jim Rosborough. "We spent an awful lot of time together because I was always checking him into classes every day. The interesting thing to me was that he struggled academically. That was not because he wasn't smart. It was just because there were other things more important to him, and basketball was one. But this dude goes overseas and probably within a month of being in Italy, he's fluent in Italian. He's very smart, intelligent, giving. Everything you would want. I really am proud of Joseph and what he's done."

And that last part includes his return to Arizona basketball. At the age of 39 in the fall of 2013, Blair decided to launch a coaching career, which meant heading back into the classroom to finish that bachelor's degree he abandoned 17 years earlier. Meanwhile, Blair joined Sean Miller's staff as an unpaid undergraduate assistant coach. The key thing with that: The still very-much-in-shape Blair could instruct and practice with the Wildcats big men, notably sophomore seven-footer Kaleb Tarczewski.

"First of all, he's a great guy," Tarczewski said of Blair during the 2014 postseason. "I look at him as a personal friend more than just a coach. Basketball-wise, he's helped me tremendously this year. It's been nice having a guy who has been through it before, who has played professionally at my position and who has the knowledge to bounce ideas off of him. He's a big guy, so it's tough sometimes, but it makes me better. He's a great basketball player still, even though he's getting older."

That last remark was a playful jab, which is indicative of the kind of good relationship Blair established with the Wildcats in his first season. And Blair was having so much fun, and showing so much promise as a coaching prospect, that he decided to try a second season.

Having earned his degree in May—graduating in the same class as Jason Terry, another back-to-school Wildcat—Blair returned to the team for the 2014–15 season as a graduate assistant. "He was a great addition to this past year, especially with our frontcourt players," Miller said. "I think J.B. will continue to be an asset for us.... I've talked to him at great length that I think he'd be a terrific coach, whether that be in college or the NBA, because he has such an incredible way with players. They love him."

Blair, who came to Arizona from Houston, Texas, averaged 10.4 points and 6.5 rebounds during his UA career, playing in 104 games and starting 66. At 6'10" and 265 pounds, he had soft hands. He was tough in the low post, shooting 61.3 percent from the field. He was the 35th overall pick in the 1996 NBA Draft.

"Joseph was a hell of a player when he was with us," Rosborough said. "People hated to play against him and [power forward] Ben

Davis. Joseph was a stud. His hands were as good as I've seen on a big guy."

Although Blair never earned a spot on the All–Pac-10 team (he was honorable mention as a junior), he was well on his way as a senior. Blair was averaging team highs in points (14.7) and rebounds (8.9) when he was declared academically ineligible for the spring semester—not by the NCAA, but by the standards set by the Arizona board of regents. At the time, Blair was also helping raise his toddler son, Juordyan.

By the time Juordyan was ready to begin college, Blair figured it was his time to finish. "I have three kids," he said in 2013, "and if I'm going to push education, the best way is to lead by example."

76 Russell Brown: Assists 'R' Him

Russell Brown played at Arizona before it became Point Guard U under Lute Olson. However, he should never be left out of the discussion.

Consider this: no other point guard in Arizona history (including Steve Kerr, Damon Stoudamire, Mike Bibby, Jason Terry, and plenty of others) can match the play-making numbers of Brown, whose name is prominently listed in the assists section of Arizona's record book.

- Most assists in a game: 19, vs. Grand Canyon, December 8, 1979 (The mark also stands as a Pac-12 record.)
- Most assists in a season: 247, 1978–79 (27 games)
- Most assists in a career: 810, 1977–81 (107 games)

On five different occasions, an Arizona point guard has registered at least 15 assists in a game—and Brown authored each of those efforts. His 810 career assists is unassailable. The next-highest mark is 670 by Mustafa Shakur from 2003–07. He is also the only player who led the Wildcats in assists all four years of his career.

By the numbers, he's the ultimate point guard for Point Guard U.

"He was the best passer ever," backcourt mate Joe Nehls was quoted as saying in the *Arizona Wildcats Handbook*. "When people list the best point guards [at Arizona], they forget to mention Russell Brown, which is unbelievable. Kerr can shoot the ball and Stoudamire had the range and the quickness, but Russell Brown was like a little of them both."

Amazingly, Brown never was selected an All–Pac-10 player despite his monstrous assist totals. He was overlooked because he wasn't much of a scorer, finishing with a career average of 6.6 points per game. He did not have to score, however—not with a shooter like Nehls and a dominant inside player such as Larry Demic on the roster.

Yet Brown could score when called upon. When Arizona upset UCLA in 1979 at McKale Center—a game Fred Snowden called the best win of his career—Brown had 19 points. He had a double-double of 17 points and 15 assists against Cal that same season, as a sophomore.

Brown was also one of Arizona's top California recruits when the Wildcats ventured into the Pac-10 from the WAC in 1978–79. A product of Inglewood, California, Brown was tempted to sign with UCLA but came to Arizona because of an indirect relationship with Snowden via a Detroit past.

"I wanted to go to UCLA, was recruited by UCLA, but I was their second choice behind Arte Green of New York," Brown is quoted as saying in the book *Tucson: A Basketball Town*. "I had an uncle who went to Wayne State University in Detroit with Coach

Snowden, and that relationship helped with my choice to attend Arizona."

Brown's relationship with Snowden continued after both left Arizona. Brown became a district manager at Baskin-Robbins, serving under Snowden, who was an executive in that company before becoming the executive director of the Food 4 Less Foundation before his death in 1994.

Brown, 54, lives in the Los Angeles area today. He continues to play basketball, in an over-40 league in his community.

77 Lincoln Richmond

The extenuating circumstances that enabled Lincoln "Linc" Richmond to become Arizona's only six-year letterman in basketball hopefully will never happen again.

Because Richmond's career with Arizona occurred in part during World War II, the Border Conference ruled that wartime competition would not count against eligibility. Similarly, the conference also allowed freshmen to compete with the varsity at that time.

And it's through those exceptions that Richmond was officially part of the Arizona program from the 1942–43 season until the 1948–49 season.

The 1942–43 and 1943–44 seasons were limited in terms of opponents because of the war. The latter consisted of only 14 games and was strictly played against air force bases and military establishments such as Davis-Monthan and the Marana Air Base.

Arizona played its home games at Tucson High School's gymnasium during the war because the U.S. Navy utilized Bear Down Gym to house its personnel and equipment during the war.

Richmond missed the 1943–44 and 1944–45 seasons while serving in the army. Upon his return, Richmond also lettered in football in 1946 and baseball in 1946 and 1949. He batted .400 in 1946 and led the Wildcats with a .341 average as a senior in 1949.

His claim to fame, however, was in basketball, in which he became the first Arizona player to score more than 1,000 points in his career; he finished with 1,186.

In his first season back after military service, he led the Wildcats with 21 points in a 77–53 loss to Kentucky at Madison Square Garden in New York City on March 16, 1946.

Richmond, a lanky forward from Tucson High School, was an All–Border Conference selection in 1946 and 1947. He led the conference in scoring (17.9 points a game) in 1946–47, ranking 25th nationally. That stood as the highest mark at Arizona for 13 years, until Ernie McCray averaged 23.9 a game in 1959–60.

Richmond would have scored more points in his hoops career if he had not been hampered by a knee injury (a result of playing football) in his last couple of seasons with the Wildcats. Richmond tore cartilage and ligaments in his knee after turning too quickly on a pass route during practice in 1947. The injury required surgery to repair.

Early in his last basketball season of 1948–49, he tore the ligaments again and his knee was put in a cast. Doctors told him his career was over. Yet that did not stop him from trying to play in his last season.

The *Tucson Daily Citizen* reported that year that Arizona scheduled nonconference games with North Carolina, West Virginia, Louisville, and San Francisco with the thought that Richmond would be the senior leader on the floor. Unfortunately, he missed those games because of the knee injury, and Arizona lost them all.

With Richmond playing sparingly while hobbled down the stretch, Arizona still managed to win the Border Conference title. It was Richmond's fifth Border Conference title as a letter-winner at Arizona, a feat that will likely never be matched again.

"He is greatly handicapped with his knee and nowhere near his true self, but he is still much better than most ballplayers" Arizona coach Fred Enke Sr. told the *Citizen* at the time. "Richmond was dangerous under all conditions. His terrific change of pace made him difficult to guard. He could hit from the outside. If they came after him, he could drive past them and score."

Mo Udall and Richmond became the first Arizona players to join an NBA franchise in 1948. Richmond did not land a spot, however, on the Fort Wayne Pistons' roster that season because of his knee.

"He was such a good, tough player," said Fred W. Enke in *Tales of the Arizona Hardwood*. "You'd tell him to do something and he'd do it."

Enke called him one of the best players he'd ever played with. The two were the closest of friends.

After earning his bachelor's and master's degrees in science, Richmond went on to become the head baseball and basketball coach at West Phoenix High School when that school opened in 1949. On the playing side, Richmond later played semipro baseball for the Casa Grande Apcos and basketball for the Eloy Apcos.

78 Players UA Loves to Hate

To quote Indiana Jones, "Snakes. Why did it have to be snakes?"

If not for Reggie Miller's ophidiophobia—that's a fear of snakes—who knows how a legendary career and a couple of storied programs would have been altered?

Miller was among Lute Olson's first recruiting targets at Arizona, along with guard Michael Tait and junior college forwards

Pete Williams and Eddie Smith. Olson remembers having a great shot at landing Miller, but one incident during the player's official recruiting visit helped send that plan awry.

"Every kid, before he would take a visit here, the other coaches were all saying, 'Why would you want to go out there? There's nothing but sand and snakes,'" Olson recalled. That message apparently stuck with Miller. Olson had taken the recruits to the house of his good friend Paul Weitman. They were sitting around the pool when Miller asked Weitman's eight-year-old son, Craig, if there were any snakes around. "He said, 'Oh, yeah. Come on, I'll show you,'" Olson remembered. "And that was the end of that."

Miller, of course, signed with UCLA, where he became one of the players Arizona fans loved to hate because, well, he was Reggie Miller. Maybe he was just a polarizing personality. Everybody who wasn't a UCLA fan or, later, an Indiana Pacers fan, loved to hate Reggie Miller, it seemed. "Because he was so cocky," Olson said. "But that was what made him such a great player."

Olson got in one final dig, referencing Miller's sister, Cheryl. "Of course, he was only the second-best player in his family," Olson said.

Back in those days, the majority of Arizona's most despised opponents were UCLA Bruins. Funny moment: Don MacLean, then a UCLA freshman, once extended his hand in an effort to help Jud Buechler up from the court. MacLean, in a classic grade-school move, then pulled back his arm and slicked back his hair.

"Don and I were good friends. Played against each other in high school," said Arizona guard Matt Othick. "Everybody loved to hate him. I remember him getting into fights at Nike camps. But he was competitive, man. I think he just thought, *I hold an edge on people if I'm tough on them.*

"I remember my sophomore or junior year, I dove for a ball at his feet and got it. They called a foul, and Don kicks me. I jump up and push him, and he goes, 'Oh, my bad, Mo. I thought you were [Sean] Rooks.' He was a character, a total character."

Arizona fans had further reason to hate MacLean when he broke Sean Elliott's Pac-10 career scoring record. MacLean today serves as an analyst for the Pac-12 Networks.

Othick said he ran into MacLean at the 2014 Pac-12 tournament in Las Vegas. "He goes, 'Man, I finally feel like I can go to Tucson and people don't hate me anymore,'" Othick said. "I said, 'Well, I don't know about that, Don.'"

There have been plenty of other "hated" players over the years: Oregon State's Gary Payton (the king of trash-talking), UNLV's Stacey Augmon (because of his epic matchups against Elliott), Arizona State's Eddie House (who always had something to say), anybody from Duke, Houston's Aubrey Coleman (for stepping on Chase Budinger's face), and BYU's Jimmer Fredette (who scored a Cougars-record 49 points against Arizona in the 2009–10 season).

Other Bruins that fans loved to hate were Dan Gadzuric, Trevor Wilson (mock chants of "Tre-vor! Tre-vor!" were heard all over the league), and Tracy Murray.

"I loved them yelling at me," Murray said of the Arizona fans. "I fed off that kind of stuff. I wanted to do it some more. You have to love the loyalty of the Wildcat fans, but, with me, I kind of thrived on that."

Murray was part of the team that ended Arizona's 71-game winning streak at McKale Center on January 11, 1992. "It was sweet," he said. "We had a shot the year before and failed. But that was part of the rivalry. Anything could happen when you have two of the best teams in Pac-10 history facing each other. We went at it all the time. We had a great deal of respect for one another."

79 Chris Mills

Chris Mills was the second McDonald's All-American to transfer into the Arizona Wildcats program, right behind Brian Williams.

There have been more than 20 McDonald's All-Americans in the program—and Mills may have been the most unappreciated. Underrated or unheralded? Not exactly, but Mills, a 6'7" forward, could do it all...and he did, until he ran out of eligibility. In hindsight, he could have been like today's players who come to school and leave early, but Mills chose to stay for three years.

He was a solid rebounder, averaging 7.3 a game, and was a solid scorer from all over the court. He had great range and averaged 17.2 points per game. In starting 94 games—every one he was available to—he finished fourth on Arizona's all-time scoring list with 1,619 points.

"If you want to talk about a tough, hard-nosed guy," Lute Olson said, "Chris is that guy."

Arizona had been recruiting him when he was playing at Fairfax High School in Los Angeles, but his dad got involved. And, well, the rest of the story is well chronicled. Mills went to Kentucky, but was later declared ineligible by the NCAA to play at UK after a lengthy investigation that resulted in sanctions against the school's basketball program. One infraction was against then–Kentucky assistant Dwane Casey, who allegedly sent $1,000 to Mills' father, Claud. Eventually, Mills transferred to UA where he had to sit out the season before becoming eligible.

Olson said Mills called him to say he'd like to come to Arizona but Olson told him, "We tried hard to recruit you the first time and I'm not going to recruit you anymore. But if you want to come, we will take you. We were not going to re-recruit you."

Olson said he only spoke to Mills' father once in that time, and it was when Mr. Mills called the basketball office asking when his son would be landing in Los Angeles upon his return home. "We might say hello in passing but that was it," Olson said. "He was close to Bobbi and she had him wrapped around her finger." Bobbi had that way about her. "'Claud, you dress so well,' she'd say," Lute remembered.

As for Chris, Olson said Mills could do everything. He was a double-double machine, finishing with 30 in his 94-game Arizona career. He was the Pac-10 player of the year in 1992–93, averaging 20.4 points and 7.9 rebounds a game.

"At a time when we really needed somebody to step forward and take charge, Chris did it," Olson said in a *Los Angeles Times* article. Whatever we need—scoring, rebounding, leadership—Chris provides it. With five freshmen getting playing time, we had to have someone step up.

"Since I've been here [Olson had then been at UA for about 10 years], we haven't had a player who does the things he does. Everybody knows about the things he does on the court, but what they don't see is the kind of atmosphere he creates on this team. We've had a number of outstanding leaders, including Sean Elliott. But nobody's done as good a job as Chris is doing."

It was Mills' early-rookie-season debut that proved to people he was a player to be reckoned with. He had 25 points in a win against Notre Dame in the preseason NIT in New York and followed it with 29 points and 13 rebounds in UA's defeat of Arkansas in the tournament final. Mills was named MVP of the NIT—and this from a team that had Sean Rooks (31 points, 10 rebounds) and Brian Williams (10 points, eight rebounds).

What may have spurred Mills on was Arkansas' mistake of leaving its scouting report on UA. Olson found it and "purposely or accidently," Arizona player Matt Muehlebach left it for Mills to see. "As I remember it, the scouting report dogged [Mills] a little bit for some odd reason," Muehlebach said.

At the time, Mills was just happy to be playing again after having to sit out. "That felt really good," Mills said after the game. "I feel comfortable at Arizona. There was a lot of pressure on me when I was in Kentucky. Our personnel wasn't as strong as it is here. We have all of the inside guys, and the guys on the outside are very good. So it's like I'm in there playing a role now. I don't have to try to be the key man; I can go out there and I can do whatever it takes to help the team win."

He did just that throughout his career, although in his junior and senior years UA fell to East Tennessee State and Santa Clara in the NCAA Tournament's first round.

"He was the toughest player I ever played with," Muehlebach said. "He was the only guy I wouldn't fight, except for Tolbert because he was just big. [Mills] was versatile and could play shooting guard, small forward, and power forward. He was really good inside. He could dominate guys his size or smaller. He was a bit like Jud [Buechler]."

Mills went on to a nice 10-year NBA career, earning more than $37 million.

80 Learn the Traditions

Something doesn't have to be old to be a tradition.

The University of Arizona has added the "WC" hand sign to its treasure trove of traditions, a gesture that dates back more than a decade but really took off in 2013. The sign is formed with the thumb and curved index finger forming a "C" while the three other fingers point upward to make the "W."

Wild. Cat.

Former NCAA champion swimmer Simon Burnett is credited with coming up with the hand signal in 2003, according to the *Arizona Daily Star*, but it took a while before it caught on with fans and athletes. Now, it's common to see current Wildcats (and recruits)—and anyone wearing cardinal and navy—flashing a WC in photos.

Speaking of cardinal and navy...

Those weren't the school's colors until the university fielded its first football team in 1899, and a student manager got a good deal on blue game sweaters trimmed in red. His official request to change the school colors from sage green and silver was approved.

Here are some other traditions to know about and participate in:

- Be sure to yell, "Nice shot, buddy!" when an opponent misses a free throw at McKale Center.
- Understand where "Bear Down" came from. That was the last message from quarterback John Button Salmon to the team before he died in 1926 from injuries suffered in an automobile accident.
- Stand at McKale at the beginning of each half until the other team scores a basket. Sometimes it takes a few minutes, so be prepared.
- In what is supposed to last for the first four minutes of each half, yell, "Boing, boing, boing" when the opponent dribbles the basketball, shout "pass" when he passes, and "brick" when the other team misses a shot (this is mostly a Zona Zoo thing, encouraged by coach Sean Miller).
- Never just say "Steve Kerr." It should always be "Steeeeve Kerrrrrrrr!" as made famous by McKale public address announcer Roger Sedlmayr after the guard scored a basket. The crowd would echo back, "Steeeeve Kerrrrrrrr!"

- Realize that the nickname Wildcats dates to a November 8, 1914, story in the *Los Angeles Times*, when Bill Henry wrote of a 14–0 Arizona football loss to Occidental: "The Arizona men showed the fight of wild cats." Until then, Arizona teams were simply referred to as the "Varsity."
- Watch for the Ooh Aah Man. Yes, he's officially retired, but he'll still lead cheers at times from his seat behind the basket.
- Learn the words to the fight song, "Bear Down Arizona," written in 1952 by Jack Lee, who would become UA's band director.

  Bear Down, Arizona
  Bear Down, Red and Blue
  Bear Down, Arizona
  Hit 'em hard, let 'em know who's who;
  Bear Down, Arizona
  Bear Down, Red and Blue
  Go, go, Wildcats, go;
  Arizona, Bear Down

81 Loren Woods

Loren Woods may not have the Arizona career shot-block record, but he is arguably the best shutdown defender to man the post in the history of Wildcats basketball.

Woods, who transferred from Wake Forest after his freshman season, holds the single-game record for blocked shots, with 14 against Oregon as a junior on February 3, 2000, as well as the single-season mark, with 102 in the 1999–2000 season.

One more 100-plus blocked-shot season would have pushed him over Anthony Cook's record of 278. Woods finished with 186. (Channing Frye passed Woods later with 258 from 2001 to 2005.)

Woods, a 7'1" center, recorded two triple-doubles in his Arizona career, both including blocked shots. He had 16 points and 10 rebounds to go along with his 14 blocked shots against Oregon in 2000. In his senior season, he had 13 points, 10 rebounds and 10 blocked shots at Washington on January 13, 2001.

Despite these figures, Arizona fans wanted more from him at times, especially on the offensive end. Woods' stoic demeanor and seemingly effortless style made some believe that the gifted center did not always give 100 percent.

That notion drew the ire of Lute Olson, who openly criticized the fans at McKale Center who booed Woods during a game in 2001. Woods scored only 10 points on 4-of-7 shooting from the field in Arizona's 82–62 win over Washington on February 8, 2001, almost a month after he posted one of his triple-doubles against the Huskies in Seattle.

"If the crowd really wants to help us, and I assume that's why they are here, then they need to do what they can to encourage our guys," Olson told the *Tucson Citizen*. "I've been here 18 years, and I was probably as embarrassed as I've [ever] been by the crowd reaction in the first half."

Instead of taking out his frustration on the Arizona crowd, Woods was hard on himself, despite having had to work his way back from a back injury that kept him out of the last eight games in the 1999–2000 season. "I'm embarrassing myself, my family, and Arizona basketball," Woods told the *Tucson Citizen* after the Washington game.

But when Woods was on, he was really on. In fact, Woods helped catalyze Arizona's run to the national title game in 2001 by overcoming his self-doubt.

"I think about [all the negatives people talk about], but then I think about all the positive things that I've done over my career," Woods told the *Tucson Citizen*. "And I think about all the people I've met over my career and all the people I've [gotten] to know. It really doesn't matter what people say. Nobody will be able to take the Final Four from me. Nobody can say that I didn't play in the national championship game, that I didn't help my team get there."

Woods did not follow his All–Pac-10 performance in 1999–2000 with another selection as a senior. He was selected in the 2001 NBA Draft in the second round, the 45th pick overall.

Woods was on four different NBA rosters for parts of six seasons before he found his niche overseas. He has played the last eight seasons in Lithuania, Turkey, Spain, Iran, and Lebanon. He continues to be one of the top scorers and rebounders for a team in Beirut as part of the Lebanese League.

"I go out there and have fun," Woods told the *Wall Street Journal* in a 2010 interview, shortly after his playing days at Lebanon started. "My teammates feed off my energy and usually we win."

82 Harvey Mason

Harvey Mason was one of the most physically gifted and athletic players Lute Olson ever signed. There was little he could not do on the court. He proved it when he became one of California high school's all-time leading scorers, out of Crescenta Valley High in the Los Angeles area.

"Basketball was my No. 1 sport," said Mason.

It proved to be good for him—after some time—at Arizona, too. "Everybody at this level was such good athletes," Mason said, "you just couldn't get by on athleticism. And they worked so hard. There's one thing to be athletic, but everyone was so talented, too. And we had a team that was pretty much gym rats."

The roll call alone is a who's who of Arizona basketball: Steve Kerr, Sean Elliott, Jud Buechler, Kenny Lofton, and Anthony Cook—just to name a few. "Steve Kerr was our best player and he was always in the gym shooting for two hours a night," Mason said.

It got so frustrating for Mason during his freshman year that he was contemplating going home, to "play where the grass was greener." Lute had been on him plenty and he wasn't getting any playing time. Coach Olson recalls Mason not being angry but being sad. So on a plane trip back from a game, Bobbi decided to sit with him to see what was going on. She said, "Don't let Lute get to you. Don't let Coach get you down."

She sat with Mason for three hours, telling Mason that she had seen a number of athletes come and go, and what they had to do is learn how to deal with her husband. Mason eventually got comfortable. And he started to play.

He became more of a bit player, starting his junior year and parts of his senior year before suffering a severe knee injury—in practice, of all things—that helped set him on the course toward what he does today: produce music. That is, Grammy-Award-winning music, behind the likes of artists including Jennifer Hudson and Toni Braxton.

To say he's been part of some of Arizona's biggest basketball moments would be an understatement. He was there when Arizona advanced to its first Final Four, as well as to a Sweet 16. Everything had gone increasingly well as his basketball career progressed—until that devastating injury late in his final season in 1990.

"It was horrible and I was starting and we were having a great year," he said. "Then the rug was pulled out from [under] me." UA officials said he suffered an ACL injury, and that if he had a specific kind of surgery he'd be able to come back by the end of the season to finish out his career. Doctors pulled the complete ligament out of his knee. "If it was total reconstruction, I would not have been able to play.

"I played [two games afterward]. One was Senior Night—and the only reason why I had the surgery," he said. "I played and scored on a breakaway dunk just days after my surgery. In the process, [I] tore the rest of the ligaments in my knee that night. [With] that went my career. I went out with a bang. I got that breakaway dunk and it was over."

And yet, 25 years later, Mason looks back on his career as "amazing."

"I had a great time and great experience and lifetime memories," he said. "I've had lifetime relationships. In basketball I think I underachieved, but in life I overachieved."

He's thankful for all of it. He's become good friends with Olson, who is "someone I really respect."

And, he met his wife, Jeannine, a former UA volleyball player, at UA. They've been married for 22 years. Figure that she stayed with him even after he took her to a hospital cafeteria on their first date. "Hey," he said, "it was cheap food, and being a student money was tight.

"It was fine dining at the time," he said, laughing. "The hospital was a little further away, but the food was nice and the ambience was that much nicer. She was impressed."

She obviously saw the good, athletic guy had potential. Twenty years later he's won or been part of seven Grammy Awards, been coproducer for the soundtrack to *Dreamgirls,* and produced a recent version of the NCAA Tournament's "One Shining Moment."

Arguably, one could say he's been the most successful individual of all his former teammates, a cast that includes a five-time NBA champion (Kerr), a two-time NBA All-Star (Elliott), a Major League Baseball All-Star (Lofton), and the rest.

"I wouldn't go on the record for being the most successful guy because those other guys' accomplishments are way more important than mine," he said. "Goes with the territory. Musicians want to be athletes and athletes want to be musicians. Looking back at school, I knew we had a special group and knew everybody was going to do something important because of the character of who these guys were."

He sees the same thing happening with today's group of Arizona Wildcats, a team on which his son, Trey, is a member as a preferred walk-on. "I'm really proud and sometimes overly emotional about it," said Mason. "Hopefully he'll have the amazing experience I did. It feels good that he's playing for Coach Miller. He's a lot like Coach Olson in that he expects a lot from his kids. I can relate to what [my son is] going through. Seeing him out on the court is just a crazy feeling."

What Trey remembered most—from all the stories that have been told to him—was the day his father put his jersey on backward in an annual Red-Blue game. He went on the court with it reversed. Later in the game, when he was switching from one team to the other and he took off the jersey to turn it around, he got a loud cheer and cat calls.

"I was thinking, *This is going to work*," he said, referring to the cheers from the girls.

83 Eddie Smith

He is the author of a long-distance prayer and the person who may have put the charge into Lute Olson's rebuilding of the program back in 1983–84. He's Eddie Smith, also the author of *The Cornerstone of Arizona Basketball: The Eddie Smith Story*. And his last-second prayer at ASU in Olson's first season is that shot.

"I never want to make myself seem like I'm living in the past," Smith said. "I think it is good that the story comes out."

The Wildcats were 5–15 overall, only one win more than the previous year's victory total in Ben Lindsey's 4–24 season, before Smith made the winning shot against the Sun Devils that bounced on the rim before finally falling in. Arizona's 65–64 win against ASU, completing its first season sweep over the Sun Devils since 1969–70, put the Wildcats in motion toward where the program stands today.

"I don't forget the times when we were counted out of the game and gained momentum to beat the opponent," said Smith in 2014 of his memorable games. "I have to include both games at Arizona State. I had great times on all of the programs I played on dating back to high school. I am thankful that [the programs] I played for were championship programs coached by some great men."

Smith, Pete Williams, Steve Kerr, and the Wildcats won six of their last eight games that season, including the victory at ASU, to finish 1983–84 with an 11–17 record. The Wildcats won nine of their first 12 games in the next season before traveling to ASU again to open conference play.

In *The Cornerstone of Arizona Basketball: The Eddie Smith Story*, Steve Kerr contributed a foreword with Lute Olson. Kerr wrote, "I truly believe there were three people most responsible for [Arizona's] quick turnaround: One, of course, was Lute Olson. He was the architect. The other two were Eddie Smith and Pete Williams. His legacy at Arizona isn't that he scored 500 points in 1985. It's that he got the boys-to-men transition right and continues to show the way it's done."

Smith contributed to one of the most legendary comebacks in Arizona history. "This was the start of something that would set a tradition," Smith said of the game at ASU in '85. "The clock clicked down to less than a minute. They were up nine points. And remember, at that time in the game, there was no three-point line."

Smith converted on two traditional three-point plays instead toward Arizona's winning rally. He scored and was fouled with 26 seconds remaining. His free throw cut the Sun Devils lead to four. The late Bobby Thompson, an ASU guard who is the son of the former Arizona all-star tailback with the same name, missed the front end of a one-and-one free-throw situation and Williams grabbed the rebound. Arizona's Morgan Taylor made a 20-foot jump shot with nine seconds left to cut the lead to two.

Williams deflected the inbound pass and Smith emerged with the ball after a scramble. His scoop shot banked in while he was fouled by Thompson with two seconds remaining. The game was tied. A free throw would give the Wildcats the improbable lead.

"I went out to the free throw line," Smith writes. "Got my rhythm and shot the ball with a relaxed follow-through motion. It went in.... Man, that was a comeback!

"We shocked the players, their coach, their fans and the majority of the betting world."

The 61–60 victory propelled Arizona to a 12–6 Pac-10 season, its best record since the Wildcats joined the conference in 1978–79. Only two years earlier, before Olson arrived, the Wildcats had finished 1–17 in conference play. Arizona also advanced to the NCAA Tournament for the first time in eight years.

"That was some great history," Smith said. "In two years, a basketball program that was in the basement made the NCAA Tournament. It was a great feeling being there, although I would have liked one more year playing and returning back to the tournament."

These days Smith is an educator and motivational speaker, who resides in Stockbridge, Georgia. He has matured plenty from the gang member he was as a teen in Wichita, Kansas.

"If I had to pick one word about Eddie, it would be 'character,'" Olson wrote in the foreword to Smith's book. "He exhibited the character in what was needed to succeed."

Smith reflects positively on his relationship with Olson in the book, which includes plenty of memorable moments with the coach. There were times when Olson was firm with Smith, including the time the coach called the player into his office after a fight broke out in a pickup game at McKale Center shortly after Smith arrived on campus. Olson told him to get it together and learn to play within the team concept or leave, Smith writes. That was a significant event that contributed to Smith's maturity and what he has become today.

"Based on my experiences, I make myself available to mentor other young men," Smith said. "Relational leadership helped shaped my life and I know that without relational leadership, the young men and women today are left to their own devices.

"I know that without the coaches in my life, I don't think I would have made it as far as I have. It is my responsibility to give to those that respect my time and contributions."

84 George Rountree: A Different Breed of Cat

To say George Rountree has had an impact on the University of Arizona men's basketball team would be a major understatement. He may have averaged just 9.3 points per game in the waning heyday years of the Fred Enke coaching era. But more than five decades later he's still making an impact. As he puts it—and he's being modest—he's given "a couple of million" to the athletic department and university's College of Law.

He's been a staple around McKale Center and the College of Law through the years. In early 2014, he pledged $800,000 to help renovate the 40-year-old building. The 80-year-old attorney from Wilmington, North Carolina, "loves" UA, from which he graduated in 1955 after serving as team captain in his senior year and coaching the freshman team while he attended law school.

Rountree credits Arizona for much of his success. "When I entered Arizona in September of 1951, I was just a kid who had difficulty expressing thoughts," said Rountree to the *Tucson Citizen*. "I stuttered frequently and was very unsure of myself. When I got out of law school, I was a different breed of cat. I was ready to make something of myself because people believed in me, and those people had Arizona connections."

He helped build the Hall of Champions, and in it is the George and Sylvia Rountree Mezzanine. He also has a UA building named in his honor: Rogers Rountree Hall, named for him and fellow attorney James Rogers.

"I would hope my legacy would be that if you give a former player the opportunity in an appreciated environment, he'll give back," Rountree said. "You would get a huge response [in return]."

Rountree suggested Arizona should get former UA student-athletes to return annually to UA to counsel them on their futures. "Have them come in and talk about how to be successful in the business world," he said. "You have to use the same feelings that made you a good athlete to be a success in the real world. You have to work hard and work harder than the next guy. You have to be focused." He does that now when he talks to law students each year at UA.

In talking about his past and Arizona's era of the 1950s, Rountree said UA hasn't given the era it's proper due. "They haven't paid enough attention to anybody in the 1950s," he said. He talked about turning in his jersey after his senior year and graduating "without a 'thank you' or 'fuck yourself' or a 'drop dead.'"

Rountree added that soon after leaving UA he was sent a lifetime pass for every Arizona athletic event because he had lettered for three consecutive years. That lasted about five years. According to former teammate Bill Reeves, who worked for the UA Alumni Association, only 400 passes were given and then they gave five-year passes.

"Then that lifetime pass was revoked," Rountree remembered. "That happened to Jack Howell, Leon Blevins, Roger Johnson, Leo Johnson, Teddy Lazovich, Hadie Redd, and a number of us. Everybody whom I knew. That is no way to treat people the best they could."

Rountree said goodwill didn't come until about 1977, when Reeves was working for the alumni association and held a function to gather players from the 1952–53 season. It was the last time UA won the Border Conference. "That was the first time anyone at Arizona had anything nice to say about us," Rountree said.

Rountree acknowledged that things changed once Cedric Dempsey became athletic director. The goodwill continued through Jim Livengood and still continues now through Greg Byrne.

Rountree continues to give back to the university he loves.

85 Bennett Davison

Bennett Davison was a rarity in the history of the Arizona basketball program. Rarely did coach Lute Olson dip into the junior college ranks for a player, but he did for Davison, a 6'8", 205 pound forward who could do so many things, including play the center position.

In fact, he was Aaron Gordon before Gordon was—an Arizona one-and-done NBA hopeful. "Yes, we're kind of similar in terms of build and kind of spring-loaded," admits Davison, who was part of Arizona's national title team in 1997. "Everything we do is spring-loaded. He's far more advanced offensively than me, but I did get there three or four years later in my professional career."

Davison spent 12 years playing overseas and is now back in Northern California, where he grew up. Years later he's still one of the more famous people from his small hometown of Sebastopol. "I guess semifamous," he said, laughing. "There's Novo Mesto, Slovenia, Sebastopol, Tucson: those are the only places where people will recognize my name."

In Tucson, and some other parts of the college basketball world, they will never, ever forget Davison. After all, he was the player who had the courage to muss Olson's hair after UA won the national title in 1997. The cameras caught the unscripted moment. He did it on a whim and perhaps as a challenge from Josh Pastner (although John Ash and Jason Stewart were part of the challenge to get Lute's always-perfect hair messy).

"They asked, 'What are you going to do? You have to do something crazy,'" Davison recalled. "Of all people, Josh said to go mess up Coach's hair. He said it and, well, it turned out to be one of those things where you don't prepare. They just happen."

That's who Davison was: the on-a-whim player and the "jokester." Has there ever been anyone at Arizona more funny in terms of antics? Probably not. Figure the late night in Oregon, at the airport. There, he and Jason Lee were dared into riding in the baggage carousel after the team's 11:00 PM flight. Sounded good at the time, and the entire airport was quiet. Players offered up money for the prank, but Lee backed out. Davison didn't. Eventually airport officials, none too happy, started yelling at him, saying it was a $10,000 fine and that he was breaking the law. "The worst part is," Davison told the *Los Angeles Times*, "I only collected about two bucks."

Davison laughs now, but that's who he is and was. "I'm 38 years old and still do stupid stuff like that," he said in 2014. "Things don't change. I don't care [about] the age. I embarrass my girlfriend and kids and they ask why I do things. But you have to have fun in life. It's always fun to do stupid little things, and that's what I'm famous for."

Shenanigans aside, he was also a key to UA's title run, defending players like Kansas' Raef LaFrentz and Kentucky's Ron Mercer along the way. "My job was to rebound and defend. I thought I was a good role player," he said. In making his college decision, "It was between Arizona and Oregon, and I could have been a star at Oregon. I thought [Arizona] was the right choice. I've had great relationships and have made good friends. They still roll out the red carpet when I go back to Tucson. The two years I was there were just two magical years when everything seemed to go right for us."

86 Joe Turner: Mr. Happy

"Smiling" Joe Turner, as he was called by Arizona fans and teammates because of his jovial demeanor, wasn't having any fun while playing against USC at the L.A. Sports Arena in 1986, during his sophomore season.

The 6'9" center from Bakersfield, California, went to the free-throw line with no time remaining and the Wildcats trailing 63–61. Turner, a 55 percent free-throw shooter that season, had been fouled by USC's Rich Grande before the buzzer, after frantic shots by freshmen Sean Elliott and Anthony Cook did not go in.

Turner banked in his first attempt, drawing an incredulous response from the USC crowd. The fans became louder as he prepared for the second shot, which bounced off the rim...and out.

"I was nervous," Turner told the *Los Angeles Times*, "and, when I banked in that first free throw, it didn't help me any."

USC coach Stan Morrison told the *Times* that he gave up on prayer after Turner sank the first attempt. "I became an atheist," Morrison joked. "There was no God. But we got it back [with the miss]."

Turner and his teammates can laugh about that sequence now, but at the time it meant the game.

Turner averaged only 3.1 points and 2.8 rebounds during his four-year career at Arizona (1984–88), but those numbers don't really tell the story. Most of Turner's value at Arizona was in the locker room, or with his teammates in a social setting. He kept things loose, which helped the Wildcats' bond grow stronger.

In the book *Tales from the Arizona Wildcats Locker Room*, Turner paints himself as Arizona's version of Yogi Berra.

Here are some classic stories:

- Turner, talking to a broadcaster about Alabama-Birmingham, answered the question of "Where is UAB?" by saying, "UA be in Tucson."
- A waitress once asked him if he wanted "soup or salad" and he responded by saying that sounded good. He wanted the "super salad."

- And then there's the time Lute Olson had Turner diagram on the chalkboard in front of his teammates how he blew a defensive assignment that helped New Mexico defeat Arizona 59–58 in 1984. Turner's drawing of the key was so small it was hardly noticeable on the massive chalkboard. He looked at some of his teammates for assistance, but Olson told him, "Don't look for help."

  "We left the locker room just falling out laughing," former Arizona center Pete Williams said. "And you know that Coach Olson just wanted to scream."

Turner had his quirks, but he is intelligent. He was a businessman before coaching the girls team at his alma mater, Foothill High School in Bakersfield, California. He has also coached the boys varsity team there since 2007.

And he's going to be leaving another legacy. Turner's daughter, Jade Turner, a 6'4" middle blocker from Foothill High School, signed a letter-of-intent with the Wildcats volleyball team in November 2013.

It looks like Turner's smile will be back in McKale Center once again.

87 Jawann McClellan: Tough Career, Tough Person

A snapshot of the last days of the Lute Olson era might be Jawann McClellan breaking down on the shoulder of his former coach on Senior Day in 2008.

Olson was like a father figure to McClellan, who lost his father, George, to a heart attack shortly after his freshman season in

2004–05. That was a troublesome period in McClellan's life because he was also struggling with academic issues and injuries to his wrist and knees. At one point he contemplated leaving UA to go to the NBA.

Olson was finishing a year of a leave of absence on that Senior Day in 2008 because of health reasons. McClellan, who contemplated transferring closer to home in Houston after his freshman

Jawann McClellan and coach Lute Olson share an emotional good-bye after the senior's last game, in 2008.

season, was filled with emotion knowing his time at Arizona had not been easy and was almost over.

Still, it didn't have to be. He could have appealed to the NCAA for one more season because his wrist injury caused him to miss all but two games in his sophomore season after returning from academic problems. "I don't have anything against the program, but I'm not going to appeal," he told the *Tucson Citizen* in a 2008 interview. "I've grown up so much. I just think it's time to go play elsewhere. I have to do something to take care of my mom. The program has to rebuild with new kids coming in next year."

McClellan, a McDonald's All-American out of Houston Milby High School, went undrafted in 2008 and was headed to Belgium to play professionally before opting to spend the bulk of the 2008–09 season in the NBA D-League. However, injuries ended McClellan's career late that season and he turned to coaching.

He finished his fifth season as assistant coach at Houston's Yates High School, under Greg Wise, the father of Nic Wise, McClellan's former Arizona teammate.

The injuries that precluded him from playing in the D-League were unfortunate because McClellan was at his healthiest at Arizona during his senior season. He started to show the form that merited him Mr. Texas high school basketball honors at Milby in 2004. He averaged 8.4 points and 3.6 rebounds as a senior. The most important stat? Minutes played. He averaged 35.1 minutes that season, well over the 25.7 average for his Arizona career.

Interim coach Kevin O'Neill gave McClellan a chance to play extensively and deemed McClellan the team captain entering the season. It was then when O'Neill called McClellan a Bruce Bowen type for his ability to lock down defenders.

"We clicked from day one," McClellan said about O'Neill to the *Tucson Citizen*. "And we don't talk about basketball. We're both guys who tell it like it is, hard-nosed people. We joke and laugh away from the game. He says I have a career in coaching, and it's something I want to get into."

O'Neill used McClellan's resolve from his personal problems early in his career as an example to motivate the Wildcats. "Nobody could have given up more of themselves to make the team better," O'Neill said. "Jawann has been solid and a great leader."

McClellan may have played in only parts of three years under Olson, and finally flourished without his father figure as a senior, but he is appreciative of the life lessons he learned in Tucson. He mentioned to reporters when he left the game in 2009 that he learned at Arizona what it took to be tough to manage life's challenges. He said the difficult but enriching experience made him mature. It also prepared him to become a coach.

"It's been up and down here, but I've had a lot of fun," he told the *Tucson Citizen*. "I don't regret my decision in coming [to Tucson] because things happen for a reason."

88 Attend the Pac-12 Tournament in Vegas, Baby

For years, Arizona basketball fans have been notorious for traveling in support of their Wildcats. Of course, some places are better than others in that East Coast destinations aren't the easiest places to get to or visit for a game. But Arizona does a great job when the game is a less-than-two-hour plane ride away. Arizona typically had a good showing in Los Angeles for the annual Pac-10 Conference postseason tournament, but it wasn't until the tournament was moved to Las Vegas that you could really tell how much UA loved its Cats. Yes, Vegas had something to do with it, too.

In the last couple of years, when UA was the prohibitive favorite to win the tournament, UA fans have turned out in droves, filling out the MGM Grand Arena to about 80 percent, with the opponent having the rest. To say the crowd was one-sided would be an understatement. And as each game became more important, more fans from Arizona showed up.

A 2013 *Los Angeles Times* article noted: "Either the Wildcat fans really love their team or they really love gambling." Well, it could be a mix of both.

For the 12,900-seat MGM Arena, Arizona easily sold out its allotment of 1,600 all-session tickets. And when Arizona was locked in as the No. 1 seed, the single-session tickets for the Wildcats sessions were quickly sold out.

Las Vegas was a sea of red throughout the 2014 tournament. Everywhere you turned—in the lobby of the MGM, on the sidewalks of the famous Strip, at the airport, and on the road—UA was representing. Some fans came without tickets. They went to enjoy the atmosphere and maybe score some seats for a game.

"I told Larry Scott when we had the discussions about the Pac-12 Tournament being moved to Las Vegas that we would show up in force," said UA athletic director Greg Byrne. "Sean [Miller] and I thought we may have 40 to 50 percent of the fan base. However, our showing far exceeded our expectations, and it speaks volumes about the passion of our fan base and the support that is out there for the University of Arizona."

89 He Touched the Ball

If you didn't get to the first two years of the Pac-12 tournament, you sure missed plenty of drama. Most recently you missed the got-to-be-there intensity of the championship game between Arizona and UCLA, one in which the Bruins raced out to a quick early lead before Arizona stormed back in the second half only to lose in the final seconds. All you could have seen in the arena was red, save for some powder blue shirts here and there. No. 1 seed Arizona was upset by No. 2 UCLA and first-year coach Steve Alford.

A season earlier, UCLA came away with a huge win on a controversial call when senior Mark Lyons was called for a double-dribble in the final minutes of a hotly contested game. Arizona eventually lost 66–64. UCLA was helped by the call—which turned out to be a bad one—and a technical foul was assessed to Sean Miller for arguing with the referee that UCLA had "touched the ball" (which, of course, would have negated the double-dribble call).

In his press conference, the always-intense Miller said "he touched the ball" seven times, in what has now become a famous postgame clip on YouTube. The coach did admit it was "on him" that he got the technical foul, but he was adamant that he was right. Replays showed that he was.

What was the explanation for the call? "They don't talk to me," Miller said of the officials. "So much of what's happened is, you're in March and everybody is being super evaluated. The coaching box, the bench standing up. Everyone is really, really tight because so much is at stake. It's just difficult, man, when you invest hundreds of hours, in Solomon [Hill]'s case, thousands of hours. If I cuss, and I'm out of control and I've been warned, then shame on me. But when I say, 'He touched the ball, he touched the ball'—because quite frankly I thought maybe two of them could have gotten together and say, maybe he did touch the ball—that technical right there is hard to swallow. When you lose by two and you gave them two, and you're the coach, you have to take that burden, and I take that with me."

A month after the game, it was learned Pac-12 coordinator of officials Ed Rush told referees he would give $5,000 or a trip to

Cancun to anyone who "rang up" Sean Miller up with a technical or ejected him from the game. Rush later stated he had said it in jest, but he couldn't overcome the scandal and eventually resigned. The referee involved, Michael Irving, did not referee an Arizona game in 2013–14, but is still a referee in the Pac-12.

All the craziness may have started in Vegas, but it's not exactly what happens in Vegas stays in Vegas.

90 Red-Blue

You never know what you're going to see when you go to an Arizona game. Heck, had it not been for the Lute Olson All-Star Classic, one would have never seen this array of talent on one court at one time: Steve Kerr, Sean Elliott, Miles Simon, Gilbert Arenas, Luke Walton, and so many more.

There were a few reunions, and UA fans loved them. They got to see, among other things, former UA player Pete Williams—even at the age of 40—prove that he could still compete with the younger players.

The past was always fun to revisit, and the game was more about hugs and handshakes than dunks and dishes. It was that way when UA celebrated the 25-year reunion of its first Final Four team (1988) and the 20th reunion of the second Final Four team (1994).

It's always been that way for Arizona fans, who have made UA's exhibition games a special place. The players haven't disappointed either. Figure that in the mid-1980s if you didn't get to a Red-Blue Game you missed out on seeing UA player Harvey Mason removing his shirt and then switching from Red to Blue, showing his physique. "Some of the fans got kind of excited," Mason said, laughing. "They kind of enjoyed it. And I'm thinking, *This works....* That got the game started."

Through the years it's either been the Red-Blue Game or the White Out game that has stirred the emotions of fans. There seems to be a certain energy. In 2013, Arizona assistant coach Damon Stoudamire, in his first year at UA, gave a speech to say hello and tell the crowd it was good to be back as an assistant. "I played on a lot of teams. I've played for a lot of coaches. I've played with a lot of great players; I've played with Hall-of-Fame players," Stoudamire said to a packed McKale Center at the Red-Blue Game. "But the memories—and I hope this current team is listening—the memories that you have of college, [they] will never go away. Because if you go to the NBA, you will never get this right here. You'll never get it."

As for the White Outs, it's been four years now. Arizona fans come decked in their best white attire, giving the arena an impressive shine. The White Out almost ended after the third year. After two consecutive losses, Arizona coach Sean Miller declared he was all but done with the annual event.

"The white-out theme that we have, I think we're going to retire it, put it in a package, and let someone else do it," Miller said on the Pac-12 teleconference call days later. "It hasn't worked out very well for us the last two years."

Later that day, Miller said maybe UA would change the theme to a "polka dot" event. UA athletic director Greg Byrne, not wanting to say either way, said the idea of the game going away would be made later.

It returned in 2013–14 and Arizona broke the perceived curse, defeating UNLV 63–58.

91 Anthony Cook

As dominant as Anthony Cook was as a low-post defender for Arizona, he was as tenuous as a professional player, hampered by injuries. Cook endured an injury-filled, vagabond existence as a pro, which was unfortunate, but it did not define him as a basketball player. His contribution toward making Arizona a Final Four program under Lute Olson was significant.

A four-year starter for Olson, Cook was the perfect complementary player to slashing forward Sean Elliott. Cook, a wiry 6'9", 205-pound post player from the Los Angeles area, averaged 12 points per game and shot 57.5 percent from the field in his career, mostly because of high-percentage shots off put-backs and clear looks because Elliott drew multiple defenders.

"He was very bright," Olson said. "He wasn't one to practice a lot on his own but Sean Elliott made him work. A.C. was a great shot blocker and a very good rebounder. He was a good team player."

Cook was often forgotten behind the All-American Elliott, popular Steve Kerr, and affable Tom Tolbert. "He's one of those players who has not gathered the type of accolades he deserves," former USC coach George Raveling told the *Los Angeles Times* after one game in which the Trojans were burned for a career-high 31 points and 12 rebounds by Cook in a 93–70 loss in 1989. "He wins a lot of games for them down in the trenches—blocking shots, rebounding. He does all the things that only a coach or a mother is going to appreciate."

Shot blocking was Cook's strength at Arizona. His long-reaching arms made it difficult for opponents to get a clear view of the basket. He still holds Arizona's career record in blocked shots with

278, 20 more than Channing Frye. Cook and Frye are the only Arizona players with more than 200 blocked shots in a career.

Former UCLA coach Jim Harrick, whose predecessor, Walt Hazzard, tried to recruit Cook to Westwood, raved about Cook during the standout's senior season. "He's the most overlooked guy in the West, and maybe in America," Harrick told the *Los Angeles Times*. "You look at Dennis Rodman and John Salley and you see Anthony Cook. He's going to be the surprise of the NBA Draft.

"Anthony Cook will block your shot, stick it right back in your face, and then he'll run right back down to the other end of the floor and dunk on you. He's a big-time player, and nobody ever talks about him."

Cook was drafted by Phoenix in the first round as the 24th pick overall in 1989. He was immediately traded to Detroit, but he spurned the Pistons' offer and opted to play professionally in Greece instead. He returned to the United States the following season, and was traded to Denver. In 58 games over the 1990–91 season, his longest playing stretch in the NBA, he averaged 5.3 points and 5.6 rebounds per game.

He missed 23 games that season after tearing a ligament in his lower right leg and opened training camp the next season by seriously injuring his right shoulder. Though he played in 22 games in the 1991–92 season, he was ineffective and ultimately underwent reconstructive surgery on his shoulder, missing the rest of the year.

During the 1992–93 training camp, Cook suffered a ruptured patella tendon in his right knee, had reconstructive surgery, and missed the entire season. He was then traded to Orlando, and after appearing in just two games with the Magic for a total of two minutes, he was traded to Milwaukee.

Cook looked nothing like he did at Arizona. His weight had increased to 250 pounds by the time he got to Milwaukee. The injuries took a toll on him physically and his playing time diminished. After a season in France, he played 11 games for Portland in 1995–96 before being waived three months before the season ended.

It was a difficult end to a career that started off so strong and promising. Looking back, injuries stopped him whereas opponents could not, despite his gangly appearance.

"Flex for us, Anthony," Olson said in a press conference after Arizona defeated Cornell in a first-round game of the NCAA Tournament. "Show these guys how big you really are.

"You should have seen him when he first came to us," Olson said to the press. "We used to think we were playing with four guys, but then we'd find out that Anthony was standing sideways. He's the only player we've had who needed suspenders with his trunks."

92 Two-Sport Players

Quarterback Ortege Jenkins, standing on the sideline during a football practice, called over to a reporter from a local newspaper. "Here's what you should do," Jenkins said. "Take a picture of me in my shoulder pads and basketball shorts, with a football under one arm and a basketball under the other. Then, above the picture, it can say, WHAT *CAN'T* HE DO?"

Jenkins, never hurting for confidence—and the author of one of the most audacious plays in Arizona football history, the 1998 flip into the end zone to beat Washington in the final seconds—actually did play two sports for the Wildcats, albeit briefly.

He played in 13 basketball games—for 36 total minutes—during the team's 1997–98 national championship season. Although he wasn't with the team at the end, he is in the official team photo, which was taken at the start of the season.

Fendi Onobun

There have been Arizona football players who you look at and wonder, *What would he be like on the basketball court?* Tight end Rob Gronkowski comes to mind. Wouldn't it have been fun to see Gronk smash defenders like peanut shells underneath the basket?

It worked the opposite way for burly power forward Fendi Onobun. He had a body that screamed "TIGHT END," but he never put on the cleats during his four seasons with the Wildcats.

Football came later. After his UA hoops career came to an end in 2009 and he earned a degree in interdisciplinary studies, Onobun (6'6", 250 pounds) went back to his hometown and played a season of football at the University of Houston. Onobun was selected as a tight end in the sixth round of the 2010 NFL Draft. He has been part of six organizations through the 2013 season.

"I gave my heart to my teams and did whatever I could to make them better," Onobun told the *Tucson Citizen* about his Arizona basketball career. "I'll be honest and say that my career here wasn't what I expected, but at the same time I'm so blessed and thankful for what I have achieved."

On the court, Onobun persevered through four seasons of uncertainty and lack of opportunities. He played 157 minutes in 16 games as a freshman, giving up a redshirt year after Arizona players had several injuries. He played just 60 minutes in 14 games as a sophomore.

As a junior, he suffered a shin injury that eventually was diagnosed as a tibia fracture, yet he still played in 21 games.

By the time he was a senior, he was the lone player left from the heralded 2006 recruiting class that included Marcus Williams (who left for the NBA after his sophomore season) and J.P. Prince (who transferred to Tennessee). Even head coach Lute Olson (who retired) and assistant Josh Pastner, who recruited Onobun to Tucson, were not around in the end.

He played his last two years under interim coaches Kevin O'Neill and Russ Pennell. Onobun averaged only 6.3 minutes per game as a senior.

"He's going to be a successful young man," Pennell said at the time. "I've tried to get that across to him. I know his career hasn't been what he wants it to be here. But I told him that 'You'll learn more about yourself in your life [because of this].... When you're 40 years old you'll think back and say "I'm the man that I am now because of those things."'"

Jenkins is one of a handful of Arizona athletes in the past 30 years or so who played basketball in addition to another sport. Other quarterbacks who dabbled in basketball were Craig Bergman (who played 38 minutes on the 1988 Final Four team), Peter Hansen (who saw action in seven games across two seasons from 1999 to 2002), and Ryan O'Hara, who joined the hoops team in 2003–04 because of injuries to Lute Olson's squad. O'Hara played briefly in six games.

"My experience was awesome," said Hansen, who eventually followed his father into football coaching, including working under Jim Harbaugh at Stanford and with the San Francisco 49ers. "The best part being I have two teams of friends I keep in touch with. Another great part of coming to hoops after three seasons of football was the travel meals. Football is buffet style in the hotel. Basketball was nice restaurants in whatever town we were in."

Sometimes, the talent went the other way—from basketball to another sport. Point guard Kenny Lofton is the greatest example, although he played just a handful of games for Arizona baseball coach Jerry Kindall. Lofton, using his elite athleticism, went on to a 17-year career in the major leagues, amassing 2,428 hits, 622 stolen bases, and countless leaping catches against the fence that will be played in highlight packages in stadiums across the country for many years to come.

Another is Tony Clark, a 6'8" forward who played only the first semester of basketball in the 1990–91 season, including a tantalizing play in which he soared under the basket for a double-pump scoop shot against Notre Dame, before ultimately pursuing pro baseball. Clark, the second pick in the 1990 baseball draft behind Chipper Jones, went on to a 15-year major league career. He also rose to executive director of the Major League Baseball Players Association after the 2013 season.

Kelvin Eafon is the best case of a basketball player helping another sport. A bulldog of a scholarship guard for two seasons

Of all of Arizona's two-sport athletes, Kenny Lofton is perhaps the best known. Quick on the hardwood, he was even quicker around the bases.

under Olson, he then joined Dick Tomey's football team full time. He was brilliant as a bruising senior running back in the team's 12–1 season in 1998, rushing for 532 yards and 16 touchdowns.

Tomey always credits Eafon with being the fiery, emotional heart of that team, which finished No. 4 nationally. Eafon's basketball teammates still recall a chewing out he gave them in the locker room after a 1996 loss at Stanford.

And, of course, there are the countless number of players who played multiple sports throughout the early days at UA, when such a practice was more common. Fred W. Enke was brilliant in football and basketball. Linc Richmond as well. Joe Skaisgir was unbelievable in basketball and baseball. UA has had a long history of storied multiple-sport athletes.

93 Ricky Anderson: The Ultimate Practice Guy

He was part of one of Arizona's best recruiting classes in the Lute Olson era.

He's also part of another exclusive club in being a part of the only father-son combination to have played for the Hall of Fame coach. He's Ricky Anderson, the lanky, jack-of-all-trades forward who visited Arizona on the same weekend as Richard Jefferson and Luke Walton. That class also included Michael Wright and guard Travis Wilson (who later transferred). When Arizona had everyone signed, sealed, and delivered, recruiting analyst Bob Gibbons said he was ready to rate the class as No. 1.

"I'm impressed with Arizona's bunch, in terms of quality and character and the integrity of the people Arizona signed," Gibbons told the *Tucson Citizen* at the time. There was some question if Anderson would be part of the mix, however, when he failed to get a scholarship after Walton and Jefferson committed. Olson typically gave scholarships to those who visited and committed first, and Walton and Jefferson did just that. Wright and Wilson came later, but eventually Arizona had a scholarship and was able to sign Anderson, whose father, Gary, played for Olson more than 20 years earlier, at Long Beach City College.

"I had an incredible time at Arizona," said Anderson, a 6'9", 225-pound forward from Long Beach. "My freshman year I started five times or so and played with Jason Terry. He was a guy with great heart and a guy who cared. Eugene [Edgerson] and Justin Wessel taught me everything."

Well, not everything. Anderson came in with a keen knowledge of the game already, as his father coached a bit at Long Beach City

College. He was also a pretty good bowler, table tennis player, volleyball player, and these days, yoga instructor.

Yes, yoga instructor. He teaches yoga along with basketball and volleyball at Santa Ana (California) Junior College and Long Beach City College, 12 years after finishing up his playing days at UA. As it turns out, he might be working for his former teammate Jefferson, who contacted Anderson after he opened up a yoga school in Southern California. It's those types of friendships that he'll always remember, including joining Walton in a winter basketball recreational league. And, of course, they won the title.

"I got the call from Luke and he was like, 'We need you,' so I was out there hitting three-pointers again," Anderson said of the 2014 competition. "I'm not too quick. I could never move laterally, as Coach O would say, but I was jumping OK. And, damn, it felt good. Playing with Luke again and winning the league is something I will never, ever forget. We hadn't played together for about six years. It was like old times at Arizona."

Old but glorious times, when Arizona made deep runs into the NCAA Tournament (he was part of five of them). He redshirted the year UA played in the 2001 final and was instrumental in Arizona reaching the Sweet 16 and Elite Eight.

"Being part of that No. 1 team in the country was great—it's like being on cloud nine," he said. "I'd have to say being at Arizona and all that was probably the best time of my life, in basketball and life."

Yet it wasn't always so rosy. Olson, seemingly, was always on him. *Always.* "Rumor was I was probably the one guy who probably got yelled at the most," he said. "He was on me a fair amount. He knew my mom and my dad."

Anderson, however, knew why—or at least now he does. If Olson stopped yelling, he said, that would have been a problem. It would have showed that he didn't care. "He wanted me to succeed, and I did," he said. "I think he did that for a good reason. I did have negative feelings at the time—when he yelled a lot it frustrated me—but once I grew and redshirted and became a junior he backed off. He knew I was maturing. He did it in a way to be a better person, man. I respect that in Coach O. It was all a learning experience.

"I knew he was one of the best leaders coming from Long Beach. He'd challenge his players with competition.... That developed confidence. He led by example. He never talked that much. He never rambled on at half time. That's what made him an unbelievable coach. He didn't just talk, he just *did.* That's what made him a great leader."

94 Spit Into a River

Lute Olson was not superstitious as a coach. Well, he did have one ritual. He always arranged for someone to bring him a bucket of popcorn and some Red Vines into the locker room before games. So there's that—and the fact that he (almost always) wore a red tie.

"It wasn't like it was a case of not washing clothes or anything," he said of his superstitions. That would be very unbecoming of such a dignified coach whose good looks and sartorial splendor were always the envy of ESPN's Dick Vitale. But you know what else seems unbecoming and undignified? Spitting.

Yeah, spitting.

Arizona's 1994 team borrowed a custom from Kansas coach Roy Williams, who used to spit into the Mississippi River for good luck. He started that in 1982, when he was a North Carolina assistant, and he did it again in 1993 when he led the Jayhawks to the Final Four, going through St. Louis.

The Wildcats began their 1994 NCAA Tournament in Sacramento, and on one of the team's early morning walks—that was another Olson ritual—a team manager, aware of Williams' spitting history, suggested that a little expectoration couldn't hurt the team's luck. And so the distinguished Olson gathered up some saliva and—*ptui!*—spit into the Sacramento River.

"Everybody did it," Olson said. "Some of them weren't enthused about it."

He got that right. Twenty years after the fact, point guard Damon Stoudamire, reminded of the tradition, made a face and said, "That was stupid."

Countered Joseph Blair, his 1994 teammate and 2014 colleague on the Arizona coaching staff, "It worked. Whatever works."

The second-seeded Wildcats cruised past Loyola-Maryland 81–55 in a first-round game and then defeated Virginia 71–58 to advance to the Sweet 16. That took Arizona to the Sports Arena in Los Angeles.

"That was a tradition beyond Sacramento," Olson said. "We'd take that [morning] walk, and sometimes it was hard to find a river. We probably had to go over one of the bridges and spit on a freeway, probably."

The Wildcats kept winning, beating third-seeded Louisville 82–70 and then top-seeded Missouri 92–72 to advance to the Final Four in Charlotte, North Carolina. Finally, Arizona's luck ran out against Arkansas in a regional semifinal.

Perhaps the most famous superstition during the Olson years came from Jason Terry, who was known for sleeping in his uniform the night before games. Fans always have their superstitions, too. Watching a game from the same place. Not changing socks after a Wildcats win. A lucky hat.

You might also want to try spitting into a river.

If Lute Olson did it...

95 A.J. Bramlett

A.J. Bramlett went up for a two-handed dunk over Donnell Harris in practice... and down came glass. Lots and lots of glass.

"The whole backboard just shattered. It wasn't like one that just cracked. All the glass fell," Bramlett said. "Everyone was pretty surprised, myself included, and kind of excited about it. And then I looked down at my arm and it was sliced open to the yellow and white meat. So the excitement kind of took a turn there for a second with all the blood.

"Still, it was one of the coolest moments I have ever had on the basketball court. It wasn't like I was 300 pounds, so I don't know exactly why it happened... but I got a cool scar from it."

Patched up in the trainer's room with several stitches, his elbow still shows the memory of that practice in February 1997. He didn't miss any playing time, which was good. Really good. That crazy practice moment—arguably just another notch in the confidence belt for the lanky, athletic 6'10" sophomore center—was the beginning of a great stretch of basketball that ended at a different backboard in Indianapolis, where Bramlett helped cut down the nets after Arizona's national championship.

"A lot of people like to point to when I broke the backboard in practice, but I don't think anything mentally went off or anything like that," Bramlett said. "I was just starting to play better at that time, getting some more momentum and confidence in my offensive game, especially in the last few games of the Pac-10 season. Going into the tournament, I felt as good as I have ever felt in an Arizona uniform and in my ability to help the team win."

Coach Lute Olson often talked about confidence being the missing piece during Bramlett's first two seasons at Arizona, but Bramlett did not lack that during the 1997 NCAA Tournament.

He pulled down 16 rebounds in the first-round game against South Alabama. He followed up with 12 points and 15 rebounds against the College of Charleston.

In the stunning Sweet 16 upset of No. 1 Kansas—one of the greatest victories in school history—Bramlett had 12 points and 12 boards against the Jayhawks' superb 6'11" towers Scot Pollard and Raef LaFrentz. Pollard, who averaged more than 10 points per game, didn't score one.

At the team's walkthrough that morning, Olson had laid out a challenge to his big men. "The post guys were going through their shooting and I asked them to stop," Olson recalled saying after the win over Kansas. "I brought out four towels and laid them on the floor and asked them, if anyone felt like they needed to surrender to step forward."

There was no surrender in Bramlett, who later had 10 rebounds against No. 1–seeded North Carolina in the Final Four. Bramlett was the tournament's leading rebounder with 10.3 per game, and he posted two of his three double-doubles for the season in the NCAAs.

Bramlett continued improving his career arc, averaging 10.4 points and 7.4 rebounds as a junior, and 14.2 points and 9.4 rebounds as a senior. He ranked seventh in Arizona career blocked shots (104) and eighth in rebounds (817) through the 2013–14 season.

He was a second-round pick (39th overall) of the Cleveland Cavaliers in 1999, playing in eight NBA games before playing overseas for several years, mostly in Spain.

But it's those several weeks in 1997—from the shattered backboard to the national championship—that never fail to bring a smile to his face. "That was some of the best basketball I played in my career," Bramlett said. "To do it in that run, when we needed it the most, that means a lot to me and it's fun to watch. When they show those games on TV, I usually play pretty well," he added with a laugh. "I get to show my little boys that daddy played well."

96 Jim Rappis: The Bionic Man

One of the gutsiest players in Arizona basketball history was appropriately nicknamed "Guts" by his teammates because of his fortitude through many injuries.

Jim Rappis injured his left heel with 5:57 left in the first half in the 1976 West Region semifinal—one of the most thrilling games in Arizona history as the Wildcats beat Jerry Tarkanian and UNLV 114–109 in overtime—but Rappis continued to play despite being hobbled throughout.

He finished with 24 points and 12 assists against the Runnin' Rebels. And his 12 assists were more than what UNLV produced *as a team*. His injury limited him to only four points against UCLA in the regional final, which the Wildcats lost 82–66 at Pauley Pavilion.

Rappis, a member of Fred Snowden's first and heralded recruiting class in 1972–73, was also known as "the Six Million Dollar Man" because of those injuries. If only Rappis could have become the world's second bionic man.

He fractured an ankle as a freshman and played only nine games. He suffered a ruptured appendix at the beginning of his sophomore season. He then had a series of ankle injuries but managed to play in 24 of 26 games.

He was forced to use a cane off the court as a junior because of another ankle injury. On the first day of practice as a senior,

Rappis was in the hospital for a spinal disc operation. He missed only one game.

After his effort against UNLV in the 1976 Sweet 16, Rappis was lauded by Snowden as being the "epitome of courage."

Rappis was one of the last members of Snowden's Kiddie Korps to sign with Arizona in 1972. One of Snowden's assistants, Jerry Holmes, was responsible for recruiting Rappis out of Waukesha, Wisconsin. According to the book *Tucson: A Basketball Town*, written by former teammates Eric Money and Bob Elliott, Rappis was swayed because of the other talent Snowden and his staff recruited to Tucson.

The book details Rappis' recruiting trip to Georgia, on which he was introduced to the Bulldogs' only two black players. "We were playing and I remember thinking, *I'm the best player on the floor*," Rappis said. "*I don't want to be the best player on the floor. I want to win.*"

Rappis became a two-time selection on the Western Athletic Conference's All-Academic team. His performance, despite his injured heel against UNLV in 1976, earned him a spot on the All-West Regional Team.

"Rappis reminded me of a boxer," Elliott told the *Tucson Citizen* in a 2001 interview. "The more you hit him, the better he got. He thrived on adversity. I think it gave him more energy to focus and play better. He was gutty."

Rappis was selected in the fifth round of the 1976 NBA Draft by Milwaukee, his favorite team from childhood. Unfortunately, more leg injuries precluded him from playing in the NBA.

97 Reggie Geary: The Defender

There was Damon Stoudamire, Khalid Reeves, and, well, Reggie Geary: two NBA lottery picks in the first two and a future NBA player and eventually a pretty good coach. And not once during the 1992–94 stretch did Geary feel left out.

"I never felt like a third wheel with the 1994 team or any other team," said Geary. "I felt I was always a valuable member of a team of 12 players. I had a role that had developed that I was going to do my very best to fulfill for the success of the team. Damon and Khalid were NBA lottery talents, literally, and all the attention they received was well deserved and without question. My role was to guard the best player on the other team most nights, be the third point guard on the floor, and to be solid and athletic."

He also liked to think he was a coach on the floor at all times, even with Stoudamire and Reeves by his side. "I wanted to be the guy who Coach Olson could rely on consistently," Geary said. "I felt if I did my job that my time for greater recognition, which was never the goal, would come when I became an upperclassman, and it did."

Geary ranks fourth in all-time steals (208) and sixth all-time in assists (560) at Arizona. He could defend smaller guards and defend taller forwards. He was the team's four-time defensive player of the year and a first-team All–Pac-10 Conference member. He could do it all—except dance (according to his Wildcats teammates).

"The way the Tucson community embraced me when I was a player and even after has been unbelievable, and I believe it's because they always appreciated my hard-nosed [play] and my team efforts on the court," Geary said.

Looking back, there is much to remember. "I have some great memories," he said. "From my very first game in front of the McKale faithful, where I scored 14 points versus Arkansas as a freshman, to the Final Four, where I performed well and stepped on to the national stage for my defensive efforts, to holding Jalen Rose to four points versus Michigan, to hitting five three-pointers versus Syracuse in front of 30,000-plus in the Carrier Dome. But if I have to pick just one, my personal favorite might have to be leading my team as a senior to a preseason NIT Championship and defeating an Allen Iverson–led Georgetown team in New York."

Iverson had 40 points—but shot 12-for-27 from the floor, including 2-for-7 from beyond the arc. No other Hoya player had more than seven points.

Geary followed his Wildcats career with a nice professional career, playing two years in the NBA (Cleveland, San Antonio) and a number more in the Continental Basketball Association and overseas. He played with former UA teammate Chris Mills in Cleveland.

"It was a childhood dream to play in the NBA," he said. "Chris took me under his wing my rookie year and again played the role of big brother, schooling me on the ins and outs of the NBA game. After receiving a better offer to join the San Antonio Spurs the following season, I was able to work myself into the playing rotation and even started a couple games. Night in and night out playing against and guarding the world's best players—Michael Jordan, Gary Payton, John Stockton, Kobe Bryant, Jason Kidd, and Steve Nash."

His NBA career was cut short after being diagnosed with a thyroid condition that almost went undiagnosed. But he recovered and played seven more seasons before retiring.

"Being a professional athlete was an unbelievable experience for me and my family," he said. "What helped prepare me for the pro level were the daily battles against so many great teammates at Arizona in practice every day, the great competition found in college basketball in the 1990s, and because of the guidance of Coach Olson and his staff."

He was so well thought of that Olson asked him back to be an assistant coach in 2008 after having been part of the program as a recruiting and basketball operations coordinator.

It got crazy in 2008, on his second tour with the program. "That was a difficult time for UA basketball," he said. "Once Coach O decided to retire due to his health, it was a very sad time. A man who had played such a *huge* part in not only the success of the basketball program but really putting the university and Tucson on the map, would no longer be around."

He said he was hoping to get hired as the interim coach when Olson retired abruptly that fall of 2008. He was out with assistant coach Russ Pennell having a quick bite to eat when Jim Livengood called Pennell into his office.

"Russ knew that I, as a former player, was hoping for the opportunity to at least speak with the administration about the position of interim for the remainder of the season. I was already known at Arizona and had just completed two seasons as a head coach in the NBA Development League," Geary said. "After his meeting, Russ came to me first in the office with the news, acknowledged my disappointment in not even being spoken with [about the job], and asked for my support. Russ is a great coach and a good family man, and I was happy to work for—and with—him, coaching a team Tucson would be proud of."

That team reached the Sweet 16 in what was a remarkable accomplishment.

98 Walk-ons and Unknown Stars

There were a couple of pioneers on the Arizona basketball team through the Lute Olson years—Craig McMillan (the first McDonald's All-American), Sean Elliott (the first two-time All-American), Cliff Johns (the first Native American to make the team). And there was Brian Nelson, the first walk-on.

Nelson making the team made such big news in the fall of 1991 that all the early questions to Olson in the first few moments of the Pac-10 Conference preseason media day were about Nelson, a native of Illinois. Olson was taken aback by the questions, in part because Nelson, being a walk-on, was rarely going to play. He just happened to be Olson's first at UA. Weeks after, Nelson quit.

Johns' distinction was he was the first walk-on to make it through a complete season. It happened by chance when Johns, who played at Winslow (Arizona) High and attended Northern Arizona, decided to transfer to UA and attempt to walk on. Olson, already having tried to bring in a walk-on just a couple of years before, told Johns he couldn't do it.

But on a trip to an Arizona recreation center, assistant coach Jim Rosborough saw Johns play and he looked pretty good. Johns was convincing enough to get him a chance to play with Khalid Reeves, Reggie Geary, and Damon Stoudamire.

"I had to prove myself," Johns said. "I had to go to certain lengths. That's just how it is." He did.

There have been other walk-ons since him—and a few successful ones, too. In 1993, Andy Brown and Jason Richey came in together. Richey eventually left after UA's Final Four run in 1994 and had a nice career at San Diego State.

After learning under Lute Olson as a player and then assistant coach, Josh Pastner (right) went on to become head coach at the University of Memphis.

"It was an excellent experience," said Richey. "The treatment I got with the players, coaches, and fans, it felt like a home for me. I got some great competition and that was one of the reasons why I thought I had to move on. I wanted to play but I felt I learned a lot there. My game got better."

How could it not? He faced Stoudamire, Reeves, and Geary every day in practice.

Brase

At the age of two, Matt Brase had a basketball in his hand. It was also about the age he and his family moved to Tucson, Arizona. When you're the grandson of Lute Olson, of course that's what you do.

Eighteen years later, Brase fulfilled his lifelong dream of becoming an Arizona Wildcat, playing for his famous grandfather.

"It was unbelievable," he said of his experience. "I was very fortunate to grow up in McKale and around his program since before I can remember. My grandfather is an amazing man on and off the court, and someone who I have always looked up to and tried to emulate. Being able to observe him as a young kid, going to his basketball camps, working his basketball camps, playing for him, and working for him is a truly special relationship that I have been able to have with him."

Yet it almost didn't happen. Brase, who is 6'6", played at Tucson's Catalina Foothills High and eventually went to Central Arizona College. After two years there—he was a team captain—he wasn't sure what he was going to do. It was either go to a smaller Division I school, a Division II school or, well, who knows?

"While I was at Central Arizona College I would always come back to Tucson in the summers and play at McKale with the current players on the team and some former players that would be in town during the summers," he said. "The summer after my final year of junior college, I was undecided on where I would continue my career. While talking with Hassan Adams one night he said I should come and play at Arizona. He said I was good enough to be on the team and that I should ask my grandfather about walking on."

At the time, local product John Ash was on the team as a walk-on. "He told me about what he went through and encouraged me to go that route as well," Brase continued. "I thought about it for a few days and then brought it up to my grandfather."

Olson writes in his book, remembering telling his grandson, "'You know, Matt, you've been playing, not sitting. If you come to Arizona, you're only going to get a few minutes now and then. I know that sounds exciting to a lot of guys, but then they get here and the reality is that they practice hard but don't a chance to play.'"

Brase said he was fine with it. Who better to learn the game from than his grandfather?

"I was just excited to be a part of it," Brase said.

He played in 26 games, 70 minutes total, in two seasons. He was part of two NCAA Tournament teams, including UA's Elite Eight team of 2005.

"There were a lot of great memories," he said. "The experience from playing in a program of that magnitude is an incredible journey. My senior season [2004–05] was amazing, to watch Salim Stoudamire and Channing Frye lead us to a Pac-10 Championship—Salim hitting the elbow jumper to beat ASU and my grandpa passing John Wooden for Pac-10 wins in the same game—and the Elite Eight ending with the infamous Illinois game."

All his experiences have helped shape who he is today. He's currently the director of player development for the Houston Rockets after serving a couple of years as a graduate assistant under Kevin O'Neill and Russ Pennell at Arizona. He then followed Pennell to Grand Canyon University to be an assistant coach.

"Growing up in a basketball family, I lived in the gym," he said. "As a kid I would go to practices and watch film with my grandpa. And then having the opportunity to be with him constantly for three seasons [two as a player, and one on staff] was pivotal in my growth in the game of basketball. He has always been there for me and supported me. He is always available when I need to talk about things. We have conversations all the time on the current Wildcat teams, and also the Rockets."

"Of the thousands of players who play, hardly any of them can say they went to a Final Four," he said. "That experience was tremendous for me. It helped me."

That was the case for Bret Brielmaier, who was later awarded a scholarship. He wanted to eventually become a coach and wanted to learn from one of the best in Lute Olson. Brielmaier played in 92 games, eventually starting in 11. He played 905 total minutes.

There have been plenty of others: Jason Ranne, Jason Lee, Peter Hansen, and Ortege Jenkins.

The most famous walk-on may well be Josh Pastner, who came in 1996 and went 42–0 when he actually played (just 98 minutes). After years of numerous roles at Arizona, most notably an assistant, he is now the head coach at the University of Memphis.

99 Bill Reeves

Bill Reeves may have been Arizona's first big man post player in the post-WWII era. He was clearly a player who had the numbers for it.

He was especially impressive on February 1, 1956, when he grabbed a school-record 26 rebounds in a 68–53 win over Santa Barbara in Bear Down Gym. "I did it against Cal [wait for it, wait for it]...Santa Barbara," he said, laughing. "I always hesitate for effect."

Of course, so people would think it's the University of California...Berkeley, a rival of Arizona's in the Pac-12 Conference. But the record is nothing to be unimpressed with; in fact, it's one of the longest-standing records in school history.

Reeves, who is 6'6"—tall for those times—said he didn't remember the night all that much. "I remember that they weren't very tall and it was their first or second year in Division I," said Reeves, now 79. "I just seemed to get all the rebounds that night."

He does recall a teammate coming up to him and saying, "'Man, you have a few rebounds,' and they brought it up the next day. Jiminy Christmas, I just didn't realize it at the time."

One of Arizona's all-time best players, Joe Skaisgir, equaled the total six years later almost to the day, January 31, 1962. "He was a heck of a player, a good baseball player, too," Reeves said.

Reeves was pretty good himself. He finished with 825 total rebounds and still holds the school record for season average rebounds, with 13.2 per game. And he ranks third in career rebounds at 10.7 per game.

"It was a lot of fun," he said about his career. "It wasn't like it is today when you're playing 365 days a year. But I did really enjoy it."

Former UA standout Ernie McCray wished he could have played with Reeves. He was a freshman when Reeves was a senior, but back then freshmen could not play on the varsity. He called the freshman team the "Wildkittens," knowing he was capable of playing on the varsity, but couldn't.

"I think we would have dominated the boards," McCray said. "Bill had a tenacity on the court, that blue-collar approach to playing—scratching and crawling and fighting for rebounds. Bill is one of the best rebounders I've seen in an Arizona basketball uniform." Reeves attributed his abilities to Allan Stanton, then the JV coach at UA. "Had he taken over the varsity like he wanted to [instead of going] to law school, we would have won the Border Conference a couple of times," Reeves said. "He had a way of getting us motivated."

Getting motivated to eat was never a problem, though. Teammate George Rountree recalled a trip UA took to Salt Lake City. At one breakfast Reeves had a slew of food around him—pancakes, eggs, bacon, the whole works. There was so much food on the table that his teammates put their own plates on his table to make it look like he had eaten for a family.

"Fred said to me, 'Damn, you eat like Notre Dame and play like podunk,'" Reeves said, laughing.

100 Michael Tait: He's Gone

Guard Michael Tait played in 32 games, starting in 28 of them. But in the middle of the 1984–85 season he decided to leave the program. With that, he officially became Lute Olson's first big recruit to transfer. At the time, he was also Olson's biggest recruit, part of the recruiting class that included Pete Williams, Eddie Smith, and Steve Kerr. In fact, it was Tait who convinced Williams to sign at Arizona to begin with.

Transfers

The circumstances are always different for the individuals, but Arizona, even though it's a haven for blue-chip basketball players and has been for more than 30 years, has seen its share of departures. Of course, it's had its influx of transfers, too.

Whether it's injury or playing time or homesickness or just not the right fit, Arizona has seen players come and go.

It's had 30 transfers and a bevy of incoming players who have had impact, as well as players who have come and gone, never sticking around long enough to even make the media guide. A couple of guards—Orlando Vega and Richard Hollis—were two unbelievable talents who just didn't fit in (both under Lute Olson).

Only one outgoing transfer, Will Bynum, has been able to make a significant impact at his second destination (Georgia Tech), and in the NBA. He finished his seventh year in the NBA in 2014.

He transferred the weekend of New Year's in 2003. There was no explanation; he was just gone. The lack of playing time was suspected, although Bynum later said the decision to leave wasn't easy. He did say he wanted to be closer to his mom, Rose, who had been diagnosed with diabetes just months earlier. At the time he was a junior playing alongside Salim Stoudamire and just ahead of Chris Rodgers.

Just a month later, Dennis Latimore left while Arizona was playing some of its best basketball in 2003, eventually losing in the Elite Eight. Latimore transferred to Kansas. "It was a tough decision to leave, because I loved Arizona, the fans, and the coaches," Bynum told the *Tucson Citizen* from the Final Four when he was playing with Georgia Tech in 2004. "There was nothing wrong with the situation. I play the same amount of minutes that I played at Arizona. There was nothing different. It was my mom's [health]."

Bynum is one of the success stories. In fact, there are few that even compare to Bynum when it comes to success after UA. Ruben Douglas, who didn't want to sit and wait while Gilbert Arenas was becoming a star, left for New Mexico and became an honorable mention All-American in leading the nation in points per game (28.0).

Etdrick Bohannon may or may not be a success story. He left UA after 1992–93, transferred to Tennessee and then Auburn University–Montgomery. He played in 26 NBA games for five different teams over four seasons, finishing in 2001. J.P. Prince was another transfer who left UA and landed at Tennessee. He has since played overseas.

The transfer list is long—with one player an incoming transfer and an outgoing transfer all in the same year. That would be Luke Recker, the former Indiana star who left Arizona just months after arriving on campus after his then-girlfriend suffered serious injuries from an automobile accident while on vacation during the summer. He was injured and slowed after recovering from a broken wrist. He transferred to Iowa, but speculation was that he left because he too saw an up-and-comer in Arenas and realized he wasn't going to see time. Playing time and happiness are always factors.

Quynn Tebbs left in 1999 to be closer to his then-ailing grandfather, who was diagnosed with leukemia. He was part of the 1997 national championship team. "There will always be a connection just because of what we were all part of," Tebbs told the *Tucson Citizen*.

Others could have stayed to be part of a good run at a national title, such as Angelo Chol, who left Sean Miller's program in the spring of 2013, deciding he'd rather be close to where he played in high school, in San Diego.

"Nothing against Coach Miller. I have a lot of respect for him," Chol told the *San Diego Union-Tribune*, "but at the same time it was hard. I felt like I had to keep looking over my shoulder, keep looking at the bench every time I did something to see if I would get subbed out. It wasn't a fun way to play. I want to be comfortable when I'm out there. I was never able to get into a rhythm. You can't do much in eight minutes per game."

University of Arizona Men's Basketball Early Departures & Transfers, 1983–2012

Early Departures	Years at Arizona
Gilbert Arenas	1999–2001
Jerryd Bayless	2007–08
Mike Bibby	1996–98
Chase Budinger	2006–09
Aaron Gordon	2013–14
Jordan Hill	2006–09
Andre Iguodala	2002–04
Richard Jefferson	1998–2001
Grant Jerrett	2012–13
Nick Johnson	2011–14
Brian Williams	1989–91
Derrick Williams	2009–11
Marcus Williams	2005–07
Michael Wright	1998–2001

Transfers	Years at Arizona
Sean Allen	1991–92
Daniel Bejarano	2010–11
Etdrick Bohannon	1992–93
Will Bynum	2001–03
Angelo Chol	2012–13
Eric Cooper	1985–87
Ron Curry	1988–89
Ruben Douglas	1998–99
Kelvin Eafon*	1994–96
Mark Georgeson	1987–89
Travis Hanour	2000–01
Richard Hollis	1983
Rolf Jacobs	1985–87
Robertas Javtokas	1999–2000
Zane Johnson	2007–09
Jarvis Kelly	1993–94
Dennis Latimore	2001–03
Laval Lucas-Perry	2007–08
Beau Muhlbach	2003–04
J.P. Prince	2005–06
Luke Recker	1999–2000
Jason Richey	1993–94
Casey Schmidt	1989–91
Michael Tait	1983–85
Quynn Tebbs	1997–98
Orlando Vega	1989
Jesus Verdejo	2004–05
Traves Wilson	1998–99
Jeff Withey	2008–09
Andrew Zahn	2000–02

* concentrated on football only at Arizona following two seasons of basketball.

In Tait's sophomore season, Olson decided to return Brock Brunkhorst to the point guard position after a season at the shooting guard spot. Brunkhorst had been a holdover from the Ben Lindsey/Fred Snowden days.

Brunkhorst had been moved to the shooting guard position because of Tait's arrival. (Kerr was a freshman that year.)

"I struggled with that," Brunkhorst told the *Tucson Citizen*. "I was moved because he brought Michael in, and he didn't have another two guard that could do anything."

After Olson's first season, Olson spoke to the players and Brunkhorst asked to be moved back to the point guard spot. Olson said their competition would determine who would win the job. "I told Michael that Brock wanted to play the point guard spot, so there would be a battle," Olson said. "Brock wanted that challenge and took on that challenge. That probably scared Michael a bit."

Brunkhorst won out.

"Steve [Kerr] was playing very well, and Craig McMillan was coming in," Brunkhorst said. "But Tait was his recruit. But Coach Olson said he would play the best player. That's all I needed to hear."

He won the starting job that season, and two months later Tait was gone.

"I hurt my knee in Hawaii," Brunkhorst said. "Coach [Ken] Burmeister asked Coach Olson, 'Do we call Michael?' Coach said, 'I'm not going to take him back.'"

Tait landed at Clemson, where he had a nice career and ultimately became a fifth-round pick in the NBA Draft. In the NBA, however, he didn't stick.

Olson said he'd often hear from Tait later in his career. "I'd hear from him every so often and he'd say that he had made a big mistake in leaving," Olson said. "He knew he had made a mistake, that he should have stayed and that he got some bad advice."